Prologue
to
Sociology

Prologue to Sociology

Robert Boguslaw
Washington University, St. Louis

George R. Vickers
Brooklyn College,
City University of New York

Goodyear Publishing Company, Inc.
Santa Monica, California

Library of Congress
Cataloging in Publication Data

Boguslaw, Robert.
    Prologue to sociology.

    Includes index.
    1. Sociology.   I. Vickers, George, joint
author.   II. Title.
HM51.B72   301   76-21551
ISBN 0-87620-677-1

ISBN: 0-87620-677-1
Y-6771-3

Current printing (last digit):
10 9 8 7 6 5 4 3 2 1

Interior design: A Good Thing, Inc.
Cartoons: David Christianson
Cover design: Christy Butterfield

Printed in the United States of America

Contents

Part Three   201

Preface

The sociologist Karl Mannheim once observed that, "it is not men in general who think, or even isolated individuals who do the thinking, but men in certain groups who have developed a particular style of thought in an endless series of responses to certain typical expectations."[1] If there is truth to this observation, then this book reflects the particular style of thought developed by a group of students and faculty at Washington University in St. Louis during the late 1960s.

Both authors met at Washington University in 1968, but they had traveled quite different paths in getting there. One, a full professor, had spent many years in government-funded "think tanks." The other, a participant in the civil rights and student movements of the early and mid-1960s, was clearly looking for new battles to fight as a graduate student. At Washington University, both found other faculty and students who had traveled similar paths. The department of sociology at Washington University was experiencing the turmoil and pain that had become endemic to most universities during those hectic days, but there was also a sense of intellectual excitement that too often is missing from campuses today.

This sense of excitement stemmed from a confrontation of ideas and a unity of purpose that welded students and faculty into a somewhat contradictory whole. The unity came from a common "humanism" that saw the faults in American society and sought ways to achieve effective social change. The confrontation came from the diverse intellectual traditions in which that humanism was rooted. Traditional "functionalist" and energetic "behaviorist" sociologists were challenged by "phenomenologists," who in turn were confronted by more or less orthodox Marxists. For the students, who knew little about these traditions, the experience of this confrontation resulted in their questioning the assumptions of each tradition and, ultimately, in their achieving a certain synthesis of the elements of each. The label "critical sociology" probably best describes the nature of this synthesis, but so many sociologists today call themselves "critical" that the word may have lost much of its distinctive meaning.

In their current teaching and writing, many former students and faculty of Washington University continue to expound and develop the ideas nurtured during those days. In this volume, we present some of the foundations on which that work is based. In years of teaching at several universities and extended stays in various European countries, we have found that American undergraduates, unlike their European counterparts, are singularly unprepared to cope with the philosophical, theoretical, and methodological issues that lie at the root of any science of society. American students are taught facts, but the source and meaning of those facts too often remain obscure.

This text presents for undergraduates the central issues that divide sociological thinking. We have no illusions. These are difficult issues, and high school and college education in this country often does not prepare students to deal adequately with these issues. We have tried to be as simple and clear as possible, but the issues themselves are often complex. Accordingly, what we have written will seem almost embarrassingly elementary to some, and hopelessly advanced to others.

This volume is the first step in a larger project, which will extend the ideas we discuss to the full range of topics normally covered in an introductory sociology book. Thus, although we view this text as complete and self-contained, it is also incomplete and open-ended, in the sense that it is part of a larger projected work. For those who are familiar with sociological thinking in other parts of the world, the issues we discuss will seem indispensable to any responsible introduction to sociology. Conversely, the discussion of elementary statistics and research techniques may strike intellectuals in other cultural settings as inappropriate. But our primary target is the American student and teacher. We hope that our efforts will lead to a dialogue that will allow students, and perhaps their teachers, to understand somewhat better the position of others with whom they may disagree.

Without the advice, assistance, and support of many others, we could not have completed this work. Paula Barron, Norman Birnbaum, Sol Levine, Kenneth Neubeck, Deborah Offenbacher, Peter Rossi, Marty Liebowitz, Mary Beth Gallagher, Patricia Tummons, Paul Piccone, and Jonathan Turner all read portions of earlier drafts. Their comments and criticisms were invaluable. We owe a profound personal and intellectual debt to friends and colleagues like Tamar Pitch in Italy, and Pedro Cavalcanti in Portugal. Hetty DeSterke, Sophia Goodman, and Wanda Boguslaw helped prepare the manuscript. David Christianson is an unbelievably perceptive illustrator, and his cartoons accurately capture a key feature of each chapter they precede. Susan Steiner, Sue MacLaurin, and Jim Levy of Goodyear Publishing Company were a constant source of assistance and support. We would probably never have undertaken this work without the sensitive, highly intelligent, and persistent persuasion of Alfred W. Goodyear. Most of all, we acknowledge the colleagues, both student and faculty, who have passed through Washington University's Department of Sociology during the last decade or so. Without their humor, intelligence, thirst for knowledge, and aspirations for a better world, there would be nothing to write about.

Note

1 Karl Mannheim, *Ideology and Utopia* (New York: Harcourt, Brace and World), p. 3. First published in 1936 in the International Library of Psychology, Philosophy and Scientific Method.

Introduction: What is Sociology all about?

Textbooks in most scientific disciplines seem to be virtually identical in format. A textbook in physics or chemistry often begins with a one-sentence definition of the field of study and goes on to provide a simple and coherent introduction to the "facts" discovered by the use of the "scientific method." It describes the methods of scientific research appropriate to the field, the findings that have resulted from the use of these methods, and the various theories put forth to explain the findings and to guide further research. Many sociology texts follow this model.

Chemistry, physics, and astronomy are natural sciences (that is, they study nature), while sociology, political science, and economics are social sciences (that is, they study society). The scientific method that has emerged from the study of astronomy, physics, and chemistry involves very strict requirements for systematic observation and analysis. In the broadest sense, to be "scientific" requires that we observe events through the use of methods that are agreed upon and can be used by others to test theories that claim to explain or predict the events we observe.[1] Underlying these requirements is the fundamental assumption that natural phenomena cannot change of their own accord. Planets cannot change their own orbits, but must be acted upon by some other force; molecules cannot change their own structure, but they may change according to certain laws of physics and chemistry.

Are there similar laws that govern human behavior? Is human behavior determined by genes, or by history, or by social structure, or by other factors outside the control of individuals? Or can human beings voluntarily change their behavior?

What will happen on your date next Saturday night? Will you be a success or failure in your chosen career? What will decide how things come out? In seeking to answer such questions, sociologists often disagree about whether the method of the natural sciences is appropriate for the social sciences, or whether it must be modified to take into account the differences between natural and social phenomena. Some even argue that sociology cannot be a science in the sense we have described.

Sociologists use a wide variety of methods of research, and they have many conflicting theories to explain their findings. Indeed, they often disagree about just what the "facts" are. Because of these and other disagreements, responsible and serious textbooks in sociology cannot provide a simple, unidimensional introduction to the discipline, as textbooks in the natural sciences do. A basic textbook in sociology should show how these disagreements affect the problems studied and the findings that result from research. This text provides an introduction to the major views on sociology as a science and offers a systematic introduction to the sociological theories, methods, and findings reflecting these views.

The Sociological Perspective

C. Wright Mills once said that someone who possesses the "sociological imagination" is able to understand history and biography and the relations between the two in society.[2] By *biography,* Mills meant those conditions and circumstances an individual experiences uniquely as his own. *History,* for Mills, refers to those broad changes in existing social structures that affect the character and direction of whole societies. Personal biographies are lived within history. The importance of Mills's distinction lies in the fact that individuals, in living out their personal biographies, often experience history as a succession of personal troubles rather than as public issues caused by changing patterns of social structure.

Mills asserts that it is the challenge and the task of the sociological imagination to distinguish the personal troubles that result from individual biographies and those that result from historical developments over which the individual has little control. Karl Marx poses the same issue in even stronger terms when he argues,

> Men make their own history, but they do not make it just as they please; they do not make it under circumstances chosen by themselves, but under circumstances directly encountered, given and transmitted from the past.[3]

College students who get an *F* on one test after another may experience a sense of personal failure. They may begin to wonder about their ability to do college-level work and may decide to drop out of school. College instructors know that all individuals do not have the same abilities and may also view poor performance by a student as a sign of individual failure. In both instances, the "cause" of failure is identified with characteristics of the individual student.

To a sociologist, however, poor performance on tests might be a result of social rather than individual causes. A social relation exists independently of the unique characteristics of the individuals affected by it. For example, class size exists independently of the personal characteristics of pupils in a classroom. Before accepting an explanation based on personal failure, a sociologist would want to know what patterns and regularities exist with respect to performance on tests. If students from urban high schools generally perform worse than students from suburban high schools, the sociologist would want to know whether there are differences in classroom size, amounts of money spent for education, or other differences between urban and suburban schools. If students from poor families generally perform worse than students from wealthy families, the sociologist would want to know whether wealthy parents provide more emphasis on education and better study opportunities (such as a separate room and more books) than do poor parents. If national tests of performance in basic skills such as reading, writing, and arithmetic show a steady decline in performance over a period of years, the sociologist would want to know whether there were broad changes in educational philosophy, curriculum design, teaching methods, or other changes related to the decline in performance.

Sociology, then, is the study of social relations that affect human behavior. Sociologists hope that their studies will lead to a better understanding of the individual, of society, and of the relationship between individuals and society.

Sociology and Science

In using a sociological perspective to study actual problems, sociologists try to be scientific. For most of us, the word *science* conveys an image of laboratories, experiments, equations, and other operations. We also assume that science deals with "facts" and that all scientists can agree on the facts. In sociology, however, there are often explicit disagreements about the facts, and there are explicit disagreements about the appropriate scientific method. Before we examine these disagreements, it is important to understand that there is a great deal of disagreement about facts and methods in *all* scientific disciplines.

Introductory texts in disciplines like chemistry, physics, or astronomy characteristically suggest to the beginning student that the discipline is characterized by a single paradigm to which all practitioners subscribe. Such a paradigm defines the focus of study, the categories for inquiry, the kinds of data relevant to these categories, and the methods for gathering relevant data. This idea is really quite misleading, since important areas of disagreement are necessary if scientific progress is to occur but there must also be a broad area of agreement to serve as a basis for any specific discipline.

Thomas S. Kuhn argues that any science is dominated by a specific paradigm at a given point in time.[4] He uses the term *normal science* to describe the period during which scientists accumulate knowledge to expand and refine the dominant paradigm. While accumulating knowledge, scientists occasionally discover *anomalies,* or things that cannot be explained within the dominant paradigm. If many anomalies are discovered, a *crisis* stage is reached, in which some scientists reject the dominant paradigm and seek a new one that can account both for those things explained by the old paradigm and for the anomalies. When a new paradigm replaces the old one, we can speak of a *scientific revolution.*

This view of the history of scientific thought challenges the common belief that scientific progress is the result of the gradual accumulation of knowledge that refines and expands a basic scientific method common to all scientific disciplines. For Kuhn, the emergence of a new paradigm is at least in part a political process. One paradigm wins out over another, not so much because it is better than another (although it may be), but, more importantly, because its supporters have more power than the supporters of another. The paradigm whose supporters control the most important journals in a field is likely to gain dominance over paradigms whose supporters lack access to such journals. Similarly, positions of leadership in a discipline are given to supporters of the dominant paradigm, and this adds legitimacy to their support. Supporters of different paradigms seldom try to understand the basic points of their competitors, but instead try to discredit the validity of competing paradigms.

Thus, a scientifically "good" paradigm cannot gain dominance without a political struggle, and a scientifically "bad" paradigm can gain dominance through political means. Although not all scientists accept Kuhn's view of how scientific revolutions occur, his explanation does point up the fact that disagreements rage within all scientific disciplines.[5] The fact that these disagreements are not often presented in introductory texts may say more about the strength of the dominant paradigm within that discipline than it does about the amount of actual disagreement.

Sociological Orientations

Contemporary sociology has become a battleground for competing models of existing reality and rules of the scientific game, as well as for fundamental philosophical differences and value conflicts. We will describe the battleground throughout this book. The major competing orientations are categorized according to the way their supporters define the nature and purposes of sociology as a science.

All sociologists hope that their work will

lead to a better understanding of human behavior and human society and that such improved understanding can be used to improve society. There are at least three major categories of disagreement, however, about how to gain a better understanding. These categories represent sharply divergent views about the nature of sociological problems, the appropriate unit for study, and the appropriate procedures for gathering information, as well as different value orientations.

The Pure-Science Orientation

The dominant view of sociology is that it is a pure science. Differences between sociology and such natural sciences as physics and chemistry are seen as differences of degree. Supporters of this view argue that the purpose of sociology is to discover the general laws governing human behavior. They insist that sociologists strive to achieve the rigor of the natural-scientific method in their research, and that sociologists avoid having their values bias their research.

A fundamental premise of this view is that there is an inherent order to social life, that social relations reflect this underlying order, and the task of sociology is to discover the general laws that govern this order. As sociologists perfect their methods of study, human behavior will be able to be predicted with greater accuracy, and our knowledge of the social world will be similar to our knowledge of nature, it is claimed.

The Applied-Science Orientation

Norman Campbell has observed that there are two forms or aspects of all science. In one form, science is a pure, intellectual exercise, the aim of which is to study the needs of the mind, not of the body. It "appeals to nothing but the disinterested curiosity of mankind." [6] In its other form, science is a body of useful and practical knowledge and a method of obtaining it. This second form is emphasized by those who believe that sociology is an applied science. Supporters of this view argue that value orientations cannot, and should not, be ignored in the research process.

In this view, society is seen as a somewhat fragile thing, characterized by both order and conflict. The pursuit of disinterested curiosity is seen as a luxury that ignores the immediate and pressing importance of most social problems. Applied scientists seek to define the practical problems of society in sociological terms and to discover realistic solutions to these problems.

The Critical-Science Orientation

A third major orientation views sociology as a critical science. Supporters of this view believe that the interaction between individuals and society is a complex process—one that is fundamentally different from the world of nature alone. They argue that the methods of the natural sciences are not appropriate for studying society. Human beings act, in part, according to their values, and values are shaped, in part, by society. Thus, for critical scientists, social relations must be examined in terms both of the historical processes that have shaped the present, and in terms of the future goals that motivate human actions in the present.

Supporters of this view believe that society is constantly undergoing change and that no invariant order can be assumed. Critical scientists argue that the purpose of sociology is to discover the sources and directions of social change, in order to create new social relations.

A Word of Caution

Before going on to the approaches, concepts, and methods of sociology, we must enter a word of caution about the distinctions we have drawn among these three orientations. In making views of sociology as a science the criterion for organizing the three categories, we are deliberately focusing on assumptions, theories, and methods. However, some sociologists would argue that sociology is not a science of any kind. Any kind of science requires an assumption that human beings behave rationally and that social life operates according to rational rules, they would say. If this assumption is incorrect, then sociology can never be a science. The most it can hope for is an understanding of history and society as a series of unique circumstances.

If our assumption that human society is a fundamentally rational enterprise is incorrect, then the categories we have described may indeed be inappropriate. But the test, we think, should be the value of this view for understanding and explaining social life and objective reality in society.

There are also many sociologists who, while agreeing that sociology is a science, would disagree with the divisions we have made. For example, there have always been disagreements among sociologists about the political implications of research, and some people might wish to classify theories according to the degree of support or opposition they offer to the existing structure of power and privilege in a society.

We agree that it is possible to make such divisions, but we think that such an approach obscures the actual areas of agreement and disagreement. For example, Auguste Comte was no less a critic of the France of his day than C. Wright Mills was of America in the 1950s. At the same time, some sociologists, like Comte, have been concerned with making society work better, while others, like Mills, have sought basic changes in the structure of society.

Disagreements are not the only characteristic of sociologists. While

Comte, Marx, Weber, Durkheim, and Mills have disagreed about the sources, functions, structure, and consequences of the division of labor in society, they agree that the division of labor is a fundamental feature of all societies. We believe that it is essential to recognize such points of agreement, as well as to understand the disagreements. It is this belief that has led us to our description of the major orientations of modern sociology.

Plan of the Text

In chapters 2 to 4, we describe the pure-science, applied-science, and critical-science orientations of sociology. In each case, the major works that serve as a model for those who support the orientation are discussed, and their view of the problems sociologists study is analyzed. Some of the theories and methods used by supporters are also described.

The theories and methods used by supporters of different orientations are not mutually exclusive. Therefore, chapters 5 to 8 examine in greater detail the basic types of theories and methods employed by sociologists. Some of these are more appropriate to one orientation than another, and we explain the reasons for this.

Finally, in chapters 9 to 11, we look at some of the basic categories of analysis used by sociologists to see how different orientations view human behavior and human society. We show how various concepts are shaped by the different orientations, and how these concepts lead to quite different findings about the nature of social order and the sources of social change.

At intervals throughout the text we have introduced a discussion of certain important issues in sociology. These discussions are labeled part 1, part 2, and part 3. In the chapters immediately following each of these discussions, we indicate the relevant body of theory and research findings from various sociological perspectives.

Summary

The scientific method developed in the natural sciences assumes that the phenomena studied cannot change of their own accord. Some sociologists believe that the natural-scientific method can be used to study human behavior and human society, but other sociologists believe that the ability of human beings to change their behavior voluntarily means that a different scientific method must be used. All sociologists study the social relations that affect patterns and regularities of human behavior. Unlike personal relations, social relations exist independently of the unique characteristics of the individuals affected by them.

Most natural sciences are characterized by paradigms defining the focus of study, the categories for inquiry, the kinds of data relevant to these categories, and the appropriate methods for gathering relevant data. Thomas Kuhn has argued that scientific progress often occurs as a result of political struggles between different paradigms, rather than as a result of the slow accumulation of knowledge within a paradigm. This process is particularly characteristic of the development of sociological thinking.

Sociology is characterized by several competing orientations similar to scientific paradigms. The *pure-science* orientation seeks to find general laws of human behavior, and tends to believe that the scientific method of the natural sciences can be used in the social sciences. The *applied-science* orientation seeks practical solutions to immediate social problems. The *critical-science* orientation seeks to discover fundamental processes of change that shape the problems and prospects of existing societies.

For Further Study

Excellent summaries of classic studies in pure sociology can be found in John Madge, *The Origins of Scientific Sociology* (Glencoe, Ill.: Free Press, 1962). Summaries of more contemporary studies appear in Bernard Rosenberg, ed., *Analyses of Contemporary Society*, vols. 1 and 2 (New York: Thomas Y. Crowell, 1966, 1967). Standard journals in this tradition include the official *American Sociological Review* and the *American Journal of Sociology*.

Specific examples of applied sociology can be found in such books as Paul F. Lazarsfeld, et al., *The Uses of Sociology* (New York: Basic Books, 1967); Phillip Hammond, ed., *Sociologists at Work: The Craft of Social Research* (Garden City, N.Y.: Free Press, 1965); Alvin Gouldner and S. M. Miller, *Applied Sociology: Opportunities and Problems* (New York: Free Press, 1965); and Arthur Shostak, *Sociology in Action* (Homewood, Ill.: Dorsey Press, 1966). Also see the journals, *Social Problems* (the official publication of the Society for the Study of Social Problems), *Social Policy,* and the *Journal of Social Issues.*

For an interesting collection of articles written from what may be seen as the critical sociology perspective, see David Horowitz, ed., *Radical Sociology: An Introduction* (San Francisco: Canfield Press, 1971). Other useful articles in critical sociology can be found in journals such as *The Insurgent Sociologist* (Eugene, Oregon: Department of Sociology, University of Oregon), *The Inter-*

national Journal of Sociology (White Plains, N.Y.: International Arts & Sciences Press), Science and Society (New York: John Jay College, City University of New York), Berkeley Journal of Sociology (Berkeley: Department of Sociology, University of California at Berkeley), The Human Factor (New York: Graduate Sociology Student Union, Columbia University), Telos (St. Louis, Missouri: Washington University), Theory and Society (Amsterdam: Elsevier Publishing Co.), The Monthly Review (New York), Liberation (New York), New Left Review (London), Our Generation (Montreal), Radical America (Cambridge, Mass.), Review of African Political Economy (London), and Review of Radical Political Economics (Ann Arbor). A periodical that will be of interest to those concerned with either applied or critical sociology is Society (New Brunswick, N.J.: Rutgers University).

Notes

---

1 See, for example, Alfred North Whitehead, *Science and the Modern World* (New York: Macmillan, 1925).

2 C. Wright Mills, *The Sociological Imagination* (New York: Oxford, 1959).

3 Karl Marx, *The Eighteenth Brumaire of Louis Bonaparte* (Moscow: Progress Publishers, 1934), p. 10.

4 Thomas S. Kuhn, *The Structure of Scientific Revolutions* (Chicago: University of Chicago Press, 1962).

5 For a detailed analysis of this view see George Ritzer, *Sociology: A Multiple Paradigm Science* (Boston: Allyn & Bacon, 1975).

6 Norman Campbell, *What is Science?* (New York: Dover, 1952), p. 1.

part
one

There is a familiar America. It is celebrated in speeches and advertised on television and in the magazines. It has the highest mass standard of living the world has ever known.

In the 1950's this America worried about itself, yet even its anxieties were products of abundance. The title of a brilliant book was widely misinterpreted, and the familiar America began to call itself "the affluent society." There was introspection about Madison Avenue and tail fins; there was discussion of the emotional suffering taking place in the suburbs. In all this, there was an implicit assumption that the basic grinding economic problems had been solved in the United States. In this theory the nation's problems were no longer a matter of basic human needs, of food, shelter, and clothing. Now they were seen as qualitative, a question of learning to live decently amid luxury.

While this discussion was carried on, there existed another America. In it dwelt somewhere between 40,000,000 and 50,000,000 citizens of this land. They were poor. They still are.[1]

With these words, Michael Harrington reawakened Americans to the existence of widespread and severe poverty in the United States. *The Other America* was published in 1962, and the issues it raised quickly became the center of a national debate about the extent, causes, and solutions to the problem of poverty amid affluence. The ultimate question all the politicians, journalists, activists, and social scientists sought to answer was, How can poverty be eliminated? They often disagreed—not only about the answer to this question, but even about *how* to answer it.

Poverty had become a political issue in the 1960 presidential campaign, when John F. Kennedy won a crucial primary campaign in West Virginia where there was serious economic depression. After his election, Kennedy continued to speak out about problems of poverty and unemployment. He managed to pass some legislation to stimulate the economy, provide federal assistance to depressed areas, and retrain the unemployed, but he did not call for an all-out attack on poverty until a few days before his assassination.

It was President Lyndon Johnson who officially declared a "war on poverty." The legislative basis for this was The Economic Opportunity Act of 1964, which created an Office of Economic Opportunity (OEO). A variety of social scientists, community activists, and politicians were brought to Washington to develop and administer programs authorized by the legislation. There was a Community Action Program to finance local antipoverty boards in poor communities by mobilizing the poor; there was a Head Start program to make nursery schools available to help poor children develop basic educational skills comparable to those of other children; there was a Job Corps and Neighborhood Youth Corps to provide training and jobs for poor youths; there was Volunteers in Service to America, a domestic "peace corps" sending young people with skills into poor areas to assist in antipoverty work. All these programs were centrally coordinated by the OEO.

There were many critics of the war on poverty. Conservatives often attacked the programs as a federal giveaway that put money into the hands of the poor, blacks, and militants. Radical critics complained that the OEO programs neutralized the militancy of leaders of the poor by drawing them into government activities. Many local politicians complained that the direct federal funding of local antipoverty boards weakened their own political power. Despite these criticisms, the OEO programs were initiated and carried on through the late 1960s, until President Nixon transferred them to other government departments during his administration. Did the War on Poverty succeed? In 1969, Michael Harrington took a new look at "the other America" and concluded that there had been very little progress in eliminating the ills he had described seven years earlier:

> The Other America was published in March, 1962. Now, almost seven years later, the condition that book described is objectively not quite as evil as it was; politically and morally, it is worse than ever. For despite a long, federally induced boom and an "unconditional" war on poverty, tens of millions of Americans still live in a social underworld and an even larger number are only one recession, one illness, one accident removed from it.[2]

Poverty in America

There are many reasons for the limited success of the war on poverty.[3] Most of these reasons are rooted in the fact that there is no simple or easy answer to the question, How can poverty be eliminated? The sociologists, economists, and other social scientists who joined the War on Poverty quickly discovered that, before they could answer the ultimate question, they had to answer several prior questions: What do we mean by "poverty"? What are the characteristics of the poor? What are the causes of poverty?

What Do We Mean by Poverty?

Before it is possible to develop programs to eliminate poverty, it is necessary to know how many people are poor. Before it is possible to find out how many people are poor, however, it is necessary to agree on a definition of "poverty." As sociologists quickly discovered, this is no simple matter. As they debated the meaning of poverty, sociologists argued about whether "objective," "subjective," or "relative" definitions were more correct, and about the implications of different definitions. These disagreements reflect fundamentally different conceptions about the nature and purpose of sociology as a science.

Figure 1 shows official government figures, indicating that between 1959 and 1973, the number of people living in poverty dropped from 39.5 million to 23.0 million. Between 1973 and 1975, however, the number of poor people increased to 25.9 million. These government figures are based on a poverty index developed by the Social Security Administration. This index is calculated by taking the Department of Agriculture's estimate of the cost of a low-budget, nutritious diet for households of various sizes and multiplying this food budget by three, based on the assumption that food typically represents one-third of the expenses of a low-income family.[4] In 1970, for example, the poverty level for a family of four was set at $3,968. In 1975, the poverty level for a family of four was $5,500.

In 1970 the Bureau of Labor Statistics estimated that an urban family of four required an income of about $6,960 to maintain a *low* living standard, and about $10,666 to maintain a modest but adequate living standard.[5] Thus, if the Bureau of Labor Statistics estimates had been used instead of the estimate of the Social Security Administration, the government would have listed many millions more people living in poverty.

What Are the Characteristics of the Poor?

Once a definition of poverty is set, it becomes possible to estimate the number of poor people. But before it is possible to initiate programs to eliminate poverty, it is necessary to know the causes of poverty. And in order to evaluate the causes of poverty, it is necessary to know something about the characteristics of people who are poor.

About 8 percent of white persons and 31 percent of black persons in the United States were officially "poor" in 1973. About 22 percent of persons of Spanish origin were poor. About two-thirds of these were Mexican-

figure 1
Characteristics
of the
Low-Income
Population:

Low-Income Persons by Family Relationship—1959 and 1973

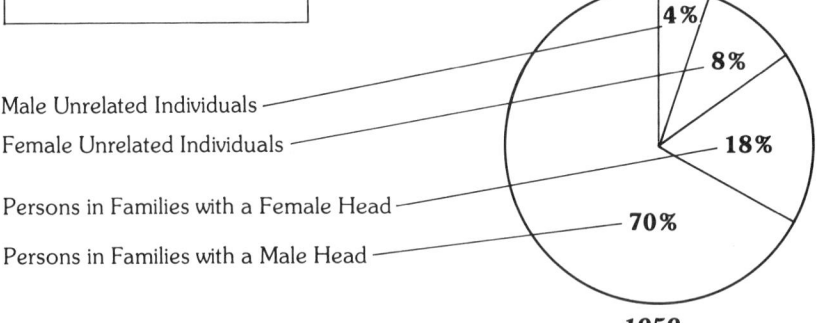

Male Unrelated Individuals

Female Unrelated Individuals

Persons in Families with a Female Head

Persons in Families with a Male Head

4%

8%

18%

70%

1959
Number of low-income persons: 39.5 million

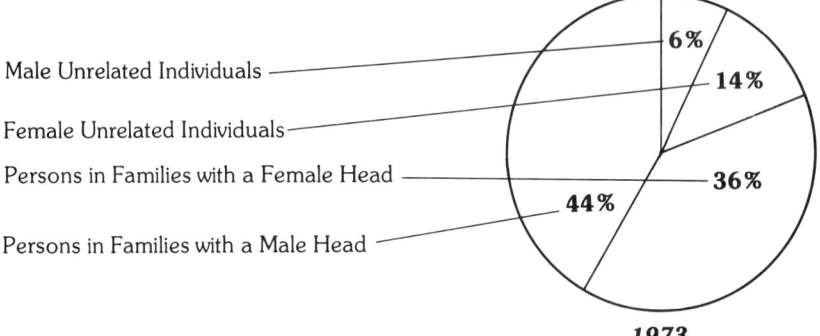

Male Unrelated Individuals

Female Unrelated Individuals

Persons in Families with a Female Head

Persons in Families with a Male Head

6%

14%

36%

44%

1973
Number of low income persons: 23.0 million

Source: U.S. Social and Economic Statistics Administration, Department of Commerce, Bureau of the Census, *Current Population Reports,* series P-60, no. 98 (Washington, D.C.: Government Printing Office, 1975), pp. 1–2.

Americans, most of whom lived in five southwestern states (Arizona, California, Colorado, New Mexico, and Texas). About 15 percent of all poor persons were 65 years of age or over.[6] Poor people have shorter life expectancies, higher infant mortality rates, more illnesses, more physical disabilities, and higher rates of mental disorders than people who are not poor. In short, their chances to stay healthy and alive are fewer than those of people who are not poor.[7]

When sociologists tried to interpret the meaning of these characteristics, once again there were many disagreements. They had to determine which characteristics were important in creating poverty, and which were created by poverty—which were the symptoms, and which the disease. Are people who are physically and mentally ill likely to become poor, or are people who are poor likely to become physically and mentally ill? Does lack of education lead to poverty, or does poverty lead to lack of educational opportunity? The disagreements among sociologists about these questions reflect their different conceptions of the nature and purpose of sociology.

What Are the Causes of Poverty?

Nowhere are the disagreements among sociologists more evident than in their analyses of the causes of poverty. Some sociologists have emphasized the common social and psychological characteristics of poor people, such as

> living in crowded quarters, a lack of privacy, gregariousness, a high incidence of alcoholism, frequent use of physical violence in the training of children, wife beating, early initiation into sex, free unions or consensual marriages, a relatively high incidence of the abandonment of mothers and children, a trend toward mother-centered families ... the predominance of the nuclear family, a strong predisposition to authoritarianism, and a great emphasis on family solidarity ... an ideal only rarely achieved. Other traits include ... a sense of resignation and fatalism based upon the realities of their difficult life situation, a belief in male superiority which reaches its crystallization in machismo or the cult of masculinity, a corresponding martyr complex among women, and finally, a high tolerance for psychologcial pathology of all sorts.[8]

The sociologists noting such characteristics argue that they constitute a "culture of poverty" that is passed down from generation to generation and keeps people locked in a condition of poverty. They argue that to eliminate poverty, it is first necessary to destroy the culture of poverty and then to replace it with a culture of "making it" in the mainstream of American society. Other sociologists have rejected the idea of a culture of poverty. They argue that the so-called culture is a set of attitudes and behavior that grow out of the actual conditions of poor people, and that poverty is rooted in the broader structures of inequality in American society.[9] Income and wealth are unequally distributed in our society, and many sociologists think that poverty is caused by the conditions that allow such inequality to exist. They claim that only by reducing or eliminating inequalities of wealth and income will it be possible to eliminate poverty.

Sociology and the Problem of Poverty

As this discussion suggests, social scientists have not been able to agree about how to eliminate poverty. Some, like economist Milton Friedman, do not believe that it is possible or desirable to eliminate either poverty or inequality, but they have proposed ways of alleviating poverty. Others have argued that massive intervention by the federal government can improve the living standards of the poor while leaving intact the basic sources of inequality. Still others have argued that poverty can be eliminated only by fundamental changes in our economic, political, and social institutions.

While these different solutions reflect ideological and political differences among their supporters, they also reflect different ways of defining and analyzing the problem of poverty. These differences, in turn, grow out of fundamentally different conceptions of the nature of sociology. In the next three chapters, we will examine in detail basic orientations to sociology and see how these orientations affect the sociology of poverty and other issues of widespread concern.

The issue of poverty is typical of the kind of concern that pure, applied, and critical sociologists all share. Other concerns range from the definition of sex roles and the raising of children to global issues of war and peace. Social relations may involve two persons or two billion. Underlying all levels of sociology and within all orientations are a number of questions that confront everyone engaged in sociological work: Shall I devote my efforts to discovering the nature of the existing order in the social universe? Shall I work under artificially controlled conditions such as a laboratory, or in a relatively uncontrolled, real setting? Shall I work to gratify my own curiosity, or to satisfy the requirements of some client? In any case, how can I obtain financial support for my work? Shall I accept support from anyone who can afford to pay for my services? If not, how shall I make appropriate distinctions between "good" and "bad" support?

Increasingly, there has developed a widespread concern about the quality of life in human society—a concern that transcends narrow interests. There is a feeling that not enough has been done to improve the conditions under which human beings exist on this planet. Scientists in general, and sociologists in particular, have been seen as being preponderantly in the service of those holding economic and political power. As a remedy for this state of affairs, a growing number of sociologists have felt the need to do applied research on a broader range of issues, and to work to help improve the quality of life.

For some sociologists, a shift in research focus is not enough. They insist upon defining a more action-oriented role. Without necessarily rejecting the traditional orientation, they argue that the sociologist must become actively engaged in constructing new forms of social order, not simply in describing or uncovering existing forms.

Should I become a secondary change agent, who works through such primary agents as administrators, union leaders, community organizers, and community leaders? Should I be close to the action and know it intimately? Should I be able to move in and out of action settings? Can I retain the freedom to criticize, dissent, and reformulate ideas and programs? Is my focus on organizations, entire communities, or specific institutions? If so, can I focus on a Cuban hospital, or a Chinese school, or an American welfare organization, or a factory? To what extent is each of these a "human service" organization? What is the nature of bona fide human services? How can sociology help insure that their precise character be clarified and that effective means are developed to provide them?

Implicit in these questions are problems such as the relevant unit of analysis and change. Organizations, institutions, and groups can be seen as part of larger configurations or systems embracing not simply a given community or even a country, but a vast complex of interrelated economic and political power factors. The reference group can be seen not simply as an organization or institution, but in terms of the people for whom services are to be provided.

If I value the needs of all people, do I nevertheless have an obligation to place special emphasis on the needs of those who are deprived? Can the relevant needs of common people be met by existing human service organizations and social institutions without changing crucial elements of the larger social system? What are the undesirable rigidities of the large social system, and can one proceed to reconstruct the system? What forms of social effort can result in needed change without an accompanying self-destruction?

To what extent is it possible to learn the answers to these questions from previous sociological theory and research, if our concern is not primarily with what *has* existed or what *now* exists but with what *can be*?

Notes

1   Michael Harrington, *The Other America* (New York: Macmillan, 1962), p. 9. Copyright © Michael Harrington 1962, 1969.

2   Michael Harrington, "The Other America Revisited," *The Center Magazine,* Center for the Study of Democratic Institutions (January 1969).

3   For a detailed discussion of these issues, see Helen Ginsburg, ed., *Poverty, Economics, and Society* (Boston: Little, Brown & Co., 1972).

4   For a more detailed description, see *Poverty Amid Plenty: The American Paradox. The Report of the President's Commission on Income Maintenance Programs* (Washington, D.C.: Government Printing Office, 1969).

5   See Ginsburg, *Poverty, Economics, and Society.*

6   U.S. Bureau of the Census, *Current Population Reports*, series P-60 no. 98, "Characteristics of the Low-Income Population: 1973" (Washington, D.C.: Government Printing Office, 1975). pp. 1–2.

7   For a description of other effects, see Kurt B. Mayer and Walter Buckley, *Class and Society* (New York: Random House, 1969).

8   Oscar Lewis, quoted in Elizabeth Herzog, "Facts and Fictions about the Poor," *Monthly Labor Review* (February 1969): 42.

9   For examination of the debate over the "culture of poverty," see Charles Valentine. *Culture and Poverty: Critique and Counter Proposals* (Chicago: University of Chicago Press, 1968).

Sociology as a Pure Science

Before the social scientists participating in the War on Poverty could propose ways of eliminating poverty, they had to define poverty, estimate the number of poor people, describe the characteristics of poor people, and analyze the causes of poverty. One way to accomplish these tasks would have been for them to use their common sense. They might have defined poverty as, "not having enough money to purchase minimal needs"; estimated that the poor are a small minority of the total population, although concentrated in inner cities and some rural areas; described poor people as chronically unemployed, ill, untrained, or lazy; and analyzed the causes of poverty as bad luck, laziness, or lack of skills. The problem with such a set of answers is that we still would not know what "minimal needs" are, how small a minority the poor are nor exactly where they live, what proportions of poor people are unemployed, ill, untrained, or lazy, or which causes accounted for each proportion. Moreover, another sociologist might come up with a different set of "common-sense" answers.

Of course, no sociologist would be content to offer such answers to these questions. Although all of us may have personal opinions about the nature and causes of poverty, sociologists want to discover the truth about poverty. How can we know a "true" answer from a "false" one? Many sociologists would respond by saying that the truth is not influenced by the wishes and values of an individual, and that anyone who observed the same events in the same way would arrive at the same answer. They would say that sociology is a science that discovers truth by using the scientific method. Or, as one sociology text puts it, "by social science we mean those bodies of knowledge compiled through the use of the scientific method which deal with the forms and contents of man's interaction."[1] Science is a way of systematically observing, classifying, and interpreting the world. When we speak of "the scientific method," we are usually referring to a specific set of procedures for seeking knowledge, based on certain assumptions developed in the natural sciences.[2] Not all sociologists subscribe to these procedures. Those who do, view sociology as a pure science. In this chapter, we examine the natural-scientific method and the way it has been adapted by some sociologists.

The Natural-Scientific Method

In these closing decades of the twentieth century, it is probably not necessary to defend or justify the application of science to any human activity. We live in a scientific age, and the vast majority of all the scientists who have ever lived are probably alive today. In an age when science is the predominant way of arriving at truth, it is important to remember that it has not always been so. Although we can trace scientific thought back to ancient Greeks such as Aristotle and Archimedes, throughout most of history, nonscientific ways of thinking have prevailed. Until relatively recent times, people assumed that their lives were determined by fate, by God, or by other forces beyond their comprehension. It was not until after the Middle Ages that science began to replace these earlier ways of thinking.

Assumptions of Science

The starting point for scientific thought is the belief that there is an underlying order to nature and that it is possible for people to comprehend that order. How do we know about nature? Through our senses—the senses of sight, hearing, and touch, and, to a lesser degree, those of taste and smell. Everything we know about the world comes, ultimately, from these senses. If we could not see, hear, or feel, we would have no reason to believe that there was an external world.

Although our senses permit us to perceive an external world—a world outside ourselves—the actual experience of seeing an object or hearing a sound is an event that takes place in the mind of an individual. It is "I" who sees the object or hears the sound. Is the external world, then, merely a thought—an idea within each individual? While "thoughts" coming from our senses seem to be internal, the "thoughts" we call sensations are different from other kinds of thoughts, such as memory, or reasoning, or will. First, we have much less control over our sensations than we do over our thoughts. Second, other people agree with us about sensations more than they do about other thoughts. It is for these reasons that our sensations lead us to believe in the existence of an external world.

Our belief in the external world is based on the fact that other people agree with us about sensations, but what reason do we have to believe that other people exist? The answer seems to be that our belief in other people is based on an analogy between the behavior of their bodies and the behavior of our own. Our senses make us aware of our hands, feet, and other parts of our bodies. We also know that certain changes in our bodies are connected to purely internal feelings. For example, if I bring my hand too near a hot body, my hand quickly moves away, and this sudden motion is accompanied by the feeling of pain. I perceive other objects that appear very similar to my body, and these other objects behave similarly to my own body. I explain these similarities by calling such objects "other persons."

In short, the possibility of science depends on the following assumptions about the distinction between an internal and external world:[3]

1 **A person is a thing that "wills," a thing with volition inside of it.**

2 **People believe in an external world because of messages they receive through their sense organs. These messages are independent of their wills and are verified by other persons who say they receive similar messages.**

3 **A person believes in the existence of other people because the behavior of his or her body is similar to theirs.**

The Method of Science

These assumptions imply there are things that all people can agree about, and these things give rise to our belief in an external world. Moreover, we believe that the judgments universally agreed upon give us information about the external world. *Science, then, is the study of those judgments concerning which universal agreement can be obtained.*

What kinds of judgments are these? If you were alone in your room reading this text, and if the book fell from your desk to the floor, making a loud noise, would that event be a proper subject for science? No, because there could not be universal agreement about that event, since only one person was in the room. It would be possible, however, for everyone to agree that if a book were pushed over the edge of the desk, it would fall to the floor and make a loud noise. In short, it is possible to reach universal agreement not about single events, but about relations between events. The kinds of relations about which it is possible to reach universal agreement—the actual subject matter of natural science—are conditional relations. They are presented in statements that *if* one event occurs, *then* another event will happen.

A scientific law is a statement that, whenever one event occurs, it is accompanied by another event. In other words, a law is a statement of invariable association. Perhaps the kind of scientific law most familiar to us is one stating a cause and effect relationship. Such a law not only asserts invariable association, but also prescribes the order of association. Whenever event *B* happens, it is preceded by event *A;* and if *A* happens, it is sure to be followed by event *B*. When such a relationship exists, we say that *A* is the cause of *B,* and *B* the effect of *A*.

Not all scientific laws assert cause and effect, however. For example, birth invariably precedes death, but we do not say that birth is the cause of death. Cause-and-effect relationships are one kind of scientific law, but in general, scientific laws simply state invariable relationships. We decide that relationships are invariable—and we therefore call them laws—when we have many examples of the existence of the relationship and no examples in which the relationship does not exist. A single negative case may disprove a law of science or force us to find a more general law to account for the apparent discrepancy as well as for the original observations.

The mere discovery of scientific laws is not the final goal of science. The goal is to explain these laws. Scientists explain laws by means of theories. There are, for example, a number of laws about the physical properties of gases, such as air and hydrogen. Two such laws state that the pressure exerted by a given quantity of gas on its container varies with the volume of the container and the temperature of the gas. Boyle's law states that the pressure is inversely proportional to the volume, so that, if the volume is halved, the pressure is doubled; Gay-Lussac's law states that at a constant volume, the pressure increases proportionately to the temperature. These, and similar laws, are explained by the dynamical theory of gases. According to this theory, a gas consists of an immense number of very small particles, called molecules, flying about in all directions and colliding with each other and with its container. The speed of flight of these molecules increases with their temperature, and their impact on the walls of the container tends to force the walls outward. By the motion of these molecules heat is conveyed from one part of the gas to another in the manner known as conduction.

This theory explains the laws in the sense that, if we assume the theory to be true, we can deduce the laws from the theory. This theory also explains in the sense that it adds new ideas to our understanding of the laws. It explains the laws of gases in terms of more general laws of all moving bodies, by asserting that there are such things as molecules that make up gases and other substances and are subject to such laws. Finally, such a theory predicts and explains new laws not yet observed. Thus, once the existence of molecules is postulated, we can predict that, when the number of molecules of gas in a container is very great, the behavior of the gas may be different than when the number of molecules in a container is very small. Such a prediction was confirmed by the discovery that the laws of gases change when a gas is highly compressed.

The natural-scientific method, then, involves the search for invariable relations between events—relations that can be expressed as laws about which universal agreement can be obtained, and which can be explained by theories.

Given the assumptions of science, the kinds of relationships about which universal agreement can be obtained are those that are independent of human will or volition—those that involve the external world of nature. What about relations among human beings? Can the natural-scientific method be employed to study human behavior and human society?

Positivism and the Science of Society

For Auguste Comte (1798–1857), often called the "father of sociology" because he coined the term *sociology* in his book, *The Positive Philosophy,*[4] the answer was a resounding yes. Human progress, he believed, derives from intellectual evolution through three stages— the theological, the metaphysical, and the positive stages. Comte claimed that when human beings first attempt to understand events, they tend to explain any changes that occur by saying that they were produced by the immediate action or intervention of supernatural beings (the theological stage). In the next stage of development, people substitute abstract forces for supernatural beings as causes (the metaphysical stage). Finally, they try to explain events by discovering laws of "invariable relations of succession and resemblance" rooted in the phenomena themselves (the positive stage).

Comte argued that intellectual progress tends to take place in one discipline at a time, so that knowledge enters the positive stage in some fields sooner than in others. He believed that the positive stage was reached first in the "lower," less complex disciplines that deal with inorganic phenomena, such as physics, and only later in the "higher," more complex disciplines dealing with organic phenomena. The most complex field, according to Comte, was that of social physics (or what he later called "sociology"), and it was then time for sociology to enter the positive stage.

The method Comte proposed for moving sociology into the positive stage was modeled on the method of the natural sciences. Comte called this method "positivism." He advocated observation, comparison, experimentation, and the study of history as the essential components of this method. While he recognized that controlled experiments are usually not possible in the social world, he claimed that a type of experimentation is possible by comparing abnormal states of society with normal states.

The study of society, for Comte, can be divided into two parts—statics, or the study of social order, and dynamics, or the study of social change. He believed that society is like an organism that requires the smooth interdependence of all its parts. For this reason, he viewed social order as an inherent characteristic of human society. By social change, Comte meant little

---

more than evolution, and in his view the history of society was a history of linear progress toward greater order and harmony.

The purpose of Comte's efforts is revealed in the term positivism. He felt that much of the previous work of philosophy had a "negative" character, tending to discredit existing social institutions. It did not, however, offer any replacement. He thought that a "positive" philosophy was needed to demonstrate the need for harmony among the parts of society and to show that social change can take place only according to the evolutionary process built into the social order. Because of this emphasis, Comte's work has a fundamentally conservative bias when viewed in applied or political terms. The ideal situations, he thought, would be for scientists to diagnose the ills of contemporary society and prescribe changes in line with the basic evolutionary processes. Just as sailors trust their lives to astronomers, who tell them how to calculate their position and plot their course, a scientific sociology would be able to tell people how to plot their course on the social sea.

As it was first developed by Comte, sociology was seen as a more complex science than physics or astronomy, although the basic method of all sciences was thought to be similar. More recent formulations of positivism call for a narrower interpretation and see sociology as an identical science, at least in terms of method, with such natural sciences as astronomy and physics. Perhaps the most influential sociological positivist in the twentieth century has been George Lundberg. Lundberg argued that, in order for sociology to become a science, it must observe systematically, classify systematically, and interpret systematically.[5]

Observation. Although everyone is constantly involved in the act of observing, very few people observe systematically. If, for example, all members of a sociology class are asked to observe and report what happens in the classroom during a half-hour period, a wide variety of reports can be expected. Some will focus on the words of the instructor, and even here there will be disagreement, unless a tape recorder is used. Other observers may attempt to characterize the instructor's manner of delivery, or physical gestures and tone of voice. Others may focus on members of the class, and some may focus on the architecture of the building or the arrangement of furniture within the room. To be scientific, according to Lundberg, it is necessary to develop rules for making these observations, so that different observers report the same thing.

Classification. Once observations have been made, the next step is to organize them in some useful fashion. Scientists call this process *classification.* It involves using symbols to represent phenomena that recur in the world observed. In everyday life, we are confronted with many ready-made classifications, some of which have a scientific basis, while others are clearly based on prejudice. For example, some objects in our environment are classified as rocks, stones, or flowers. Others are classified as men, women, children, or adults. Still others may be classified as Negroes, Jews, or foreigners. We also find classifications based on occupation (physician, plumber, and so on), education (high-school graduate, college graduate) and many others. Lundberg argues that, by using classification, scientists can manipulate symbols and create concepts, which then direct and control the way in which phenomena are perceived. For examples of sociological concepts, see chapters 9 to 11.

Interpretation. With the aid of concepts, it is possible to generate hypotheses—testable statements about events. When these hypotheses are made more general and verified, they are called laws. When scientists use a particular set of logical procedures to connect a set of laws, they form theories.

Lundberg notes that in the natural sciences, observation, classification, and interpretation are organized into two principal activities—the experimental method, and the construction of theory. The process of establishing scientific knowledge begins with an experiment or set of experiments in which all possible relevant factors are controlled and manipulated according to a set of techniques that is agreed upon and that will ultimately reveal the relationships among the factors. The experiment may begin with hypotheses, or a hypothesis may be developed during the research process. After the hypothesis has been proved or disproved, theories may be constructed to explain the relationships that have been found. If the theory is a good one, successful predictions can be made, and facts and hypotheses that seemed to be independent can be related to each other.

It is not always possible to meet the strict requirements of the experimental method in the social sciences. It is often physically impossible to control and manipulate all the potentially relevant factors (the independent variables) that might affect the phenomena under study (the dependent variables). If we wanted to study the factors influencing performance on tests by students, for example, it would be difficult to control all the independent variables. How much sleep you had the night before an exam, whether or not you had a fight with your parents or spouse, the weather, your health—all these are factors that might influence your test performance and are difficult for a social scientist to control or manipulate.

Social sciences get around this problem by using statistical manipulation of variables to approximate the requirements of the experimental method. The key element of such statistical manipulation is the principle of random sampling. It is usually not possible to include every single instance in which a phenomenon being studied occurs. Random sampling is a procedure for selecting a manageable number of instances in such a way that every instance has an equal chance of being included or excluded from study. The assumption is that, if some of the instances selected are biased in one direction by factors that do not affect all instances, these will be offset by other instances that are biased by opposite factors. Random sampling allows the use of statistical techniques similar to those used with the experimental method, and it thus allows us to talk about cause-and-effect relationships.

Sociology as a Pure Science

The main efforts of positivist sociologists like Comte and Lundberg have been directed toward making sociology a science, and their model for sociology is the natural-scientific method. Although Comte recognized that social behavior is more complex than the behavior of inanimate objects, he believed that the basic method of the natural sciences was appropriate to study social behavior. Lundberg takes a narrower view; he denies any significant difference between social behavior and the behavior of inanimate objects.

It is also characteristic of those who view sociology as a pure science to emphasize the disinterested pursuit of knowledge for its own sake. In describing this emphasis in the natural sciences, Norman Campbell observed that

> the motive of our study is supposed to be intellectual curiosity without any ulterior end; and . . . our criterion will always be the satisfaction of our intellectual needs and not the interests of practical life . . . Science, like everything else, has its limitations; there are problems, even practical problems, on which science can offer no advice whatever.[6]

In very similar terms, George Lundberg once cautioned against expecting too much help in solving social problems by means of scientific methods.

> Finally, a word should be said to those who find the methods of science too slow. They want to know what we shall do while we wait for the social sciences to develop. Well, we shall doubtless continue to suffer. Executives will continue to decide on the basis of guess and intuition and to mistake their own voices for the voice of the people or of God. The nations will doubtless continue to rage and the people to imagine vain things. Life went on also in the days before anesthetics, vaccines and sulfa drugs. These days also had their immediate and pressing problems. A few people, however, devoted themselves to research which could not possibly solve the current difficulties, but which have transformed our world. We do not abandon cancer research because the patients of today may not be saved by it. We shall probably become much sicker before we consent to take the only medicine which can help us[7]

The medicine is science, and this science is pure. What makes sociology a science, for Comte and for Lundberg, is the common method it shares with the natural sciences. What makes it pure is its focus on searching for basic, underlying causes and general laws of human behavior, rather than on finding practical solutions for immediate and pressing social problems. The ideal, pure scientist in this view is the value-free scholar, engaged in the disinterested pursuit of knowledge for its own sake, careful not to let personal opinions or desires interfere with or distort the research process.

Examples of the Pure Science Approach

Although it is easy enough to define the pure science orientation abstractly, it is more difficult to imagine just *how* one goes about studying a sociological problem from this perspective. Moreover, any general orientation is usually modified when put into practice, so it is important to compare actual empirical studies with the general orientation. There are several classic studies that exemplify the pure-science orientation to sociology.

Suicide

Emile Durkheim (1858–1917) was the first person to be called a professor of sociology in France, and several of his books have had a lasting influence on sociologists around the world. One of them—*The Rules of Sociological Method*—deals with the prospects for a genuine "social" science, distinct from the physical and biological sciences. In it, Durkheim argues that the data of a social science consist of "social facts"—ways of acting, thinking and feeling, external to the individual, and endowed with a power of coercion, by reason of which they control him.[8] Social facts are such things as legal and moral regulations, religious beliefs, and financial systems. Social facts influence behavior; they are like molds that shape the actions of individual persons.

To show how a social science could be built upon the study of social facts, Durkheim undertook a study of a phenomenon which, although apparently an individual behavior, is actually influenced by social facts. He reported his study in a book called *Suicide*.[9]

Durkheim gave three reasons for choosing suicide as the focus of his study: (1) suicide can be defined easily;(2) there are many statistics available on the subject; and (3) suicide is an issue of considerable and lasting importance. After examining several common definitions of suicide, Durkheim argues that the term *suicide* should be "applied to all cases of death resulting directly or indirectly from a positive or negative act of the victim himself which he knows will produce this result." [10]

After proposing a satisfactory definition of suicide, Durkheim proceeds to show that suicide is not an arbitrary act by individuals, but a social fact that is shaped by the characteristics of different societies. If we take the total number of suicides for a given country, we can calculate the suicide rate and this rate stays remarkably constant from year to year. Indeed, Durkheim presents figures showing that the death rate varied more from 1841 to 1860 than did the suicide rate. On the basis of these figures, he argues that there must be some social reasons for people to commit suicide, rather than purely individual reasons.

Durkheim next examines three nonsocial explanations for suicide: The first is that suicide results from mental illness. He compares the rates of various forms of mental illness with the suicide rates, and finds that there is *no* relationship between the two. The next explanation he examines is that suicide is related to factors such as race, age, climate, temperature, time of day, and season of the year. He succeeds in eliminating each of these as causes. Finally, he examines the explanation that suicide results from imitating others, and he shows that this explanation cannot account for the suicide rate.

Some people who live in luxury commit suicide; others do so in the midst of poverty. In one case noted by Durkheim a soldier committed suicide after being punished for a crime he did not commit; in another case, a person committed suicide because a crime he had committed went unpunished. Since the most varied and contradictory events of life can serve as reasons for suicide, Durkheim concludes that none of them is the specific cause. Instead, he argues that there are really three different types of suicide—egoistic, altruistic, and anomic.

Egoistic Suicide. Durkheim observed that Protestants have a higher suicide rate than do either Catholics or Jews in countries in which the latter two groups are a minority. In countries in which Catholics are a majority and Protestants a minority, the suicide rate among Catholics rises, although it is still less than the rate for Protestants. Durkheim explains this by arguing that Protestantism is a less strongly integrated religion than Catholicism; it allows more freedom for individual thought and has fewer required beliefs and practices. This is also the case with respect to Judaism, he argues. Since Jews are usually a minority group, and a persecuted one at that, they tend to live in close proximity to each other and to form a more tightly integrated group than do either Catholics or Protestants.

Durkheim concludes that "egoistic suicide" is committed by individuals who are insufficiently integrated into groups. The influence of society provides a meaningful purpose for our existence, and helps formulate our individual goals. If an individual is not integrated into a closely knit group, there is less purpose to existence, and the possibility of committing suicide increases.

Altruistic Suicide. Durkheim also observed that suicide rates are higher among soldiers than among civilians. Officers have higher rates than noncommissioned officers, who in turn have higher rates than enlisted soliders. Old-timers in the army are more likely to commit suicide than recent recruits, and elite troops are more likely to commit suicide than those in such units as engineers, ambulance corps, and administration. Men who have reenlisted in the army are more likely to commit suicide than those enlisting for the first time, and volunteers have higher rates than conscripts.

These relationships led Durkheim to conclude that there is a type of suicide almost the opposite of egoistic suicide, called "altruistic suicide." Altruistic suicide occurs when an individual is too strongly integrated into a social group. Sometimes suicide is felt to be a responsibility or a duty, when continuing to live would involve the loss of respect or honor, and there is great social pressure for the indivdual to commit suicide. Examples from ancient times of this form of suicide include the Hindu women who killed themselves when their husbands died, and the Danish warriors who killed themselves to avoid the "disgrace" of dying of old age and sickness.

Anomic Suicide. It has often been noted that suicide tends to increase during periods of economic crisis. Does this occur because life has become more difficult? Durkheim notes that if this were the explanation, suicide rates would decrease when conditions began to improve. But this does not happen! Moreover, he observed that there was relatively little suicide in such poverty-stricken places as Ireland and Calabria, and the suicide rate in dismally poor Spain was one-tenth the suicide rate in France. Indeed, in those areas of France containing the greatest number of people with independent means, the suicide rate was the highest.

These findings led Durkheim to conclude that it is not crises of poverty that cause suicide. Instead, crises of any sort (including sudden affluence) give rise to an increase in the suicide rate. Sudden, fundamental changes in the social order destroy an individual's previously existing goals, and, if the society does not provide new goals for the individual, a state of normlessness called "anomie" develops. Conditions of anomie occur when there have been rapid changes in society or in an individual's position in society. Suicide occurring under these conditions is called "anomic suicide." Thus, divorce or widowhood increases the likelihood of suicide by suddenly shattering a pattern of life that was routinized in marriage.

After examining the statistical data on suicide rates, and formulating concepts of different types of suicide, Durkheim returns to a consideration of the theoretical implications of his study. He argues that the study of suicide presents evidence of general, social laws affecting individual behavior.

> The relations of suicide to certain states of social environments are as direct
> and constant as its relations to facts of a biological and physical character
> were seen to be uncertain and ambiguous. Here at last we are face to face
> with real laws, allowing us to attempt a methodological classification of types
> of suicide.[11]

In discussing the implications of his study for ideas about social normality
(behavior that is "normal" and "good," as opposed to that which is "abnormal"
and "bad") Durkheim also argues that the disinterested pursuit of underlying
laws of behavior by the pure scientist is preferable to the arbitrary determi-
nations of morally committed people.

> The common flaw in these definitions is their premature attempt to grasp
> the essence of phenomena. They presuppose propositions which, true or not,
> can be proved only at a more advanced stage of science ... Instead of aspiring
> to determine at the outset the relations of the normal and the morbid to vital
> forces, let us simply seek some external and perceptible characteristic which
> will enable us merely to distinguish these two orders of facts.[12]

The Adolescent Society

In 1957, sociologist James S. Coleman began a research project that was
eventually published under the title *The Adolescent Society*.[13] In defining his
research problem, Coleman hypothesized that adolescents have "social climates" of their own making, and that these climates are quite different from
those found in adult society. They determine the kinds of activities that will
be regarded as important and the kinds of achievements that will result in
high status. For example, in one school, only success in sports activities may
be important for boys, and only popularity may be important for girls. In
other schools, other things like academic success may be important. If a
student who does not do well in sports enrolls in a school where success
in sports is absolutely essential for high status, there may be serious consequences for his entire school experience, and even for his subsequent
professional and personal career. So learning about adolescent society and
its social climates can be seen as a significant area for sociological investigation.

Coleman's specific research goals, then, were: (1) to understand the
nature of these social climates and their effects upon students; (2) to learn
why one kind of climate exists in one school, while a totally different kind
exists in another. Coleman decided to study ten different high schools in
northern Illinois. He and his research staff prepared a questionnaire to be
filled out by every student in each of these schools. In addition to data obtained
from the answers to these questionnaires, he collected information from

school records about the grades, I.Q. scores, and attendance of each student. Although he collected information about individual students, his units for analysis were not individuals but the status systems in high schools—how some students became more important than others. He was interested in learning how these status systems developed and what effects they had.[14]

Although he did not get satisfactory answers to all his questions, Coleman did report a number of interesting results. He found that there was not much variation among the ten schools with respect to the importance of scholastic achievement. In none of them did academic achievement count for as much as other activities in the school. In every school, the boys named as best athletes and those named as being popular with girls were far more often mentioned as being in the leading crowd and as the ones to imitate than were the boys named as best students. Among girls, the most important qualities were being best dressed and being popular with boys, rather than doing well as a student. Coleman concluded that the adolescent cultures exert a strong deterrent to academic achievement. He saw this as evidence of the failure of American society to recruit the most able persons into adult intellectual activities.

From the perspective of contemporary American life, one may wish to reexamine Coleman's classic study. It may well be that the adolescent subcultures he observed were admirable training grounds for adult life in America, where the greatest rewards do not necessarily go to the most successful intellectuals but to those who excel in other activities. Is it possible to view the findings of *The Adolescent Society* as evidence for the ingenuity of adolescents in dealing with the real values of adult society, rather than those to which lip service is given?

An American Dilemma

From time to time, the Carnegie Corporation has financed pure research in sociology.

> Provided the foundation limits itself to its proper function, namely to make the facts available and let them speak for themselves and does not undertake to instruct the public as to what to do about them, studies of this kind provide a wholly proper and, as experience has shown, sometimes a highly important use of their funds.[15]

In 1937 it decided to finance such a study of the blacks in America. To help insure objectivity, the foundation determined to obtain a non-American scholar from a "non-imperialistic country which had no background of domination of one race over another" to serve as general director of the study. Dr. Gunnar Myrdal, a professor at the University of Stockholm in Sweden, eventually agreed to serve in this position. He was invited to become the director of "a comprehensive study of the Negro in the United States, to be undertaken in a wholly objective and dispassionate way as a social phenomenon." [16]

Dr. Myrdal felt that the study should be very comprehensive, focusing on the social, political, educational, and economic status of blacks in the United States. It would investigate not only the actual status of blacks, but also the opinions held by various groups of Americans about the status that blacks *should* have.The result was a massive research report entitled, *An American Dilemma: The Negro Problem and Modern Democracy*, which has become a classic in the field of race relations. It used a wide variety of research techniques and existing records to obtain data. It is not possible to summarize all its findings here. But a few salient points should be noted.

The American dilemma is essentially a moral dilemma—a conflict between the values Americans hold on a very general level (what Myrdal calls the "American creed") and the values that operate in daily behavior. The American creed includes the ideals of the essential dignity of individual human beings, the fundamental equality of all people and their inalienable rights to freedom, justice, and fair opportunity. In everyday speech, America is described as the "land of the free," "the land of opportunity," "the cradle of liberty," and the "home of democracy."[17] One central conclusion of the study is that

> the American Creed represents the national conscience. The Negro is a "problem" to the average American partly because of a palpable conflict between the status actually awarded him and those ideals.[18]

Another finding of the study was the development of what Myrdal calls the "principle of cumulation" or the "vicious circle." He thinks that principle is relevant for a broad spectrum of social relations beyond race relations. The principle refers to the interdependence of all factors involved. Thus,

> White prejudice and discrimination keep the Negro low in standards of living, health, education, manners and morals. This, in its turn, gives support to white prejudice. White prejudice and Negro standards thus mutually "cause" each other... If either of the factors changes, this will cause a change in the other factor, too, and start a process of interaction where the change in one factor will continuously be supported by the reaction of the other factor. The whole system will be moving in the direction of the primary change but much further. This is what we mean by cumulative causation.[19]

What this means in practice is that if prejudice and discrimination were decreased, there would probably be an increase in black standards of living. On the other hand, if prejudice or discrimination were increased, the circle would spiral downward. Similarly, a rise in black employment would raise family incomes, housing, health standards, and education. These, in turn, would improve the prospects of blacks for getting jobs and earning a living.

One interesting feature of the study is its attempt to define the term *Negro race*. Myrdal points out that Negro race in America is defined by white people, and it is defined in terms of parentage.

> *Everybody having a known trace of Negro blood in his veins—no matter how far back it was acquired—is classified as a Negro. No amount of white ancestry, except one hundred percent, will permit entrance to the white race.*[20]

Strangely enough, this definition is almost the converse of the definition used in the rest of North and South America. "In Latin America whoever is not black is white: in teutonic America whoever is not white is black." [21]

Perhaps the most widely discussed aspect of the entire work is contained largely in its Appendix 2 ("A Methodological Note of Facts and Valuations in Social Science"). Here Myrdal observes that the social scientist is very much a part of his or her culture and never succeeds in becoming completely free from its preconceptions and biases. Despite the most honest determination to be open-minded, the social scientist is inevitably influenced with respect to the objects selected for research, the data deemed to be relevant, the methods used to record and analyze the data, and the manner in which they are presented. Specifically, various social scientists show different degrees of the following qualities:

1 **Friendliness to blacks and to their interests.**

2 **Friendliness to the South. Myrdal concluded that at the time of this study, a friendly attitude toward the South generally connoted an unfavorable attitude to blacks and their concerns.**

3 **Radicalism or conservatism. Since the dominant white group is so heavily prejudiced in the conservative direction, even a radical position might fail to result in scientific objectivity. In any case, the customary opinion that a middle-of-the-road attitude results in the greatest degree of objectivity is entirely unfounded in this area.**

4 **Willingness to deal with the Black "problem" not in isolation but as an integral part of the total complex of problems in American civilization. Greater objectivity is obtained, Myrdal concludes, the more completely an investigator is able to relate problems of blacks to the total economic, social, political, judicial, and cultural life of the country.**

5 **Readiness to study unpopular subjects and state unpopular conclusions derived from studies. Especially in communities with little academic freedom, the scientist tends to adjust to the surrounding environment, avoid controversial issues and avoid making clear, blunt statements about these issues.**[22]

In perhaps his boldest conclusion, Myrdal recalls that since the days of Benjamin Franklin, American science has been characterized by a healthy trust in "hard facts." This emphasis on empirical fact-finding has been an important factor in the "magnificent" rise of American social science. But, Myrdal tells us,

> biases in social science cannot be erased simply by "keeping to the facts" and by refined methods of statistical treatment of the data. Facts, and the handling of data sometimes show themselves even more pervious to tendencies toward bias than does "pure thought"...There is no other device for excluding biases in social sciences than to face the valuations and to introduce them as explicitly stated, specific, and sufficiently concretized value premises.[23]

Durkheim, Coleman and Myrdal all were seeking underlying laws of behavior; they all sought to prevent values from biasing their research; they all tried to adapt the natural scientific method to the study of human society. It is evident, however, that Myrdal interpreted each of these tasks in a much broader way than did either Durkheim or Coleman. Thus, even within the pure science orientation, there is room for a wide range of research activities.

The Data of Social Science

For Auguste Comte and his successors, there is really no important difference between social and natural science. The method of all sciences is essentially identical, and the goal of sociology should be to emulate the rigor of the natural sciences.

As we have pointed out, however, the scientific method assumes that the "data" of science—the events and phenomena we observe—are largely independent of human will. This assumption is crucial when we seek to discover cause-and-effect relationships. Some sociologists working within the pure-science orientation believe that this assumption is not valid for sociology, and that the data of the social sciences are fundamentally different from those of the natural sciences.

It was the philosopher-historian Wilhelm Dilthey (1833–1911) who first argued that there was a fundamental difference between the two.[24] He maintained that the human or social world is a world filled with *meaning*, and that the social scientist must be concerned, not simply with causal relationships, but with meaningful relationships. For example, consider the case of a tree chopped down by a man. A physical-science explanation of the event would deal with the relation between the force of the axe as a cause and the splintering of the wood as an effect. A social-science account of the event, however, must also deal with the relationship between the intention or purpose of the woodsman and the chopping down of the tree. The act of chopping down a tree is a meaningful action for the woodsman.

Similarly, suppose someone insults me, and I slap his face. A physical-science account of the situation would be exhausted with an analysis of the relationship between the stimulus to my muscle system and the muscular response of my body. The social scientist, however, must understand the meaning of the actions. In order to be insulted, I have to understand the words of the insult and their intent. If I understood the words as a joke, I would not be insulted and probably would respond differently. In addition to understanding the insult, I also have to have some sense of what response is appropriate in the context. While a slap in the face may seem appropriate, a kick on the shin may seem ridiculous, and a knee to the groin may be viewed as vulgar or brutal. The social scientist must understand the meanings I share with others as well as those of the insulter.

Dilthey argued that the social sciences must not only observe events, but also understand them. The process for accomplishing this understanding is to relive social events by putting oneself in the place of others. He called this process *Verstehen* (understanding). Each one of us in any given society knows what it is like to be angry or happy, to exert effort to reach a goal, or even to remember. We know how a memory can produce grief or desire, and how this in turn can lead to action. We have experienced the relation between feeling anger and clenching our fists. All these shared experiences help us to understand other people. The process of *Verstehen* grows out of such shared experiences. I see a man clench his fists; I clench my fists when I am angry; therefore, this man is angry.

It was the German sociologist, Max Weber (1864–1929),who most explicitly wedded the *Verstehen* approach with sociology as a pure science.[25] Weber argued that the task of science is to tell people, not what they should do, but what they can do. He maintained that the sociologist must not permit values to influence research. Sociology must be a value-neutral science because sociology cannot discover a full understanding of the "facts" when personal values are involved. Finally, Weber argued that sociologists should incorporate a *Verstehen* approach in the scientific method. They should start with an understanding of the values of the milieux they study, and within that framework they should follow strictly "scientific" methods of inquiry.

A number of American sociologists have attempted to embody *Verstehen* approaches in their scientific investigations, and their work has given rise to an important school of thought known as *symbolic interaction*.[26] We will discuss these approaches in chapter 7. The *Verstehen* approach is, as Weber demonstrated, compatible with a pure-science orientation. So long as a sociologist thinks the task of sociology is to discover fundamental, general laws of human behavior rather than immediate solutions to practical problems, so long as he views the appropriate means for such a task as *the* "scientific method" (with or without the *Verstehen* approach), and sees the implementation of research as value neutral or objective, then we say that such a sociologist works within the pure-science orientation.

Poverty and Pure Science

We can now return to the question with which we began this chapter. How could a sociologist working within the pure-science orientation analyze the problem of poverty? One answer is that such a sociologist might not even try to analyze a problem like poverty. Indeed, very few "pure scientists" participated in the War on Poverty, and very little of the voluminous writing about the causes of and solutions to poverty can be identified as a pure-science approach.

The reasons for this should be clear from what we have said. Poverty is usually treated as an immediate and pressing problem requiring practical solutions. As such, it does not lend itself to disinterested study. It involves hunger and suffering, and it is not easy to take a detached view of such very real emotions.

To the extent that pure scientists are concerned with poverty, they are likely to try to understand why poverty has been so constant and pervasive throughout human history. They might ask whether inequality is a basic feature of human society, leading to wealth at one extreme and poverty at the other.

Thus, for a social scientist like Oscar Ornati, reporting on research conducted with a pure-science orientation, poverty can be defined variously as subjective, objective, or relative.[27] It may also involve insufficiency, inequality, or both. Subjective poverty refers to whether a person feels rich or poor in terms of the goods and services he might reasonably expect to have. A hundred years ago, for example, people did not feel deprived if they did not have electric lights in their home. Today it is a necessity even for the poor.

Ornati tells us that poverty can be measured from an objective point of view by examining the quantity of necessities a given income can buy. But then another question arises: to what extent are persons of a given income level sharing reasonably well in the goods and services currently available in America? This is a question of relative poverty. It is possible to be poor because one has a significantly less than proportionate share of the food, clothing, housing, and medical services that are available .

Ornati notes that not even the physical sciences are of much help in defining insufficiency. No one states with absolute scientific assurance what the daily requirements are for protein, calcium, iron, or vitamins. In addition, of course, people have great differences in their ideas about what constitutes need. (To measure this difference objectively, one might prepare an estimate of what some friend or neighbor needs to get along and then compare this with the neighbor's own estimate of his needs.)

To confirm the existence of inequality, Ornati says, it is sufficient to note that the lowest 20 percent of the population gets only about 5 percent of the national income. He feels that some such inequity will always exist, whether the lowest 20 percent gets 5 or 4 or 6 percent, or some other amount. From his perspective, however, poverty could be eliminated if the income of every family in the bottom 20 percent of the population were raised to the level of standards currently regarded as minimal. Ultimately,

> whether those at the bottom of the income distribution are or are not poor depends on whether their income level is or is not, by objective standards, sufficient to cover their needs ....one can deal only with objective changes in income standards; the subjective impact of changes in income standards is beyond this study.[28]

Summary

Sociologists seek scientific explanations, rather than commonsense ones. As developed in the natural sciences, "science" is the study of those judgments concerning which universal agreements can be obtained. The possibility of such a science is based on the assumption that events occur independently of our own will or volition, and that others will therefore agree with our perceptions of such events. The natural-scientific method involves the search for invariable relations among events—relations that can be expressed as laws about which universal agreement can be obtained. These laws can be explained by theories.

The pure-science orientation in sociology began with positivism which was an attempt to use the natural-scientific method to study society and human behavior. It is called "pure" science because it seeks to discover basic causes and general laws of human behavior, rather than practical solutions to immediate problems. Pure scientists also attempt to be value free—to make certain that their own personal values do not in any way influence their scientific research.

Some sociologists working in the pure-science orientation believe that human behavior is not independent of the will of human beings, and that the natural-scientific method must therefore be altered for the social sciences.

They argue that human behavior is meaningful to people, and that the sociologists must not only observe behavior, but must also understand the meaning of the behavior to the actors. This approach is called *Verstehen* and it can be used to modify the natural-scientific method.

For
Further
Study

George Lundberg's *Can Science Save Us?* (New York: David McKay, revised edition 1961) has become virtually the Bible of pure sociology. It is available as a little paperback, 4th ed. (New York: Harper, 1968), very clearly written. The introductory text, *Sociology* which Lundberg co-authored with Clarence Schrag, Otto N. Larsen, and William R. Catton, Jr., has been through several editions and is a thoroughly competent and authoritative presentation of introductory sociology as seen from this perspective.

For a discussion of the dilemmas with which pure scientists in all disciplines are confronted, see Daniel S. Greenberg, *The Politics of Pure Science* (New York: New American Library, 1967). The author of this volume was news editor of *Science*, the weekly magazine of the American Association for the Advancement of Science. For interesting accounts of scientists who resist discoveries in scientific research, see Thomas Kuhn, "The Functions of Dogma in Scientific Research" in *Scientific Change*, A. C. Crombie, ed. (New York: Basic Books, 1963), pp. 347–469, and Bernard Barber, "Resistance by Scientists to Scientific Discovery," *Science*, 134 (Sept. 1, 1961): 596–602.

Critiques of Durkheim's *Suicide* can be found in Jack P. Gibbs, "Suicide," in ed. Robert K. Merton, and Robert Nisbet, *Contemporary Social Problems*, rev. ed., (New York: Harcourt, 1971); Jerry Jacobs, "The Use of Religion in Constructing the Moral Justification of Suicide," in *Deviance and Respectability*, ed. Jack Douglas, (New York: Basic Books, 1970).

For another classic study of adolescent behavior, see Edgar Z. Friedenberg, *Coming of Age in America: Growth and Acquiescence* (New York: Vintage, 1965). Friedenberg found that nonconformity was the least popular value among the students he studied. He suggests this is due to the task assumed by schools—to prepare students for a bureaucratic society that is suspicious of nonconforming behavior.

Gunnar Myrdal's *An American Dilemma: The Negro Problem and Modern Democracy* (New York: Harper, 1962) has been attacked for suggesting that the "Negro problem" is a moral rather than an economic one. See Herbert Aptheker, *The Negro People in America: A Critique of Gunnar Myrdal's "An American Dilemma"* (New York: International Publishers, 1946).

Aptheker insists that the oppression and superexploitation of American blacks, and the prejudice associated with these practices, exist and are maintained because they are useful to the properties interests in this country.

For a more complete discussion of symbolic interaction and other phenomenological or subjective orientations, see chapter 7 of this book.

Notes

1 Kimball Young and Raymond W. Mack, *Systematic Sociology: Text and Readings* (New York: American Book Co., 1962), p. 6.

2 For a detailed discussion of the origins, assumptions, and method of the natural sciences, *see* Alfred North Whitehead, *Science and the Modern World* (New York: Macmillan, Co., 1925); see also Norman Campbell, *What is Science?* (New York: Dover, 1952).

3 *See* Campbell, *What is Science?* p. 26.

4 Auguste Comte, *The Positive Philosophy,* translated and ed. Harriet Martineau (New York: Reproduction of 1855 edn. AMS Press Inc.).

5 *See,* for example, George A. Lundberg, *Can Science Save Us?* (New York: David McKay Co., 2nd ed., 1967); see also George A. Lundberg, Clarence E. Schrag, Otto N. Larsen, William R. Catton, Jr., *Sociology,* 4th ed. (New York: Harper, 1968).

6 Campbell, *What is Science?* p. 4.

7 Lundberg, *Can Science Save Us?* p. 143.

8 Emile Durkheim, *The Rules of Sociological Method,* trans. Sarah A. Solovay and John H. Mueller (Chicago: University of Chicago Press, 1938), p. 3.

9 Emile Durkheim, *Suicide,* trans. J. A. Spaulding and G. Simpson (Glencoe, Ill., Free Press, 1951).

10 Ibid., p. 44.

11 Ibid., p. 299.

12 Durkheim, *The Rules of Sociological Method,* pp. 54–55.

13 James S. Coleman, *The Adolescent Society* (New York: Free Press, 1961).

14 *See* James Coleman, "Research Chronicle: The Adolescent Society," in *Sociologists at Work,* ed. Phillip E. Hammond (New York: Basic Books, 1964), pp. 198–202.

15 F. P. Keppel, Forward to *An American Dilemma: The Negro Problem and Modern Democracy,* 20th anniversary ed. by Gunnar Myrdal (New York: Harper, 1962), p. xlvii.

16 Myrdal, *An American Dilemma,* p. li.

17 Ibid., p. 4.

18 Ibid., p. 23.

19 Ibid., pp. 75–76.

20 Ibid., p. 113.

21 Ibid., p. 113.

22 *See* Myrdal, *An American Dilemma,* pp. 1035–40.

23 Ibid., pp. 1041, 1043.

24 *See,* for example, Wilhelm Dilthey, *Pattern and Meaning in History: Thoughts on History and Society,* ed. H. P. Rickman (New York: Harper, 1962).

25 *See,* for example, Max Weber, "Science as a Vocation," in *From Max Weber: Essays in Sociology,* ed. Hans Gerth and C. Wright Mills (New York: Oxford University Press, 1958).

26 *See,* for example, Marcello Truzzi, ed., *Verstehen: Subjective Understanding in the Social Sciences* (Reading, Mass.: Addison-Wesley, 1974).

27 Oscar Ornati, *Poverty amid Affluence: A Report of a Research Project Carried Out at the New School for Social Research* (New York: Twentieth Century Fund, 1966), pp. 1–3, 7, 16, 120–21. Excerpted in Helen Ginsburg, ed., *Poverty, Economics and Society* (Boston: Little, Brown & Co., 1972), pp. 140–43.

28 Ginsburg, *Poverty, Economics and Society,* p. 143.

Sociology as an Applied Science

If sociologists working as pure scientists have written little on the problem of poverty, other sociologists have devoted a great deal of attention to the subject. While the problem of finding an acceptable definition of poverty is a major obstacle to developing long-term solutions, many sociologists argue that the really important fact is that society defines some people as poor. The poor emerge when society elects to recognize poverty as a special status and assigns specific persons to that category. The fact that some people may privately consider themselves poor is sociologically irrelevant. What is sociologically relevant is poverty as a socially recognized condition, as a social status. [1]

Government agencies, private organizations, and other groups have defined some people as poor and have developed programs to alleviate or cure the conditions of these people. The energy and resources available for attacking poverty can thus be applied efficiently and successfully, rather than wasted on the wrong targets, it is claimed. Lewis Coser has pointed out, however, that the approach of providing public assistance for people defined as poor has some negative consequences.

> Social workers, welfare investigators, welfare administrators and local volunteer workers seek out the poor in order to help them, and yet, paradoxically, they are the very agents of their degradation ... The help rendered may be given from the purest and most benevolent of motives, yet the very fact of being helped degrades.[2]

Coser suggests that it is necessary to eliminate the stigma of assistance, and that a guaranteed minimum income would be a first step in this direction. If everyone were entitled to an income sufficient to avoid poverty, then the poor would not stand out as a special group that received aid. This, in turn, would eliminate the sense of degradation the poor experience. We might note, however, that some forms of assistance, such as lucrative contracts, honoraria, or grants, are not seen as degrading even when they are payments for unnecessary services or simply thinly disguised gratuities. Something more than the bare fact of assistance seems to be involved in social and individual attitudes toward poverty.

While other sociologists may disagree with Coser about the specific causes of and solutions to poverty, many of them would agree that poverty is the kind of problem that sociologists should study. They think that sociology should try, not only to discover general laws of human behavior, but also to improve society by finding solutions to the practical problems that confront us every day. While they would agree with the pure scientist's insistence that personal values should not be allowed to distort research, they would also maintain that values can, and should, guide the selection of problems to be studied. The overriding objective in selecting problems must be not simply knowledge, but relevant knowledge. Those who work within such an orientation believe that sociology must be an applied science.

Applied Science Versus Pure Science

The natural sciences have always recognized a distinction between pure and applied science, and have recognized both activities as legitimate.[3] While the scientist's motivation may be primarily the desire to discover new laws and develop new theories, it is the practical applications of scientific laws and theories that have led to the growth of popular interest in scientific research. Einstein developed the theory of relativity as a work of pure science, but the development of atomic energy resulted from the application of one of the laws contained in that theory. Newton proposed the laws of motion as a work of pure science, but the development of piston engines resulted from the application of those laws. Scientific knowledge can also develop in the opposite direction. The attempt to apply the theories of relativity and quantum mechanics to develop atomic energy, for example, has led to many unexpected discoveries that have forced new examinations in pure science. Indeed, there seems to be a constant race between those attempting to apply the work of pure scientists to practical problems, and those attempting to explain the unexpected results of such applications in terms of their significance for pure science.

Thus, in the natural sciences, pure and applied science have been seen as two sides of the same coin. Progress in either aspect often leads to new developments in the other. At the same time, natural scientists have recognized that applied science poses different questions than does pure science. Whenever we become concerned with *acting* to solve practical problems, we are confronted with two issues: (1) We have to decide the *end* of our action—the results we want to obtain; and (2) we have to discover the right *means* to that end—the action that will produce the desired result. From this perspective, applied science is a way of answering the second question. It can tell us whether or not a particular action will produce a particular end. It does so by applying scientific laws to specific problems through the scientific method. Applied science, it is felt, cannot answer the first question. It cannot tell us whether or not an end is desirable. The answer to that question depends on our values, not on science. Applied science can tell us how to build atomic bombs or nuclear reactors, but it cannot tell us whether building atomic bombs is more desirable than building atomic reactors. In the natural sciences, then, applied science has traditionally been the discipline that can tell us what can be, but not what ought to be.

Applied Science and Social Science

The first explicit attempt to distinguish between pure and applied efforts in the social sciences was made by an American sociologist, named Lester Ward (1841–1913).[4] Before Ward, prevalent thinking in social science held that man should not interfere with nature by attempting to change society. Influenced by Charles Darwin's view of nature as a struggle for survival of the fittest, most social scientists believed that interference with the natural course of events was not only ineffectual, but even dangerous. They subscribed to a doctrine of laissez-faire—the belief that the interests of individuals and society coincide, and that individuals should be allowed complete freedom to pursue their own self-interests. Attempts to control behavior, since they interfered with this natural competition among individuals, were harmful.

Ward saw a fundamental inconsistency in the laissez-faire position. If its adherents had simply tried to prove that specific efforts to improve social conditions were ineffective, such a position would have forced advocates of social intervention to prove that their efforts were successful. But the advocates of laissez-faire insisted that such efforts were actively harmful. Ward argued that this meant that social intervention had *some* effect. He maintained that man is different from other animals because man is capable of understanding and controlling nature, and he concluded that "those who can see a surplus of good in things as they are, or can hope for their improvement under the laws of evolution unaided by social intelligence must be set down as hopelessly blinded by the great optimistic illusion of all life." [5]

Ward believed that law, marriage, religion, and other social institutions are means devised by human beings to improve their adaptive capacities to nature. At the same time, he felt that these institutions have developed largely unconsciously, as people have sought more efficient means of pursuing their interests. The time had come, he thought, to become conscious of these institutions and to seek deliberate change toward desired goals. To accomplish this, Ward envisioned two branches of sociology—pure sociology, oriented toward knowledge for its own sake; and applied sociology, oriented toward applying knowledge for the betterment of society.

Sociological knowledge, in Ward's view, should be used to organize society in such a way that all individuals could realize their full potential. His view of applied sociology, however, differed in one important respect from the view of applied science in the natural sciences. Ward thought that applied sociology should be concerned with what ought to be. Indeed, the ideal society would be governed by persons versed in the scientific study of society, since applied science could determine desirable ends. Pure sociology has no concern with what society *ought* to be, or with any social ideals. It confines itself strictly to the present and the past, allowing the future to take care of itself.[6]

Thus, Ward did not see a distinction between means and ends. Values were not outside the scientific method, but implicit in the method. Individuals were the building blocks of society, and whatever fostered their development and collective progress was good.

In the early decades of this century, applied sociology began to grow and spread. Most of the early efforts centered about the work place, with attempts to restructure both the structural and the human aspects of industrial organization. The "scientific management" approach, pioneered by Frederick Taylor, was an effort to standardize the production process.[7] Taylor argued that the most efficient way of performing a job was by subdividing it into the smallest possible units of time and motion. Instead of workers being craftsmen who produced entire products, each worker should perform a specialized task which, together with the work of other specialists, would add up to a finished product. The most dramatic example of this application of scientific techniques was the creation of the automobile assembly line.

One weakness of the scientific management approach was that it did not take into account human factors. It treated all individuals as essentially alike, and did not consider that some people might be better at particular jobs than others. To remedy this deficiency, another attempt at applied social science, called "industrial psychology" emerged. The purpose of this effort was to identify, "those personalities which by their mental qualities are especially fit for a particular kind of economic work." [8]

The early industrial psychologists, like many of their contemporary followers, believed that their task was to develop tests for predicting behavior and performance, without making any judgments about whether a job or operation was good or bad. The role of the scientist, for them, was to develop means but not to judge the ends served by those means. They thus returned to a pure-science orientation, distinct from the value-laden perspective of Ward. Science, in their view, is value-neutral, and the scientist is like a technician whose method can be used for evil or for good. Out of the work of the industrial psychologists came the personnel tests and intelligence tests that play so central a part in education and business today.

Still another early attempt at applied sociology grew out of experiments designed to discover ways of increasing the productivity of workers. The results of these experiments suggested that workers who feel they are treated as individuals rather than as objects are more likely to increase their productivity. The experiments also indicated that the informal groups that develop among workers on the job are crucial factors in determining productivity. These findings gave rise to an approach known as "managerial sociology," which stresses the importance of maintaining warm human relations in work settings and seeks to advise managers on ways of doing it.

By the 1930s, applied social science had become a major element in the development of scientific studies of society, and it represented a real challenge to the predominance of the pure-science approach. Shortly before World War II, sociologist Robert S. Lynd articulated the concerns of some applied sociologists in a little book called, *Knowledge for What? The Place of Social Science in American Culture.*[9] Lynd began by arguing that contemporary social science had developed two different orientations that had the effect of dividing its workers into two types—scholars and technicians.

The scholarly bloc, said Lynd, works in a world in which time moves very slowly. The scholars value "impersonal objectivity," and "aloofness from the strife of rival values", and have an intrinsic faith that knowledge is desirable for its own sake. In short, Lynd's scholar is one who works within the pure-science orientation. The technician, on the other hand, works for the practical man of affairs, in whose world time moves very quickly. The technician is not concerned with the distant past or the far future, but with the here-and-now. The characteristic attitude of this worker is, "do this, fix this, immediately."

Although it had generally been thought that these two blocs could exist independently of one another, and that they complemented each other, Lynd argued that the scholar is in great danger of lecturing on navigation while the ship goes down. The economic depression of the 1930s reversed the relative importance of the physical and social sciences, he maintained. The American dream had been spoiled because of the difficulties of dealing with human problems, rather than because of technological limitations. The challenge of the social sciences, he claimed, was to deal with these human factors.

The problem was that the scholars had collected the wrong kinds of data, according to Lynd. We had data on labor problems, but not the data needed to provide an effective program to relieve unemployment. We had legal data, but not the kind of data that could allow us to curb increasing lawlessness. We had data on business cycles, but we were not able to predict the Great Depression of 1929, even six months before it occurred. The data we had were relevant to the wrong problems. They were descriptive data, rather than "projective and predictive in the sense of being aimed at deliberate planning and control."

Because the problems of contemporary society had become so urgent, Lynd continued, it was not possible to follow the leisurely time frame of the scholar and wait until all the data were in before recommending action. In the interim, decisions would be made by "practical" persons and "hardhead-ed" politicians. These decisions would be made in response to pressure from interest groups, rather than on the basis of a scientific analysis of the problems, yet they would affect everyone in society.

In the modern world, according to Lynd, the social scientist is the equiva-lent of the person of learning. Unlike the role of learned persons in earlier times, however, the social scientist's task is not to help stabilize existing social practices and forms of social organization, but to analyze the processes of social change. The role of social sciences is to "be troublesome, to disconcert the habitual arrangements by which we manage to live along and to demon-strate the possibilities of change in more adequate directions."

The problem with most contemporary social science, he said, is that it is neither as neutral nor as "pure" as it has pretended to be. It has avoided the troublesome issues, and allowed the dominant biases in society to set the definition of the problems it studied. To the extent that it tried to improve conditions, it tended to focus on trivia by proceeding in a "general spirit of modest meliorism, seeking to make small changes for the better in various institutions to which it applies itself."

Lynd maintained that the outstanding characteristic of a *truly* well-trained scientist is the ability to distinguish significant from insignificant problems and data. Research without an active point of view becomes

> the ditty bag of an idiot, filled with bits of pebbles, straws, feathers, and other random hoardings. If nobody goes about endlessly counting throughout a lifetime the number of particles of sand along infinite miles of seashore over all the coasts of the world, why is this? Because there is no point to it, no need to complete this particular aspect of the jigsaw puzzle of the unknown.[10]

Thus, Lynd disagreed with the view of the industrial psychologists and managerial sociologists about the value-neutral role of applied scientists. He argued that it is both necessary and proper to apply values in deciding what is and what is not a significant or important problem for research. Values should not be allowed to bias the findings of research, but they are essential in formulating the problem to be studied. For social scientists to boast that they are not interested in what ought to be usually means that they have accepted the existing state of things as desirable.

The development of new techniques of quantitative measurement and the growth of applied research had led, Lynd argued, to an overemphasis on describing the current state of affairs. To the extent that sociologists were not content with such a passive role, they had become involved in slum clearance projects or other programs aimed at making slight improvements in existing conditions. What was needed, however, was an attempt to make long-term changes instead of short-range improvements.

This disagreement among applied sociologists over the role and place of values in the research process continues to the present day. While applied sociologists share a commitment to solving practical problems rather than pursuing "idle" curiosity (by which they mean pure science), they disagree about the way to apply the scientific method to practical problems.

Engineering Versus Clinical Approaches

Alvin W. Gouldner refers to this disagreement as reflecting the "engineering" versus the "clinical" approaches to applied sociology.[11] The "engineers" are those who adopt their client's definition of the problem and concentrate on providing solutions to the problem as defined. The "clinicians" view the client's definition as one of a number of symptoms to be taken into account in making their own diagnosis of the problem.

The Engineering Approach

Suppose that an industrial firm asks a management consulting organization to conduct a survey of employee attitudes because the firm wants to know whether its workers are satisfied with existing working conditions, hours, wages, and supervision. The consulting organization may agree to conduct the survey exactly as requested and prepare a report indicating the percentage of employees who are satisfied with their conditions. The report may contain some recommendations for changes in the firm's labor relations policies, and the consultants may meet with representatives of management to discuss the implications of their findings. Such a procedure represents an extreme example of the engineering approach to applied sociology, and it has been a very common practice since the 1930s.

In this example, the consulting engineer has allowed the client to define the nature and scope of the task. The applied sociologist does not ask why the firm requested the survey, what problems may have led the firm's management to feel a survey was needed, or whether those problems will continue to exist after the report is completed. The sociologist functions chiefly as a technician, employing scientific methods to achieve ends defined by the firm's management.

The danger with such an approach is that the request for a survey may reflect some deeper problem in the firm. Gouldner noted for the example given, that the network of informal communication between management and employees might have broken down, and the survey might serve as a substitute channel of communications. The survey itself would not tell the firm anything about the underlying problem of communication breakdown, and might even preserve the very tensions that made it necessary. Or it might be the case that the firm's management was having trouble with a union and ordered the survey to show that management was "on top" of employee concerns. In this case, the survey represents "scientific" information that management could use to support its position.

In any event, the applied scientist as engineer does not treat the formulation of the problem as a focus for research, but acts only as a technical extension of the client. Conventional engineers and physical scientists have usually taken this approach for granted. They try to minimize costs while performing services that meet minimum specifications, and then move on to another contract. For many physical scientists, a day of moral awakening occurred with the first use of the atomic bomb during World War II. There were worldwide denunciations of the scientists and the engineers who had worked on the development of the bomb, even by many persons who were completely sympathetic to the aims of the United States and its allies. These denunciations were not unlike those directed at the scientists who helped the Hitler regime devise more effective means for killing millions of Jews during the same era. To offer a counter-argument to the effect that the atomic bomb may have shortened the war is to accept values as relevant to the research task, and this constitutes a historic departure from conventional practice in the physical sciences.

The day of awakening for social scientists may have occurred in 1965 as a consequence of Project Camelot. This was a research project formulated by the Special Operations Research Office (SORO), a nonprofit "think tank" supported by the United States Army, much as the RAND corporation was supported by the United States Air Force, and the Franklin Institute was supported by the United States Navy. A description of the proposed research project was mailed to outstanding scholars around the world. It read, in part, as follows:

Project Camelot is a study whose objective is to determine the feasibility of developing a general social systems model which would make it possible to predict and influence politically significant aspects of social change in the developing nations of the world. Somewhat more specifically, its objectives are

First, to devise procedures for assessing the potential for internal war within national societies; second, to identify with increased degrees of confidence, those actions which a government might take to relieve conditions which are assessed as giving rise to a potential for internal war; and finally, to assess the feasibility of prescribing the characteristics of a system for obtaining and using the essential information needed for doing the above two things. The project is conceived as a three to four year effort to be funded at around one and one-half million dollars annually. It is supported by the Army and the Department of Defense, and will be conducted with the cooperation of other agencies of the government . . . [12]

For an engineer or physical scientist, the language in this document is familiar. Six million dollars for a feasibility study is certainly not excessive. In fact, it is probably miniscule when compared with the costs of feasibility studies for various kinds of military systems, such as fighter aircraft or intercontinental ballistic missiles. What do all the words add up to? For a general, they might mean a large operations room filled with computer consoles on which one could summon displays of the current "fever" chart for every country in the world. Why? "Well sir," the general might say, "it's my job to be prepared with whatever mission my commander-in-chief may assign me at any point on earth. It would be helpful if I could predict a revolution in Vietnam or Angola or somewhere in the Mideast six months or a year before it happened. I need to know where unrest is likely to occur, how it will affect the U.S. Army, and what I can do about it."

For a social scientist, such a study could mean the opportunity to work on a pure research project in the field of social change. Research funds for this kind of activity are not readily available, and it was obvious that nothing of an applied nature would be forthcoming without a considerable preliminary pure research effort. To another social scientist, it might mean the possibility of making known to the American public the precise nature of conditions in third world countries that give rise to the felt need for violent overthrow of existing governments. The role of the United States government in these situations is characteristically based on secret evaluations made by the Central Intelligence Agency or other intelligence sources. Nonsecret social science research could help open these issues for public discussion. For policy makers committed to secrecy in foreign policy, the prospect of an in-depth, open scrutiny of social conditions throughout the world and a public review of recommendations made for United States government intervention was a terrifying one.

Project Camelot was terminated by presidential order before it had really begun. Rivalry between bureaucrats in the State Department and the Department of Defense over control of funds for the research (a rivalry that may have been encouraged by bureaucrats in other agencies who felt threatened by the research) fueled potential misunderstandings to an explosive point.

For Latin Americans and for others around the world who knew the facts about the clandestine intervention of American government and industrial agencies in the domestic affairs of Third World countries, Project Camelot seemed to be simply a clumsy effort in the same tradition. For liberal social scientists, who deplored the military activities of the United States government, research for the United States Army was ethically wrong, although working for an agency such as the Department of Health, Education, and Welfare would be acceptable. Some conservative social scientists could accept the pure research aspects of Project Camelot, but would have preferred that it be financed by an agency such as the National Science Foundation or the National Academy of Sciences. Others approved the idea that it would help the American military effort. Still others preferred that significant policy issues of this sort be based on information and recommendations made by agencies like the Central Intelligence Agency.

As Irving Louis Horowitz has noted, "The problem of the relationship between pure and applied social science" was centrally involved in the Project Camelot matter— specifically, the matter of determining the "precise character of social science values in a context of extreme political and professional tensions."[13] In any event, since Project Camelot it has become clear to many sociologists that exclusive reliance on a traditional engineering approach in applied sociology is neither possible nor desirable.

The Clinical Approach

In the clinical approach to applied sociology, the sociologist adopts a broader interpretation of the task. Take, for example, the case of a hospital administrator, who notes that employee turnover in his organization is very high and that there seems to be continual friction among employees, along with a variety of other personnel problems.[14] The administrator hires a consultant firm and asks them to design a supervisory training program to deal with these problems.

After a long discussion with the administrator, the consultants feel that a training program is premature and recommend that they be allowed to study the situation. They give a personality test to the administrator, interview all the department heads, and observe the administrator as he works with other people. They conclude that some of the difficulties are due to the administrator's own behavior and make recommendations to him for changes. His handling of problem situations improves, and he develops ways of fostering cooperation among employees. He never returns to the idea of a formal training program.

A classic example of the clinical approach, one that also made contributions to pure science, resulted from a series of experiments at the Hawthorne plant of Western Electric Company in the 1920s.[15] The initial purpose of the experiments was to test the idea that the physical conditions of work, such as adequate lighting, were important in determining the happiness and productivity of workers. Two groups of workers were put into identical rooms, except that in one of the rooms the amount of light could be increased or decreased. The experimenters found that, as they had expected, productivity increased when the amount of light was increased. They discovered, however, that productivity also increased in the control group. And, much to their surprise, they discovered that productivity also increased when the amount of light was decreased.

To further investigate these surprising findings, additional experiments were conducted, using more sophisticated controls and observation techniques. The investigators eventually concluded that it was the structure of the groups of people that influenced the behavior of individual members. The experimenters had unwittingly converted a collection of individual workers into a group that was conscious of its common features. A whole series of formal and informal relationships developed within this group and served to set standards for performance and productivity. As a result of the Hawthorne experiments, a whole new area of applied sociology developed to help managers deal with informal groups at the work place. More important, in terms of pure science certain laws of group behavior were proposed, laws that stimulated new theories and experiments in the decades to come.

Social Problems and Applied Science

The differences between the engineering and clinical approaches to applied sociology may seem to involve only an ethical issue concerning the proper relationship between a sociologist and a client. In fact, however, these differences point up a fundamental conceptual problem confronting applied science—that of defining a social problem. To the engineer, a social problem is whatever the client thinks it is. To the clinician, a social problem may exist without the client's awareness. The same issue confronts all of us in everyday life.

If I lose my job, I have a problem. If you lose your job, you have a problem. At what point does unemployment become a social problem? If I have friends over for dinner and the room becomes filled with smoke, I may go outside to get some fresh air, only to discover that my eyes begin to smart from pollutants. At what point does air pollution become a social problem? If I have married friends who get divorced, they and their families have a problem. At what point does the divorce rate become a social problem?

One apparently simple formulation defines a social problem as an objective condition in society, viewed by some members of society as a problem.[16] It turns out, however, that it is very hard to justify such a definition. What, for example, is an "objective condition"?

Suppose that, for some unknown reason, the sex ratio at birth of males and females suddenly changed, and the proportion of females in the population increased sharply. Given these objective conditions, would a social problem occur? The proportion of unmarried women might increase in a way that would threaten traditional patterns of courtship and marriage. If some jobs continued to be viewed as women's work, and others as men's work, there might be too few men for male jobs and too many women for female jobs. Women might enter male occupations and encounter resistance from men. There might be serious strains on family life and mental health, as both men and women began to raise questions about what it means to be a man or be a woman. There might even be serious disruptions of political life, as the sexual makeup of the voting population changed.

All of these are possible social problems that would develop as a result of a change in objective conditions. But the change in the sex ratio would not, in itself, constitute a social problem. If people in society were flexible in their occupational, marital, and courtship practices, they might simply adapt their behavior to deal with the new conditions.

But adaptive behavior may not really solve anything. When I go outside after a dinner party and find my eyes beginning to smart, suppose I put on a gas mask. My eyes no longer smart, and I have adapted to "society as it is." Or have I? I do not enjoy the necessity of wearing a gas mask, and I may discover that many others feel the same way. I've adapted, but the social problem remains.

Because of the difficulty in finding an acceptable objective definition of social problems, many sociologists prefer a more subjective definition. They suggest that any condition defined by significant groups in society as a deviation from standards the group feels are crucial constitutes a social problem—at least for that group. Since different groups may define different conditions as social problems, however, the applied sociologist cannot escape the necessity of using values to select the problem to be studied.

Sociology as an Applied Science

From Lester Ward to Robert Lynd, there have always been important sociologists who believed that sociology should not restrict its task to the search for general laws of human behavior, but should try to solve the immediate problems confronting all societies. As is the case in the natural sciences, sociology has always included both pure scientists and applied scientists. While both orientations share a commitment to using the scientific method developed in the natural sciences to accomplish their tasks, pure scientists have tended to focus their research on the nature and sources of social order, while applied scientists have tended to focus on the forces that disrupt and threaten social order. (See Table One in chapter 4 for a comparison of pure, applied, and critical science.)

The sharpest disagreements between pure and applied sociologists have concerned the role of values in sociological research. The pure scientists have argued that sociology should be value neutral, and that the motivation for research should be the desire for basic knowledge, not the values of a particular sociologist. They argue that, since science studies those events about which universal agreement can be obtained, and since there will always be disagreements about values, value choices can never be included in the process of scientific inquiry.

Applied sociologists maintain that such a view implicitly accepts the value of existing social arrangements. Scientific knowledge, they say, can be used for good or evil, and each sociologist must allow personal values to influence the choice of problems to be studied and the kind of client to be served. However, applied sociologists differ about whether to allow the client to define the problem (the engineering approach), or to treat the client's definition as only part of the underlying problem (the clinical approach). In any case, both the choice of a client and the definition of a social problem require that applied sociologists make value choices.

While these differences between the pure-science and applied-science orientations are important, the shared commitment of these two approaches to the scientific method developed in the natural sciences, and their underlying view of the desirability of social order, limits the extent of their disagreement. There are other sociologists who reject both of these emphases (see chapter 4), and who are sharply critical of the attempt by both orientations to predict and control human behavior. C. Wright Mills summed up this criticism in a stinging attack on both orientations:

> Among the slogans used by a variety of schools of social science, none is so frequent as, "The purpose of social science is the prediction and control of human behavior." Nowadays . . . we also hear much about "human engineering"—an undefined phrase often mistaken for a clear and obvious goal. It is believed to be clear and obvious because it rests upon an unquestioned analogy between "the mastery of nature" and "the mastery of society." Those who habitually use such phrases are very likely to be among those who are most passionately concerned to "make the social studies into real sciences," and conceive of their own work as politically neutral and morally irrelevant. . . . They are, they suppose, out to do with society what they suppose physicists have done with nature. Their political philosophy is contained in the simple view that if only The Methods of Science, by which man has now come to control the atom, were employed to "control social behavior," the problems of mankind would soon be solved. . . .
>
> The use of such phrases reveals a rationalistic and empty optimism which rests upon an ignorance of the several possible roles of reason in human affairs, the nature of power and its relations to knowledge, the meaning of moral action and the place of knowledge within it, the nature of history and the fact that men are not only creatures of history but on occasion creators within it and even of it.[17]

Applied Sociology and Social Policy

The difficulties and ambiguities that confront sociologists when they try to define and analyze social problems can have serious consequences. Social scientists are increasingly asked to provide solutions to social problems, both by government and by private industry. Sometimes, very costly programs are based on sociological findings that are, at best, of questionable value. Daniel Patrick Moynihan, a social scientist who has served as assistant to the president for urban affairs, ambassador to India, and ambassador to the United Nations, has examined the history of the Economic Opportunity Act of 1964.[18] Moynihan argues that the requirement of the act that there be "maximum feasible participation" by the poor in planning and conducting antipoverty programs was a colossal mistake undermining the entire program. This requirement resulted from social science research of a dubious nature, according to Moynihan.

Many other sociologists disagree with Moynihan about the reasons for the failure of the War on Poverty, but all of them agree that the programs failed to eliminate poverty. It was a very expensive failure, and, as a result, many applied sociologists have become wary of providing solutions to social problems. In a new variation of the engineering approach to applied sociology, they hold that social science should not try to formulate social policy, but should restrict itself to measuring the results of social policy and social trends. Thus, the sociologist is again seen as a technician providing scientific advice to a client. The value dilemma is resolved by allowing society—that is, government officials and agencies—to define the nature of social problems and to develop solutions. The role of the social scientist is to inform society about whether or not the solutions work. This new approach has resulted in three main types of research—social indicators research, PPBS research, and evaluation research.

Social Indicators

Most governments have comprehensive sets of economic indicators, watched closely by both government officials and private citizens. These include statistics on national income, employment, unemployment, and wholesale and retail prices. These economic indicators do not, however, allow us to answer such questions as, Are we getting healthier? Is pollution increasing? Do children learn more than they used to? Is crime increasing? Social indicators are designed to give us answers to such questions. They are

> statistics, statistical series, and other forms of evidence that enable us to assess where we stand and where we are going with respect to our values and goals, and to evaluate specific programs and determine their impacts.[19]

The important element in developing social indicators is having comparable statistics over a long period of time, so that we can determine the direction of change. Thus, simple statistics on the number of physicians, policemen, or teachers are not social indicators, but statistics on health or crime rates are social indicators. In other words, social indicators must allow us to determine whether things are getting better or worse. Applied sociologists have begun to develop social indicators in such diverse fields as education, technology, the family, religion, leisure, health, social stratification, and social welfare.[20]

PPBS

The Planning-Programming-Budgeting System (PPBS) has been described as "a framework for planning a way of organizing information and analysis in a systematic fashion so that the consequences of particular choices can be seen as clearly as possible."[21]

PPBS was originally developed for the Department of Defense where it was used to assess the relative cost and efficiency of alternate weapons systems. From a military perspective, the problem was how to get "the biggest bang for a buck." It was introduced in all federal departments in 1965. The technique is designed to accomplish three main tasks:

1 To display information about the operation of existing government programs in such a way that it is possible to tell how much is being spent for various purposes and what is being accomplished through those programs.

2 To analyze the costs of alternate methods of achieving objectives, so that it is possible to rank each of the alternatives in terms of their cost.

3 To evaluate the benefits of achieving various objectives in comprehensive and quantitative terms, so that it will be easier to set priorities among objectives.[22]

PPBS has been applied to government planning with regard to education policy.[23] The educational level of the population may be raised by a variety of methods, including research and development in education, improvements in professional staff and administration, the addition of new equipment, the reorganization of instruction, adult retraining, education at home, and other alternatives. Each of these, in turn, can be achieved by various means. Improvements in professional staff, for example, can be made by raising standards for hiring, by retraining existing staff, by improving graduate programs, or by some combination of these. After identifying alternative possibilities, PPBS then estimates the cost and effectiveness of each alternative in order to develop a combination of alternatives that maximizes effectiveness and minimizes costs.

Evaluation Research

While PPBS focuses on planning before taking action, evaluation research is aimed at providing information about the results of social action. It is seen as a resource that can be used to modify programs and increase the likelihood that long-range goals will be reached.[24] The federal government now requires all government agencies to allocate a specific portion of all program budgets for evaluation of the program by an outside source.

One reason for insisting on independent evaluations is that evaluation research contains many potential disadvantages for a program administrator. Claims made for a given program may have been unrealistic, and evaluation research may force administrators to admit that their existing policies and procedures require change. At the same time, evaluation research may serve as a means of arbitrating disputes within an agency, or it may be used to justify decisions that have already been made. On balance, the benefits of evaluation research seem to outweigh the disadvantages, even from the standpoint of administrators.

One example of the potential of evaluation research concerns the widely acclaimed children's television show, "Sesame Street." [25] The producers of "Sesame Street" hired a consulting firm to evaluate the program. The evaluation showed that the program had succeeded in improving the reading performance of children who watched the show. The consulting firm concluded that the program had succeeded in accomplishing its objectives. However, another sociologist reviewed the data on which the evaluation was based and discovered that an important fact had been overlooked. A major objective of the program was to improve the performance of poor and minority children—to place them on a more equal footing in school with children from families that were not poor. But relatively few children from poor families watched the program, compared with children from middle-class families. As a result, the gap between the performance of poor and middle-class children might have been increasing as a result of the program. Although these findings were not conclusive, the independent sociologist wondered why the evaluators hired by "Sesame Street" had failed to explore this finding.

As this example suggests, evaluation research poses certain troublesome questions for applied sociologists. Usually, sociologists want to retain ultimate responsibility for designing and carrying out the evaluation research, although they admit the necessity for extensive communication and collaboration with both clients and potential users of their study. It is often difficult to maintain true independence when confronted with persons in an organization who have the power to interfere with the evaluation. Top administrators may fear the dissemination of unfavorable research results (in the case of the reevaluation of "Sesame Street," the producers sought to modify the new finding and "put it in perspective"), and lower level staff and operating personnel may look upon the applied sociologist as a management spy and refuse wholehearted cooperation.

Is Applied Sociology Conservative?

One distinguished sociologist, Peter Rossi, has characterized the roles assigned by Moynihan to applied sociology as being "essentially conservative." He points out that although applied sociologists know how to do very competent evaluation research, all that can be evaluated is what has already been tried. An evaluation of the Job Corps program, for example, can tell you whether a young person benefits more from the Job Corps than from staying at home, but

it does not tell you whether the Job Corps is worthwhile relative to alternative uses of the same amounts of money spent in other conceivable youth programs,

for example, subsidized apprenticeships in industry, money grants to take con-
ventional high school and vocational school courses, subsidized trips around
the world, or what-have-you.[26]

Rossi thinks that evaluation of existing social action programs will be
especially conservative when the programs have been designed by the practical, pragmatic politician.

His vision of alternative treatment will be especially myopic, restricted to that
range which he estimates to provide an acceptable amount of consensus and
discord . . . it is likely that the program advocated will be just a little different
from current practices, different enough to appear that changes are being made
and similar enough to garner support. Because we can expect that policy
makers' conventional wisdom will lead only to tinkering with existing social
action programs, evaluation research tied to such programs can only be con-
cerned with minor effects.[27]

Rossi is somewhat more optimistic about the use of social indicators.
He suggests that the continual monitoring of social trends will almost inevitably
evoke unconventional ideas about what is happening in a society. Thus, continual monitoring of drug usage would have taught us a long time ago that
marijuana has become almost as popular a stimulant as alcohol, and we
might have been better able to anticipate the behavioral consequences of
this trend. But Rossi also notes the conservative bias of social indicators.
He feels that they will tend to be more concerned with central tendencies
(major changes for the largest number) than with changes in critical subgroups
of the population. For example, early opposition to the war in Vietnam was
not found among the great masses of American people but was confined
to the better educated, the young, and the more liberal sectors of the population. President Johnson could ignore this opposition because it was not a
significant social indicator of political discontent.

PPBS has been criticized by conservative politicians and organizations
as being a tool of radicals and subversives. In 1971, the United Republicans
of California adopted a resolution opposing the use of PPBS in California
schools, charging that the system "involves a total complex of goals, objectives
and functions by government at all levels, culminating at the federal
level. . . .the PPBS system could be said to be totalitarian." [28] They also complained that the system would be used "not only for measuring and evaluating
academic standards but will be concerned equally with attitudinal and behavioral objectives for both students and their families; this will *intrude into the*
private realm of the home." [29] Finally, PPBS was viewed as "a political hazard
and could easily generate fatal changes in the American political system as
such computerized systems would *take control away from representative of-*
ficials." [30]

Ida Hoos has criticized PPBS on other grounds:

1 If, as an administrator, you do not know what you are trying to accomplish, PPBS will not help you;

2 Much of the information collected under PPBS must be compatible with certain set units of measurement established before it is collected. Facts are accepted as relevant only when they fit into a preconceived scheme and relate to the procedural goal;

3 Programs can be proven effective by manipulating the definition of "effective." In a job corps program, for example, effectiveness was calculated by counting "completions" as marks of success, and "dropouts" as failures. When dropouts started to increase, "certificates of completion" were issued every other Saturday instead of a diploma every six months, so "completions" rose, "dropouts" declined, and the program was judged more effective;

4 The analyst assumes that the program's objectives are necessarily good and worthy of attainment;

5 Despite the elaborate methodological facade of PPBS, it is based on data that are often not adequate to develop measures of social benefits and costs.

6 PPBS may represent a disastrous triumph of economic rationality over the political and social rationality which should really control government decisions about the allocation of resources.[31]

Despite these points of disagreement, the attempt to develop sociology into a policy science shows how far applied sociology has come since the days of Lester Ward and suggests the direction in which it is moving. Applied sociology began as a reaction against the abstract focus of pure science and saw the major promise of sociology in its potential to solve social problems. Applied sociologists argued that it was appropriate and necessary to employ value criteria in the selection and definition of problems. Only after the selection does sociology become a value-neutral science.

The chief difficulty plaguing applied sociologists involves the relationship of the researcher to the client. If the task of the sociologist is to find solutions to problems perceived by different groups in society, the sociologist may become simply a tool of those wishing to maintain or change the existing order. What happens to the truth under such circumstance? Are there any ethical and practical criteria that the sociologist can employ to ensure the maximum feasible social benefit of research?

The attempt to make sociology policy relevant represents one solution to this dilemma. Since, at least in theory, government is concerned with providing the greatest good for the greatest number, the improvement of government policies affecting health, education, welfare, and other aspects of life is a desirable objective. If social science research can assist or improve the development and implementation of public policy in such domains, then the long-standing goal of applied sociologists to improve the living conditions of members of society will be a concrete political reality. That is the hope of those currently working in the applied-science orientation.

Applied Sociology and Poverty

As we indicated at the beginning, applied sociologists have been deeply involved in the effort to analyze the causes of poverty and develop workable solutions to the problem of poverty. Although their work has focused on a wide variety of possible causes, and numerous solutions have been proposed, the issue generating the most intense research and debate has been the notion of a "culture of poverty."

The notion was first suggested by Oscar Lewis, who pointed out that the poor of any industrialized country resemble each other more than they resemble the well-to-do citizens of their own countries. He described a number of economic, social, and psychological characteristics that seem to be shared by the poor of most societies and maintained that this set of traits constituted a "culture" of poverty. (For a discussion of the concept of "culture" see chapter 10.) In other words, Lewis argued that the poor develop a particular set of attitudes and behavior that reinforce their condition, and they pass these attitudes and behavior on to their children, who then also remain in poverty.

Daniel Moynihan employed this notion to explain poverty among blacks. In *The Negro Family* and in other publications, Moynihan tried to show that the family life of black Americans was "disorganized," and that this disorganization was not only a result of discrimination, unemployment, and poor housing, but also resulted from a self-perpetuating subculture of poverty.[32] Moynihan's argument has been attacked on technical grounds, in terms of his analysis of the statistics, but most of the criticism has been directed to the whole idea of a "subculture of poverty." One reason the attacks have been so strong is the potential implications of Moynihan's argument.

If Moynihan's view were widely accepted in government circles, it could be used to justify the diversion of money away from programs to create jobs, better housing, and schools and into programs with a greater social work emphasis. If lack of money is the only affliction of the poor, then more money is what the sociological doctor should prescribe. If the poor live in a sick culture, then more money is not an effective remedy. Moreover, with the culture of poverty thesis, the black poor could be seen as sick and disorganized, rather than deprived and discriminated against. Moynihan's later book on the War on Poverty, *Maximum Feasible Misunderstanding,* seems to bear out these fears, since he blames the failure of the antipoverty effort on the decision to allow poor people a major role in the decision-making process.

Moynihan's critics have questioned whether the values and attitudes of the poor can be usefully thought of as a culture. Studies by Lee Rainwater[33] and Elliott Liebow,[34] for example, show that there are distinctive forms of behavior characteristic of poor people, and that the poor do hold some distinctive values different from those of the nonpoor. Both Rainwater and Liebow, however, argue that these values are secondary and adaptive. In other words, the poor generally share the values of the larger society, but they have adapted some of these values to the conditions they face. Since it is not possible for the poor, because they are poor, to achieve some of the values of the larger society, they have adapted these values in order to cope with the situations they actually confront.

The views of Rainwater and Liebow lead to implications almost directly opposite to the implications of Moynihan's views. Rather than eliminating the subculture of poverty in order to make it possible to eliminate poverty, it is necessary to eliminate poverty in order to eliminate the subculture of poverty. Rather than sending more social workers and psychiatrists to work with the poor, it is necessary to provide jobs and income so that the conditions of poverty can be overcome. The debate over the culture of poverty has not been resolved. Many government agencies and private organizations continue to assume that this culture must be "treated" while other sociological studies question the utility of the notion itself.

Summary

Even in the natural sciences, there has always been a distinction between the efforts of pure scientists to discover laws of nature and the efforts of applied scientists to use those laws to find solutions to the practical problems faced by society. Since the work of applied scientists has practical consequences, however, they cannot avoid the fact that values affect research. While the scientific method can tell us what means will achieve a given end, it cannot tell us what ends are desirable. That choice depends on values.

In sociology, some applied scientists have attempted to resolve the problem of values by acting as engineers who allow their clients to define the problem to be studied. Their task is merely the technical one of applying the scientific method to study the problem. Other applied sociologists disagree with the engineering approach and believe that they must be "clinicians" who treat the formulation of the problem as part of the research task. Either explicitly or implicitly, all applied sociologists invoke their own values to select problems for study. Once that selection is made, they try to prevent their values from biasing the results of their research.

While pure scientists tend to look for the general laws of human behavior that make social order possible, applied scientists tend to examine the social problems that threaten and disturb the social order. The definition of a social problem is no simple matter, since different groups in society may have conflicting views of what constitutes a social problem. Here, too, the values of the sociologist influence decisions about what to study and how to formulate the research problem.

One attempt to resolve the value dilemma is to allow the government to define problems and formulate solutions. Applied sociologists would then concentrate on measuring and evaluating the success or failure of policies and programs. This leaves the value choices in the hands of elected representatives of society, rather than with individual sociologists. Some sociologists criticize this approach as being basically conservative, since it allows only for slight modifications of existing structures, rather than for the possibility of fundamental changes in those structures.

For Further Study

For an authoritative, but by no means error-free or unprejudiced, discussion of Project Camelot and other military-sponsored social science research projects, written by a former official of the Department of Defense, see Seymour J. Deitchman, *The Best-Laid Schemes: A Tale of Social Research and Bureaucracy* (Cambridge, Mass.: M.I.T. Press, 1976).

For a valuable collection of articles explaining, defending, and attacking the Moynihan reports, see Lee Rainwater, and William L. Yancey, eds., *The Moynihan Report and the Politics of Controversy* (Cambridge, Mass.: M.I.T. Press, 1967). This volume includes the full text of the report itself.

For some eloquent and penetrating remarks about applied sociology in contemporary society, see M. Nicolaus, "Remarks at ASA Convention," *American Sociologist* 4 (May 1969): 154–156.

For additional material on social indicators, see Bertram M. Gross, *The State of the Nation: Social Systems Accounting* (New York: Travistock Publications, 1966); Raymond A. Bauer, ed., *Social Indicators* (Cambridge, Mass.: M.I.T. Press, 1967); U.S. Department of Health, Education and Welfare, *Toward a Social Report* (Washington, D.C.: Government Printing Office, 1969); Eleanor B. Sheldon and Wilbert G. Moore, eds., *Indicators of Social Change* (New York: Russell Sage, 1968); Andrew Schonfield and J. Shaw, *Social*

Indicators and Social Policy (London: Heinemann Educational Books, 1972).

On PPBS, see David Novick, ed., *Program Budgeting: Program Analyses and the Federal Budget* (Cambridge, Mass.: Harvard University Press, 1965); Harley H. Hinrichs, and Graeme Taylor, *Program Budgeting and Benefit-Cost Analysis: Cases, Text and Readings* (Pacific Palisades, Calif.: Goodyear Publishing Co., 1969); Harley H. Hinrichs and Graeme Taylor, *Systematic Analysis: A Primer on Benefit-Cost Analysis and Program Evaluation* (Pacific Palisades, Calif.: Goodyear Publishing Co., 1972).

For evaluation research, see Peter Rossi and Walter Williams, *Evaluating Social Programs* (New York: Academic Press, 1975).; Howard E. Freeman and Clarence C. Sherwood, *Social Research and Social Policy* (Englewood Cliffs, N.J.: Prentice-Hall, 1970).

For a valuable collection of articles dealing with applied sociologists at work in the area of public policy, see Louis A. Zurcher and Charles M. Bonjean, *Planned Social Intervention* (Scranton, Penn.: Chandler Publishing Co., 1970).

For interesting attempts by sociologists to show the relevance of pure research to applied problems, see N. J. Demerath III, Otto Larsen, and Karl F. Schuessler, eds., *Social Policy and Sociology* (New York: Academic Press, 1975).

For other works written from essentially similar perspectives, *see* Paul F. Lazarsfeld, Jeffrey Reitz, and Ann K. Pasanella, *An Introduction to Applied Sociology* (New York: Elsevier, 1975), and Mirra Komarovsky, ed., *Sociology and Public Policy* (New York: Elsevier, 1975).

For an interesting collection of applied sociological articles written from a humanistic rather than a "scientistic" perspective, see John F. Glass and John R. Staude, eds., *Humanistic Society: Today's Challenge to Sociology* (Pacific Palisades, Calif.: Goodyear Publishing Co., 1972).

Notes

1 Lewis A. Coser, "The Sociology of Poverty: To the Memory of George Simmel," in *Social Problems* 13 (Fall 1965): 141.

2 Ibid., p. 143.

3 For a good discussion of this distinction in the natural sciences, see Norman Campbell, *What Is Science?* (New York: Dover, 1952).

4 See, for example, Lester F. Ward, *Applied Sociology: A Treatise on the Conscious Improvement of Society by Society* (Boston: Ginn & Co., 1906).

5 Lester F. Ward, "The Human Mind Does Make the World Over," in

Darwinism: Reaction or Reform? Bert James Loewenberg, ed. (New York: Rinehart & Co., 1957), p. 21.

6 Lester F. Ward, *Pure Sociology* (New York: Macmillan, 1909), p. 4.

7 For a discussion of this approach, see Loren Baritz, *The Servants of Power: A History of the Use of Social Science in American Industry* (New York: Wiley, 1960).

8 Ibid., pp.1–10

9 See, Robert S. Lynd, *Knowledge for What? The Place of Social Science in American Culture* (Princeton, N.J.: Princeton University Press, 1939).

10 Ibid., p. 183

11. Alvin W. Gouldner, "Explorations in Applied Social Science," in *Applied Sociology*, Alvin W. Gouldner and S. M. Miller, eds. (New York: Free Press, 1965).

12. Irving Louis Horowitz, "The Rise and Fall of Project Camelot," in *The Rise and Fall of Project Camelot: Studies in the Relationship between Social Science and Politics,* Irving Louis Horowitz, ed. (Cambridge, Mass.: M.I.T. Press, 1967), pp. 4–5.

13 Ibid., p. 6.

14 Burleigh B. Gardner, "The Consultant to Business," in Gouldner and Miller, *Applied Sociology*, pp. 79–85.

15 For a discussion, see Loren Baritz, *Servants of Power*, pp. 76–116.

16 For a discussion of these problems of definition, see Howard S. Becker, ed., Introduction to *Social Problems: A Modern Approach* (New York: 1967).

17 C. Wright Mills, *The Sociological Imagination* (New York: Oxford University Press, 1959), p. 113.

18 Daniel P. Moynihan, *Maximum Feasible Misunderstanding* (New York: Free Press, 1969).

19 Raymond A. Bauer, "Detection and Anticipation of Impact," in *Social Indicators*, Raymond A. Bauer, ed. (Cambridge, Mass.: M.I.T. Press, 1961), p.1.

20 See, for example, Eleanor Bernert Sheldon and Wilbert Moore, *Indicators of Social Change: Concepts and Measurements* (New York: Russell Sage, 1968).

21 William Gorman, "Notes of a Practitioner," *Public Interest*, no. 8 (Summer 1967): p. 4.

22 Ibid. pp. 4–5.

23 See, for example, Henry Rowen, "Objectives, Alternatives, Costs, and Effectiveness," in *Program Budgeting and Benefit-Cost Analysis*, Harley H. Hinrichs and Graeme M. Taylor, eds. (Pacific Palisades, Calif.:Goodyear Publishing Co., 1969).

24 See, for example, Francis G. Caro, "Approaches to Evaluative Research: A Review," in L. A. Zurcher and C. M. Bonjean, *Planned Social Intervention* (Scranton: Chandler Publishing Co., 1970), pp. 403–421.

25 Thomas D. Cook, Hillary Appleton, Ross F. Conner, Ann Shaffer, Gary Tamkin, and Stephen J. Weber, *"Sesame Street" Revisited* (New York: Russell Sage, 1975).

26 Peter H. Rossi, "No Good Idea Goes Unpunished: Moynihan's Misunderstandings and the Proper Role of Social Science in Policy Making," in Zurcher and Bonjean, *Planned Social Intervention*, p. 80.

27 Ibid., pp. 80–81.

28 Quoted in Ida R. Hoos, *Systems Analysis in Public Policy: A Critique* (Berkeley, Calif.: University of California Press, 1972), p. 171.

29 Ibid., p. 171.

30 Ibid., pp. 171–172.

31 Ibid., pp. 71–77.

32 Daniel P. Moynihan, *The Negro Family*, Report of the Office of Policy Planning and Research, U.S. Department of Labor (Washington, D.C.: Government Printing Office, 1965).

33 Lee Rainwater, "Crucible of Identity: The Negro Lower-Class Family," in *The American Negro*, Talcott Parsons and Kenneth Clark, eds. (Boston: Houghton-Mifflin Co., 1966).

34 Elliott Liebow, *Tally's Corner* (Boston: Little, Brown & Co., 1967).

Sociology as a Critical Science

As we have seen, differences between pure scientists and applied scientists about issues like poverty involve different views of the nature of sociological problems and the task of sociology, as well as disagreements about the place of values in scientific research. The pure scientist would not deny that poverty is a problem, but might insist that sociology cannot solve the problem with the information currently available about the nature and causes of human behavior. The applied scientist on the other hand, once having determined that the material resources necessary to eliminate poverty were available, might see the task of sociology as one of deciding how to allocate those resources most effectively. Both orientations, employing the natural-science method or some form of phenomenological method (see chapter 7), would tend to treat poverty as the effect of causative factors, such as a "culture of poverty" or a lack of money. They would seek to demonstrate a relationship between a specific cause or causes and the specific effect. Government bodies, private agencies, corporations, or individuals could then change their policies or behaviors in order to eliminate the problem.

But what if the causes and effects cannot be separated? What if the factors producing the material resources necessary to eliminate poverty are also the factors that generate poverty? What if the most basic and fundamental ways in which American society is organized create affluence for some and poverty for others? What if poverty is built in to a certain type of society? If this is the case, then poverty cannot be eliminated by slight changes in behavior, policies, or programs. A basic reorganization of society would be required.

Many social scientists believe that this is a very real problem of contemporary America. Economist John Gurley, for example, notes that America is fundamentally structured as a capitalist society.[1] In capitalist societies, private individuals own the businesses and corporations making up the basic economy of the country, and they compete with each other in an attempt to earn a profit. The owners of a particular business control the hiring of workers, setting of priorities, and other decisions of their firm, although they may be restricted by government regulations, contracts with unions, or other rules. Gurley argues that if substantial profits could be made by eliminating poverty, private capitalists would quickly move to do so. The problem is, however, that capitalists make profits by creating poverty.

> Businesses make profits by keeping their costs as low as possible, and by charging higher prices for the products they turn out . . . . Private profit-making requires efficiency. To be efficient . . . they do not hire the worst-trained workers, the disadvantaged, the poorly educated.[2]

The very qualities that make capitalism such a successful system for producing goods also lead it to generate poverty.

> Capitalism is highly efficient, marvelously innovative, technologically progressive. Being all of these things, it has created great material prosperity for many people. But, at the same time, it has created the opposite—poverty, maltreatment of many of its people and of much of its natural environment. Consequently, these social ills aren't just problems of capitalism; they are to some extent creations of capitalism. The wealthy industrialist and the poor tenant farmer are both products of the same system.[3]

If the basic structure of a society contains conflicting tendencies, then the society must be viewed as inherently unstable and changing, rather than as static or fixed. Social change must be seen as the most fundamental social process. Moreover, according to such a view, social change comes from contradictions within the society, rather than from independent causes. These notions will be examined more fully in chapter 8. They are part of a third major orientation in sociology—sociology as a *critical science.*

The overall structure of society is seen as containing internal contradictions. Critical sociologists see the task of sociology as one of analyzing these contradictions and evaluating their consequences for the development of society.

In the case of poverty, for example, sociologists working within the critical-science orientation would attempt to determine whether there are societies, perhaps noncapitalist societies, that do not generate both affluence and poverty. They would examine the historical development of inequality in American society and evaluate the consequences of this inequality for relations between different groups in the society. They might conclude that the only way to eliminate poverty is through a fundamental reorganization of society, such that contradictions between wealth and poverty are no longer generated.

The Marxist Alternative

It was Karl Marx (1818–1883) who first systematically developed an approach to sociology as a critical science.[4] Although he was by profession a philosopher rather than a sociologist, Marx sought to identify the major forces shaping social structure and development. He argued that it was important to study real, existing societies, rather than hypothetical ones, since "the philosophers have only *interpreted* the world in different ways; the point, however, is to change it." [5]

Marx began with the proposition that the most important difference between human beings and other animals is that people transform nature to meet human needs. Human beings are producers. Although there are many techniques human beings use to transform nature, Marx argued that, in any society at a specific point in time, one set of techniques will tend to be dominant. It will involve more people and have more of an impact on the entire society. He called this set of techniques the dominant "forces of production." In one society, for example, the dominant forces of production might be hunting and gathering, while in another they might be agriculture, and in still a third, industry.[6]

Marx observed that different forms of production require that members of society coordinate and cooperate in different ways. He called these forms of coordination and cooperation "relations of production." The forces of production and the relations of production—a combination called the "mode of production"—together shape most of the other characteristics of any society, Marx argued. Thus, agricultural forces of production, together with relations of production between nobles and serfs, made up the feudal mode of production. Industrial forces of production, together with relations of production between owners and wage laborers, together make up the capitalist mode of production.

Marx went on to argue that all societies are unstable; they change constantly because of changes in the forces and relations of production. Marx devoted most of his own writing to an analysis of the capitalist mode of production and the changes occurring within it.

The Theory of Capitalist Development[7]

For Marx, capitalism is a system of commodity production. It is not a system in which men produce simply for their own needs (as was true in early agricultural or hunting-and-gathering societies), or even for the needs of individuals closely connected to them (as in feudal societies). In a capitalist system, individuals produce primarily for exchange. Every commodity, Marx maintained, has two aspects: its "use value"—the actual human needs that can be satisfied by the physical properties of the commodity—and its "exchange value"—the value the commodity has when offered in exchange for other products. Because of these two aspects, a commodity requires the existence of a market, in which goods are exchanged.

Marx argued that any product, whether or not it is a commodity (that is, capable of being exchanged), can have value only insofar as human labor has been expended to produce it. Thus, both use value and exchange value are directly related to the amount of labor expended in the production of a product.

In a market economy, there must be a medium of exchange—that is, money—that can express the exchange value of different commodities. This is so because exchange value cannot be derived from use value. If a given quantity of corn can be exchanged for a given quantity of iron, there must be some common standard applicable to both, since there is nothing intrinsically comparable in the physical properties of corn and iron.

Marx claims that the medium of exchange is based on the socially necessary labor time embodied in the production of a commodity. This is the amount of time required to produce a commodity under normal conditons of production, with the average degree of skill and intensity prevalent at a given time in a particular industry. Thus, a sudden technological improvement can reduce the socially necessary labor time required to produce a commodity and thereby lead to a reduction in the exchange value of that commodity.

In a perfect market, according to Marx, the capitalist buys labor and sells commodities at their real value. But this leads to a paradox. The capitalist "must buy his commodities at their value, must sell them at their value, and yet at the end of the process must withdraw more value from circulation than he threw into it at the starting."[8] This is only possible if labor power is itself a commodity that can be bought and sold on the market. If labor power is a commodity, then the socially necessary labor time required to produce it must consist of the commodities the worker needs to subsist and reproduce.

Marx suggested that, during an average working day, the worker produces more than is necessary to cover the cost of subsistence. Whatever the worker produces over and above the subsistence value is surplus value that can be appropriated by the capitalist. If the average working day is eight hours, for example, and the worker produces the equivalent of his own subsistence value in half that time, then the remaining four hours of work is surplus production (from the standpoint of the worker).

Capitalism is a competitive system in which different capitalists compete in the search for profit. This leads, Marx argued, to a tendency for the rate of profit to decline. The decline occurs because the main way for competitors to increase their share of the available profit is to produce at less cost then their competitors. One road to cost reduction is through technological innovations that reduce labor time. But this, unfortunately, is usually followed quickly by similar innovations by competitors. In addition, technological innovations require very high expenditures of fixed capital. Sophisticated machinery costs a lot of money. This, in turn, leads to a decline in the rate of profit. One way capitalists try to offset this decline is by reducing their variable capital costs—that is, by increasing the productivity of labor (thereby increasing surplus value), and by buying raw materials at lower prices.

The competitive struggle for profit leads to two opposing trends in the historical development of capitalism, according to Marx. On the one hand, it leads to the growing concentration and centralization of capital. Larger firms drive smaller ones out of existence and absorb their capital. Over time, there are fewer and fewer firms growing ever larger in size. This trend leads to the growth of monopoly capital.

The other trend characteristic of capitalist development is the exploitation of workers by efforts to increase their productivity and decrease their real wages. This leads to the creation of an industrial reserve army of chronically unemployed workers. There then exists a pool of cheap labor that can be called upon in times of prosperity. In general, the existence of an industrial labor pool serves to help hold down wages. It is in this industrial reserve army that the most miserable conditions of life are found.

The Theory of Class Struggle

The contradictory character of capitalism is not merely a formal process built into its structure as a mode of production. It affects real men and women, who are involved in the relations of production. The process of capitalist development described by Marx leads to a basic division in society between those groups that control capital and are able to buy the labor power of others (the capitalists), and those groups that are able to sell only their own labor power (the workers).

Marx used the concept of class to describe the relationship between the buyers and the sellers of labor power. He divided capitalist society into two classes—the capitalist class, and the working class. This simple division into two classes is a kind of abstraction that does not really exist in any society. In real societies, as Marx noted, the class structure is far more complex. There are, for example, class groupings based on newly emerging relations of production, or on those that are in the process of disappearing. Thus, within late feudal society, there were class groupings based on emerging capitalist relations of production, while in early capitalist society, there were class groupings based on declining feudal relations of production.

Another source of complication comes from the strata dependent upon the major classes. These strata tend to identify politically with the class on which they depend. Marx mentioned the managerial staff of administrative workers as an example. Still another source of complication involves the clusters of individuals, such as criminals, who are not really integrated into the division of labor. These complications lead to different class structures in different societies. Marx felt that each society must be studied in detail to discover the exact nature of its class structure at a given time.

Political power in a society tends to be organized around class relations, according to Marx. Thus, the dominant class will tend to have a disproportionate share of the political power, and other classes will be subordinate to it in differing degrees. Because of its economic and political power, the dominant class is able to propagate a set of ideas—an ideology—that justifies its dominance, and contrary ideas will not be able to gain the same prominence in media of communication. Just how this occurs is described more fully in chapter 9.

In any relatively stable society, Marx tells us, there exists a balance between the mode of production, social relations integral to that mode, and the superstructure (law, political power, religion, and so on). When a change occurs in the mode of production, a tension is set up between these forces and the existing relations of production, which resist the emerging forces. These contradictions are expressed in class conflict. The conflict ends either in the destruction of the society or in the reconstruction of the society, based on new relations of production with a new class structure.

When he examined capitalist society from this perspective, Marx concluded that the very development of capitalism contains the seeds of its own destruction. The growing centralization of production creates a more and more solidified working class, made up of the majority of the people in society. The interests of this class are fundamentally opposed to those of the ruling class of capitalists, who convert surplus value into their own private property. Marx believed that the class struggle between workers and capitalists would eventually result in the victory of the working class, which would then abolish private property and place the means of production under collective ownership. In this new stage of socialism, all members of society would be part of the working class.

Marx viewed socialism as a transitional stage between capitalism and a new society. This new society will be realized, he argued, only when the division of labor itself is abolished, although Marx provided few hints about how this might occur. He seemed to believe that the division of labor might be abolished either by allowing people to perform the entire range of social tasks (rather than only specialized ones), or by increasing automation to the point where human beings would supervise the machines that would perform the more alienating forms of necessary labor.

Critical Sociology After Marx

Marx's analysis of capitalism was based on studies he made of England, France, and Germany during the middle of the nineteenth century. Marx was not, however, a scholar sitting in an ivory tower. Because he believed that capitalist society produced misery and suffering for the vast majority of people, he helped organize and lead a political movement of the working class dedicated to the overthrow of capitalism. The movement continued after his death, and its first successful revolution took place in Russia in 1917. In the years since, the movement has become fragmented, has won other victories, suffered more failures, and continues to be a major political and intellectual orientation in the contemporary world.

Because Marxism is not only a social science orientation, but also a political ideology, it is often opposed by those who believe that capitalism is a "good" type of society. It is probably fair to say that all social theory since Marx is aimed at either refuting or supporting his analysis.[9] It is certainly the case that many of the sociologists mentioned in earlier chapters, such as Emile Durkheim and Max Weber, intended their own studies to modify or refute Marx's analysis of the nature and development of capitalism. Many sociologists currently working within the pure science orientation are also concerned with attacking his analysis (see chapters 5–8).

For those who tried to continue the form of analysis established by Marx, the Russian Revolution and the subsequent dictatorship of Stalin caused serious problems. Not only was "Marxism" suppressed and obstructed in many capitalist countries, but Stalin set out to define "acceptable" Marxism. Marxism was transformed from a critical method for studying real societies into a doctrine that had presumably discovered the laws of capitalist development. Under Stalin's influence, Marx's complex analysis of capitalism was reduced to a claim that the economic structure of society determined all other social characteristics, and Marx's examination of the contradictory tendencies within capitalist development was converted into a belief in the inevitable downfall of capitalist society.

As a result of this vulgarization of Marx's method and theories, the critical-science orientation of sociology was, for a long time, restricted to the fringes of the discipline. Beginning in the 1940s and 1950s in Western Europe, however, a few philosophers and sociologists began to reexamine Marx's own works and to apply his method of analysis to contemporary societies. By the 1970s, the critical-science orientation had become the dominant one for European sociologists, but in the United States its spread has been considerably slower.

The most important American sociologist to help develop this orientation has been C. Wright Mills, who summarized his views in a book called *The Sociological Imagination,* published in 1959.[10] Mills argued that the focus of sociology must be on biography and history, and on the intersection of these two within society. The facts of history, he noted, are also facts about the success or failure of individual men and women. "When a society becomes industrialized, the peasant becomes a worker; a feudal lord is liquidated or becomes a businessman." [11]

And yet, ordinary people do not define their experiences in terms of historical change, but instead they experience what seem to be personal troubles. Mills argued that it is the task of sociology to distinguish between personal troubles and public issues, so that individuals can see the source of their troubles in the larger history of social structures. To illustrate the problem, Mills used the example of unemployment. If only one man in a city of 100,000 is unemployed, that is his personal trouble and must be dealt with in terms of his own abilities and opportunities; when 15 million people are unemployed in a nation of 50 million, unemployment is a public issue that must be dealt with in terms of the political and economic institutions of the society at large. Other critical sociologists might suggest that people see things in personal terms for good sociological reasons. They might ask questions like: Who profits from perceptions restricted to biography? What are the implications of this for the social control of populations?

Mills was concerned that the relationship between biography and history was getting lost in the focus of most sociology in the United States, which he saw polarizing into two equally false tendencies. On the one hand were the "grand theorists" who were attempting to develop a systematic theory of the nature of man and society. Mills cited the work of Talcott Parsons (see chapter 5) as the most extreme example of grand theory, but he would certainly include many other sociologists working in the pure-science orientation. The problem with this approach, he felt, was that it took a static and abstract view of society. He complained that such an approach did little more than endlessly rearrange concepts.

The other unfortunate tendency Mills called "abstracted empiricism." He included George Lundberg in this approach, as well as many of the sociologists who studied public opinion. This approach emphasized methodology as the distinctive feature of sociology, and it focused on data collection and analysis techniques as the main interest of study. Data tended to be collected for its own sake. Abstracted empiricism placed little emphasis on the importance of theory in the selection and definition of problems.

Although Mills was very critical of both the pure-science and applied-science orientations in sociology, he still felt that sociology was a science requiring certain procedures. What he argued against was an overemphasis on theory or on methods to the exclusion of the problem at issue. Theories and methods, he cautioned, are tools to help us deal with problems, and we must always keep the problem clearly in mind. As he put it,

> social science, in brief, neither "builds up" from microscopic study nor "deduces down" from conceptual elaboration. Its practitioners try to build and to deduce at the same time, in the same process of study, and to do so by adequate formulation and reformulation of problems and of their adequate solutions. To practice such a policy . . . is to take up substantive problems on the historical level of reality; to state these problems in terms appropriate to them; and then, no matter how high the flight of theory, no matter how painstaking the crawl among detail, to state the solution in the macroscopic terms of the problem.[12]

According to Mills, sociologists who possess the sociological imagination must, as scientists, ask three sorts of questions:

> **1** What is the structure of this particular society as a whole? What are its essential components, and how are they related to one another? How does it differ from other varieties of social order? Within it, what is the meaning of any particular feature for its continuance and change?

> **2** Where does this society stand in human history? What are the mechanics by which it is changing? What is its place within and its meaning for the development of humanity as a whole? How does any particular feature we are examining affect, and how is it affected by, the historical period in which it moves? And this period—what are its essential features? How does it differ from other periods? What are its characteristic ways of history-making?

> **3** What varieties of men and women now prevail in this society and in this period? What varieties are coming to prevail? In what ways are they selected and formed, liberated and repressed, made sensitive and blunted? What kinds of "human nature" are revealed in the conduct and character we observe in this society in this period? And what is the meaning for "human nature" of each and every feature of the society we are examining?[13]

Sociology As a Critical Science

Although Mills was not a Marxist, he shared with Marx a conception of the proper focus of social science common to all those who treat sociology as a critical science. Unlike the pure scientists and the applied scientists, critical scientists do not believe the various parts of society can be studied separately and then added together to get a picture of society as a whole. Nor do they believe that society is like an organism that shapes and determines relations among its parts. On the contrary, critical scientists believe that society is constantly changing, and that the overall character of a society generates contradictions among some of the parts. In the conflict that occurs between contradictory tendencies, the overall character of society is changed and generates new contradictions.

While this conception may be difficult to grasp at first, the reasons for it are rather straightforward. If we divide society into its parts and focus attention on the individual functioning of each part, we overlook an important aspect of the function of each part—its relation to the whole. While the analysis and observation of individual parts is a necessary scientific task, it can be completed only when the part is seen as an aspect of the whole.

The critical-science orientation, then, focuses on social change as the most fundamental social process and searches for the source of change in the contradictions between parts of society. It does not treat the parts of society as independent of one another, connected only through cause-and-effect relationships. Instead, it views the parts as interdependent, related by contradiction, so that a change in any part affects all the other parts and the whole. The method employed by critical science depends to some extent on the particular problem studied, but always includes both the search for contradictions and historical analysis. The method of searching for contradictions is known as "dialectics" and will be discussed in detail in chapter 8.

While the natural-science method, employed by pure scientists and applied scientists, concentrates on problems of measurement and on establishing cause-and-effect relationships, the method employed by critical scientists concentrates on problems of comparison, history, and contradiction. Table 1 compares the three orientations in terms of their views of the nature of sociological problems, the task of sociology, the method and theory of sociology, and the use of values.

In chapters 2 and 3 we observed that, while pure scientists and applied scientists differ over the use of values in selecting and defining problems for study, both believe the actual research process is value neutral. Critical scientists maintain that the other orientations confuse value neutrality with objectivity. Although in common usage, the term "objective" implies "unbiased," that is not its scientific meaning. Objectivity involves the process of using logic to convert phenomena and experiences of social life into objects that can be studied by one or another set of procedures. (See the discussion of natural science in chapter 2.) In this sense, objectivity is common to all forms of science, and it is what distinguishes science from other forms of inquiry. Value neutrality, on the other hand, involves the process of eliminating values from any influence on the mental operations of the sociologist as a scientist. While most critical scientists would deny the possibility of value neutrality, they believe that it has nothing to do with objectivity, and that it is objectivity that is essential to the scientific enterprise.

Table One: Comparison of Orientations
Pure, Applied, and Critical Science

Issue	Pure Science	Applied Science	Critical Science
1. The nature of sociological problems	What forces make possible social order?	What forces disrupt social order?	What forces make possible social change?
2. The task of sociology	The task is to discover general laws of human behavior.	The task is to solve practical social problems.	The task is to discover the nature and direction of contradictions.
3. Methods and theory in sociology	The natural-scientific and phenomenological or subjective theory and methods.	The natural-scientific and phenomenological or subjective theory and methods.	Historical (genetic) and dialectical theory and methods.
4. The role of values in sociology	Sociology is value-neutral. Sociologists are motivated by the disinterested pursuit of knowledge and must not allow their own values to influence research.	Sociologists must and should employ values to select and define problems for study. Once the problem is defined, values must not be allowed to influence research.	Value-neutrality and objectivity are not the same. Like all sciences, sociology must be objective, but it cannot be value-neutral.

The research conducted by sociologists working in a critical-science-orientation tends to be guided by the three types of questions posed by Mills. Some studies focus on an examination and comparison of the structure of contemporary societies. Others focus on patterns of historical change within and between types of societies. Still others focus on relationships between structural change and individual behavior.

Studies of Class Structure

Mills himself conducted one of the first critical studies of changes in the class structure of the United States. In *White Collar*, he observed that major changes had occurred in the composition of the labor force during the first half of this century.[14] At the beginning of the century, farmers and independent businessmen made up a major part of the labor force. From the middle of the nineteenth century to the middle of the twentieth century, however, farmers declined from about two-thirds of the labor force to about one-eighth. The proportion of independent businessmen declined less drastically, but they became concentrated in retail and sales occupations, declining by 34 percent in manufacturing firms.

While the proportion of farmers and independent businessmen was declining, the proportion of white-collar clerical and administrative workers sharply increased. Where to be middle class once meant that you worked for yourself, the new middle class was composed of people in white-collar occupations who received a salary working for a large firm. Since the change in occupational structure also meant a change in the conditions of life experienced by these white-collar workers, Mills devoted most of his study to an examination of the styles of life of the new middle class.

A central characteristic of this life style, he observed, was that white-collar workers increasingly experience the same problems as blue-collar workers—they are quickly affected by changes in unemployment rates; their salaries are eaten away by inflation; they do not really produce a whole product that seems to belong to them. It is because the growth of white-collar occupations is a relatively recent phenomenon, Mills concluded, that this new middle class feels isolated and uncertain about life.

> *Newly created in a harsh time of creation, white collar man has no culture to lean upon except the contents of a mass society that has shaped him and seeks to manipulate him to its alien ends ... This isolated position makes him excellent material for synthetic molding at the hands of popular culture—print, film, radio and television.*[15]

Given this isolation and fragmentation, Mills predicted that the middle class would not develop distinctive political forms, but rather would tend to go along with whatever political bloc seemed to be winning. Caught between the labor movement and business, white-collar workers do not develop an awareness of a common and unique set of interests, but instead tend to identify with one or the other of the major class groupings. Just as they sell their labor to the highest bidder, their political allegiances are also for sale.

Mills wrote *White Collar* in 1951 and the trends he identified have continued and intensified since that time. Critical sociologists have given growing attention to the nature and significance of the very complex occupational structure of the United States. Anthony Giddens argues that Marx's original analysis needs to be modified on the basis of the actual development of capitalist societies since the nineteenth century.[16] In particular, he suggests, it is important to develop a greater knowledge of the relationship between political and economic power. In modern industrial societies, the government intervenes in the class struggle between workers and capitalists in such a way as to moderate and control the intensity of the conflict and to prevent it from reaching revolutionary proportions. Government also affects one of the contradictions of capitalist society—the problem of the declining rate of profit—by taking over some of the costs related to both fixed and variable capital. It assumes responsibility, for example, for much technological research and development, as well as for training and educating workers through the educational system. It also can affect the cost of raw materials through tariff policies and trade agreements.

The other weakness in Marx's formulation, according to Giddens, is that he did not sufficiently examine internal divisions in the working class. The fact that most white-collar workers are not involved in productive labor means that their wages are drawn from a portion of the surplus-value produced by blue-collar workers. This, in turn, means that their political allegiances may be closer to those of the capitalist class than to those of other workers. Giddens also notes that many occupations are reserved for different sexual or racial groups. This creates visible differences, serving to weaken class consciousness among workers. Many lower status white-collar occupations such as secretary and clerk, for example, are heavily dominated by women. They act as a buffer between blue-collar workers and higher status white-collar workers. Similarly, blacks are very often relegated to the lowest occupations, and this tends to create black-white conflicts within the working class rather than conflict between workers and owners.

Studies in Social History

Some of the most impressive studies in the critical-science orientation have been done by scholars who refer to themselves as social historians. On one level, social historians share a common mistrust of what we may think of as cross-sectional thinking. For E. P. Thompson, for example, the sociological notion of class is neither a structure nor a category. "It entails," he tells us, "the notion of historical relationship. Like any other relationship, it is a fluency which evades analysis if we attempt to stop it dead at any given moment and anatomise its structure." [17]

For Thompson, it is not possible to develop a "scientific" measure of class by isolating the concept in a laboratory setting. Class, for Thompson, always deals with real people and occurs in a real context. So it is not possible to have two distinct social classes, each with its own separate existence, and bring them into a relationship with each other.

> We cannot have love without lovers, nor deference without squires and la-
> bourers. And class happens when some men, as a result of common shared
> experiences (inherited or shared), feel and articulate the identity of their inter-
> ests as between themselves, and as against other men whose interests are
> different from (and usually opposed to) theirs. [18]

The fact of social class, in this view, is essentially based on the mode of production within which people find themselves. Awareness of this fact, or "class consciousness," ultimately occurs, but it happens differently in different times and places.

From this perspective, then, social class can be understood only as a phenomenon arising from events and processes occurring over an extended period of time. Thompson sets himself the task of writing a biography of the English working class from its "adolescence" to its "early manhood"—a period extending from about 1780 to 1832. He calls this study *The Making of the English Working Class*. In it, Thompson traces in meticulous detail how the British working class became aware of itself and its interests, and how it developed political organizations to forward these interests. Workers realized only very gradually that they were members of a common class. This awareness emerged as a result of fragmented, interrupted, but nevertheless continuing attempts by workers themselves to develop organizations to express their interests. It was through these attempts that class consciousness developed and gradually spread.

On another level, social historians are concerned with the everyday activities of ordinary people rather than with those of royalty, leaders, or statesmen. Some of them insist, for example, that

> the history of American society has been subordinated to the history of the
> American state; the reality of the American people to ideologically determined
> abstractions. The history of the American people has been subordinated to
> the history of industrial technology, of capitalism, and of related values and
> institutional arrangements. [19]

Specifically, Professor George Rawick points out, although slavery has had an ineradicable effect on life in America, virtually no serious scholars have devoted much effort to understand the private world of the slaves themselves.

> The masters not only ruled the past in fact; they now rule its written history. Like the rest of the population which did not lead "notable" lives, the slaves appear usually only as faceless and nameless people murmuring and mumbling offstage.[20]

Rawick has assembled and edited an enormous amount of material directly relating to the lives of slaves. Included in this material are autobiographies of slaves, published shortly before or after the Civil War, and interviews with ex-slaves, recorded in the 1920s and 1930s by private researchers under the auspices of the federal government. The Slave Narrative Collection, of the Federal Writer's Project of the Works Projects Administration, assembled during the years from 1936 to 1938, consists of over ten thousand pages of typescript, containing over two thousand interviews with ex-slaves. Some of this material has been made available by Rawick in his massive series now consisting of nineteen volumes entitled, *The American Slave: A Composite Autobiography*.

Using material like this as well as other sources, Professor Eugene D. Genovese, in his impressive study, *Roll, Jordan, Roll*, has provided a picture of American society and its people during the era of slavery.[21] Beyond this, however, his study contributes in a very direct way to our understanding of the contemporary world. For example, as we noted in chapter 3 the so-called Moynihan report had caused a very heated controversy among social scientists and many others.[22] The report concluded, in essence, that slavery had emasculated black men, had created a matriarchy, and had prevented the development of a strong family structure among black people. Readers were free to deduce from this that many of the difficulties confronting blacks in this country could be attributed to family disorganization. Genovese, in disputing this thesis suggests that it is based on (1) a reading of the story of the twentieth-century ghetto backward in time, and an assumption that there has been a historical continuity since slavery days; and (2) an examination of slave law and the externals of family life, rather than on what actually went on in the slave quarters.[23]

Genovese points out that, during the twentieth century, blacks went north in large numbers and encountered enormous hardships. Black men were denied employment, not only because of their lack of skills, but also because of severe racial discimination. Black women, however, could often find work as domestics. All this resulted in some disorientation of the black family, but there is no basis for concluding that the disorientation extended back to the days of slavery. On the contrary, Genovese produces considerable evidence to suggest that family life among slaves was a very powerful force, both for the slaves themselves and for their masters.[24]

Examination of plantation records shows that masters and overseers characteristically adapted their disciplinary measures to take full acount of family relationships. Selling a troublesome slave might be delayed or avoided because it would cause resentment in his family of good workers. On the other hand, a slave who was influencing his relatives in a negative way might be sold to break that influence. Some slaveholders understood the strength of these family ties so well that they argued against separation of black family members on the grounds of economic expediency. The slaves worked much better when kept together. Others, however, in commenting on separations brought about by sales, insisted that slaves did not mind being separated from their wives or husbands.

> Not content with this fabrication, some slaveholders went so far as to assert that separation of mothers from children caused only minimum hardship. Most slaveholders knew this claim to be nonsense, but they nevertheless argued that the separation of fathers from their children was of little consequence.[25]

Rawick's slave narratives are also filled with fascinating episodes relating to this issue. Here are two of them:

> ...I rec'lect one time missus sold my mother and four children but it wasn't no trade. De woman's name was Mrs. Sheppard and she was a sassy old woman. She come into my mother's cabin and grabbed her and told her she was going to take her home. Mother jes' pushed her out de door and said she wouldn't go—and she told missus she wouldn't go—so dey had to call it off—it was no trade.[26]

> ... I cannot tell in words the feelings I had at that time. My sorrow knew no bounds. My very soul seemd to cry out, "Gone, gone, gone forever." I cried until my eyes looked like balls of fire. I felt for the first time in my life that I had been abused. How cruel it was to take my mother and father from me, I thought. My mother had been right. Slavery was cruel, so very cruel.
>
> Thus my mother and father were hired to Tennessee. The next morning they were to leave. I saw ma walking around with the baby under her arm as if it had been a bundle of some kind. Pa came up to the cabin with an old mare for ma to ride and an old mule for himself. Mr. Jennings was with him.
>
> "Fannie, leave the baby with Aunt Mary," said Mr. Jennings very quietly.
>
> At this, ma took the baby by its feet, a foot in each hand, and with the baby's head swinging downward, she vowed to smash its brains out before she'd leave it. Tears were streaming down her face. It was seldom that ma cried, and everyone knew she meant every word. Ma took her baby with her.[27]

Studies of Social Relations
of Production

Although critical sociologists think that the class structure of a society influences most institutions within society, they treat the actual nature of that influence as a problem to be studied concretely in specific societies. Many critical sociological studies are devoted to an examination of different institutions and practices in society, to see just how individuals are affected by class structure.

Christopher Jencks and his associates, for example, have examined the notion that American society is devoted to equality.[28] Most Americans, they observe, believe in "equality of opportunity," by which they mean that everyone—regardless of race, sex, wealth, or other characteristics—should have the same opportunity to succeed or fail in terms of education, jobs, and so on. During the 1960s, strategies based on providing equality of opportunity were seen as the way to eliminate poverty. There were three assumptions behind these strategies:

1 *Eliminating poverty is largely a matter of helping children born into poverty to rise out of it. Once families escape from poverty they do not fall back into it. Middle-class children rarely end up poor.*

2 *The primary reason poor children do not escape from poverty is that they do not acquire basic skills. They cannot read, write, calculate, or articulate. Lacking these skills, they cannot get or keep a well-paid job.*

3 *The best mechanism for breaking this vicious circle is educational reform. Since children born into poor homes do not acquire these skills at home, they must be taught them at school. This can be done by making sure that they attend the same schools as middle class children, by giving them extra compensatory programs in school, by giving their parents a voice in running their school, or by some combination of all three approaches.*[29]

On the basis of a very careful statistical analysis of data, Jencks concludes that each of these assumptions is false. While it is true that children born into poverty have a higher than average chance of ending up poor, there still are wide differences of economic status even within families. This means that inequality is renewed each generation. Cognitive skills have relatively little to do with economic success or failure. There is almost as much economic inequality among those scoring high on cognitive tests as there is in the general population. Thus, equalizing reading scores would not reduce economic inequality. There is also no evidence that school reform can affect performance on cognitive tests.

We cannot blame economic inequality on biological differences, says

Jencks, since there is nearly as much economic inequality among people with equal test scores as among people in general. We cannot blame economic inequality primarily on the fact that parents pass along disadvantages to their children, since there is nearly as much inequality among people whose parents had the same economic status as among people in general. We cannot blame economic inequality on differences between schools, since differences between schools seem to have very little effect on any measurable characteristics of the people who attend them.

All of this does not mean that it is impossible to eliminate economic inequality or poverty,but it does mean that we cannot do so through strategies based on equality of opportunity. Instead, according to Jencks, we need to adopt strategies based on "equality of condition," designed to reduce the actual economic gap between people. This might involve reducing the wage disparities among different jobs, providing free public services to the poor, making taxes more progressive so that the poor pay less and the rich pay much more (*in fact*, rather than in theory), or even by providing a guaranteed minimum income. In short, reducing economic inequality requires taking from the rich and giving to the poor.

Samuel Bowles and Herbert Gintis have gone beyond the narrow focus of Jencks' study to examine the historical development and role of education in American society.[30] Combining statistical research with historical and dialectical analysis, they argue that the educational system is one of the mechanisms of society that teaches people to accept as natural the divisions of wealth and power embedded in the class structure. Patterns of inequality, repression, and forms of class domination are not restricted to the economic sphere, they maintain, but reappear in the major institutions of society. They identify four main functions of the educational system:

> **1** *Schooling produces many of the technical and cognitive skills required for adequate job performance.*

> **2** *The educational system helps legitimate economic inequality by reconciling the aspirations of individuals with their actual future positions.*

> **3** *The school generates rewards, and selects personal characteristics relevant to the staffing of positions in the class structure.*

> **4** *Through the patterns of status distinctions it fosters (e.g., teacher-student, upper-class/lower-class, etc.), the educational system reinforces an awareness of fine distinctions between individuals within the same group, and this is the basis for fragmentation of the working class.*[31]

Thus, they argue, a major historical role of the educational system has been to defuse and cut off conflict between classes in society. Since the forms and character of class conflict also develop and change over time, the educational system has had to be reorganized periodically to adapt to the changing class structure. George Vickers has suggested that the New Left, which appeared during the 1960s and was made up largely of white students, marked one such period of reorganization.[32] The growth of white-collar occupations, and the corresponding decline in blue-collar workers, led, he claimed, to changes in family structure and patterns of child-rearing. These white-collar occupations required different attitudes and behavior than did blue-collar jobs, and parents began to pass on these values and attitudes to their children. The educational system, however, was still teaching attitudes and values relevant to a now-disappearing occupational structure. As the children raised with these new values entered the higher educational institutions, sharp conflict broke out, resulting in the eventual restructuring of education along lines consistent with the change in occupations. In this sense, Vickers suggests, the New Left represented the growth and reintegration of capitalist society at a higher level, rather than a sign of the breakdown of that society.

Critical Sociology and Poverty

We have already mentioned the way in which John Gurley and Christopher Jencks analyze poverty and inequality from a critical orientation. Critical sociologists, like applied sociologists have devoted a great deal of attention to poverty. Most applied studies have developed recommendations for reforms in existing government policies or programs, while critical studies have concluded that only by eliminating inequality, can poverty be eliminated. At the same time, critical studies have maintained that inequality cannot be ended without fundamentally changing the basic structure of our economic and political systems.

Some years ago two social scientists working in the critical-science orientation—Paul Baran and Paul Sweezy—summarized the main arguments of this position in these terms.[33] Why is it that poverty, which recently had been written off as a phenomenon of the past, suddenly seemed to become a central issue? The answer has two parts: In the first place, as Marx pointed out in *Capital* and as subsequent experience has verified, capitalism, wherever it exists, tends to generate wealth at one pole and poverty at the other. This is the law of capitalist development that has never been accepted by noncritical or bourgeois social scientists. (Bourgeois social scientists believe that a contrary condition prevails—that there is a leveling-up tendency inherent in capitalism.)

Second, unemployment and underemployment are always at the root of capitalist poverty. The unemployed constitute what Marx called the industrial reserve army—workers who have been deprived of income and who undermine the security and bargaining power of those with whom they compete for scarce jobs.

During World War II, unemployment was really eliminated for a few years. Ten million men in the most productive age groupings were mobilized into the armed services, while total production was being expanded by two-thirds or more. All persons physically able to work were able to get jobs, despite their age, color, or sex. Several members of a family could be employed, and family incomes in the lower-income brackets rose dramatically, as did the living standards of the poor. These favorable conditions for the underprivileged and disadvantaged continued, in a somewhat weakened form, throughout the postwar boom and the prosperity of the early 1950s, which was caused by the military spending occurring in connection with the Korean War. This prosperity was misinterpreted by conventional or bourgeois social scientists, who thought that capitalism was behaving as it should behave. They had forgotten the lessons of the Great Depression of the 1930s and previous experience. They saw the future as an extrapolation of the completely atypical conditions following the greatest war in history. But "capitalism's basic law of motion, temporarily thwarted, soon resumed its sway." [34] Unemployment increased, and poverty again was with us. Baran and Sweezy undoubtedly would attribute some easing of poverty during the late 1960s to the war in Vietnam. Unemployment again increased when that war ended.

For Baran and Sweezy, poverty is not a subjective affair. Although every society has its own standards for measuring poverty, these standards are real, objective facts. Marx's concept of the subsistence minimum is relevant here. Marx did not think of the subsistence minimum as being determined physiologically, as did the classical economists. He recognized that a worker's so-called natural needs for food, clothing, fuel, and housing vary with the climate and other physical conditions of the country in which he lives and works. At the same time, other wants are a product of historical development and, to a considerable extent, depend upon the customary practice and conditions of a country. Thus, although the subsistence minimum varies historically, it can be identified and measured more or less approximately at any given time and place. Poverty is therefore defined as the condition of those members of a society whose incomes are not sufficient to pay for the subsistence minimum in that society at that time.

Using this criterion, Baran and Sweezy describe poverty in 1959—the latest year for which they had census data. In that year, they note, a "modest but adequate" level of living cost a family in any of twenty large American cities somewhere between $5,370 annually (in Houston) and $6,567 (in Chicago). But during that same year, one-fifth of the families in the country had incomes of less than $2,800 a year, another fifth had incomes between $2,800 and $4,800, and a third fifth had incomes between $4,800 and $6,500. Baran and Sweezy think the conclusion is inescapable that, by the standards of American society itself, virtually half of its population is living in poverty. It should be noted that their figures apply to residents of the twenty largest cities. Analysis of poverty in rural areas and smaller towns requires somewhat different data, since both income and cost of living are usually lower in these areas.

Sociology: Pure, Applied, or Critical?

We have now devoted three chapters to describing in some detail three different orientations of sociology. Some readers may wonder why we have devoted so much space to internal disagreements that are likely to be of very little interest to undergraduate students. Why have we devoted so much space to academic issues before getting to the "meat" of sociology—the results of research into substantive problems?

The answer is that there are different "cuts" of meat, and we must first choose the ones we want. Different orientations focus on different problems, or define the same problem differently. Most teachers of sociology implicitly or explicitly operate within one of the major orientations. This orientation strongly influences the way they define sociological theories, methods, concepts, and problems. Sociologists working within the pure, applied, or critical-science orientation often believe that their own orientation is correct, while the others are really ideologies that either support or attack the status quo. To return to the butcher shop analogy, sociologists often see the choice between orientations as a matter of differences in quality. One's own orientation is "prime," while the others are at best "approved," and at worst "rotten."

We do not mean to imply that the major orientations have no ideological characteristics. Indeed, we have tried to indicate how each is intricately tied up with an interest in maintaining or changing existing social structures. Nor do we mean to imply that sociologists can avoid choosing an orientation and simply use whichever one is appropriate to the problem at hand. We reject the possibility of value-neutrality in this sense. What we do mean to suggest is that sociologists must clearly understand that there are ways of defining and analyzing problems that are different from their own, and these differences lead to different ways of doing sociology. More important, teachers of sociology must make the effort to present the subject to students through an authentic sociological perspective—that is, they must be prepared to stand outside their own assumptions and present alternative orientations as fairly as they do their own.

In the remainder of this book, we will try to show how these basic orientations affect the theories, methods, and concepts employed by sociologists. Part 2 discusses the range of theories and methods employed, and examines how these reflect more basic orientations. In part 3, we look at three basic concepts used by all sociologists—social structure, culture, and socialization—and show how each of these is defined and used quite differently within different orientations.

Throughout the book we treat sociology as a science. Like the natural sciences, however, sociology is not static and unchanging. Just as there are fundamental paradigm conflicts in the natural sciences (Ptolemaic astronomy versus Copernican astronomy, Newtonian mechanics versus relativistics mechanics, the theory of relativity versus quantum theory), sociologists have fundamentally different ways of understanding society. During the last quarter of the twentieth century, these competing orientations will be refined and tested in the practice of sociology, and they will be judged by their adequacy in explaining social life and by their effectiveness in changing social structures, when necessary.

Summary

Sociology as a critical science focuses on social change. Critical sociologists believe that the overall character of different types of society leads to different relationships among individuals, groups, and institutions within society. The overall character generates opposing tendencies, or contradictions, within society, and social change results from the conflicts between these opposing tendencies.

Karl Marx maintained that the overall character of society is shaped primarily by its mode of production. This mode of production consists of the forces of production (technology and resources) together with the relations of production (the division of labor and relationships of authority and control). Marx argued that social institutions like government and the legal system differ according to the mode of production. The basic source of social change in society, according to Marx, is contradictions between changing forces of production and the relations of production. These contradictions are fought out through class conflict between different groups in society.

Critical sociologists attempt to use Marx's method of analysis to examine contemporary societies. They compare different societies to see how the mode of production affects individual, group, and institutional relationships. They try to understand how contradictions within specific types of societies lead to characteristic patterns of social change in institutions and in society as a whole. They examine contradictions between forces and relations of production to understand the nature and direction of changes now taking place.

See John Lewis, *The Marxism of Marx* (New York: Beekman, 1972), for an exceptionally lucid explanation of fundamental Marxist concepts. *The Communist Manifesto* appears in many collections. It is clearly written and is required reading for any understanding of the work of Karl Marx and Friedrich Engels. For an excellent biography and presentation of some core ideas see John Lewis, *The Life and Teaching of Karl Marx* (New York: Beekman 1972).

In addition, the following pamphlets by Karl Marx should prove to be very valuable: *Value, Price and Profit* (New York: International Publishing Co., 1935); *Wage, Labor and Capital* (New York: International Publishers, 1948); and *Wages, Price and Profit* (San Francisco: China Books and Periodicals, 1965).

For an excellent, simplified description of Marxist economic theory, see Ernest Mandel, *Introduction to Marxist Economic Theory* (New York: Pathfinder Press, 1973). For more sophisticated treatments, see Ernest Mandel, *Marxist Economic Theory*, 2 vols. trans. Brian Pierce (New York and London: Monthly Review Press, 1968); and Paul Sweezy, *The Theory of Capitalist Development* (New York: Monthly Review Press, 1968).

For a critical analysis of the New Left in terms of the development of advanced capitalism, see Herbert Marcuse, *Counterrevolution and Revolt* (Boston: Beacon Press, 1972).

For an important critique of Marxist practice and theory by a Yugoslavian philosopher, sociologist, and Marxist, see Svetozar Stojanovic, *Between Ideals and Reality: A Critique of Socialism and Its Future* (New York: Oxford University Press, 1973).

See Juliet Mitchell, *Psychoanalysis and Feminism* (New York: Random House, 1974) for a critical view of sexism by an author who is a Marxist as well as a feminist.

Joyce Ladner, ed. *The Death of White Sociology* (New York: Random House, 1973) is an interesting collection of articles critical of American sociology for what is seen as its white racist character.

Michael Albert's *What is to be Undone?* (Boston, Mass.: An Extending Horizons Book, Porter Sargent Publishers, 1974) provides a critique of classical Marxism, Leninism, Anarchism, and Maoism.

For what may be a disturbing view of contemporary U.S. society, see Alan Wolfe, *The Seamy Side of Democracy: Repression in America* (New York: David McKay Co., 1973). See Harry Braverman, *Labor and Monopoly Capital* (New York: Monthly Review Press, 1974) for an examination of class structure in contemporary America.

Notes

1 John Gurley, "Capitalism: The Root of the Problem," in *Up Against The American Myth,* Tom Christoffel, David Finkelhor, and Dan Gilbarg, eds. (New York: Holt, Rinehart and Winston, 1970).

2 Ibid. p. 51.

3 Ibid. p. 53.

4 Marx wrote many books, but the most important one was *Capital: A Critique of Political Economy.* See trans. from the third German edition by Samuel Moore and Edward Aveling (New York: International Publishers, 1967). An important book for sociologists is Karl Marx and Friedrich Engels, *The German Ideology,* ed. and with an introduction by R. Pascal (New York: International Publishers, 1947).

5 Karl Marx, "Theses on Feuerbach," in *Basic Writings on Politics and Philosophy,* Lewis Feuer, ed. (Garden City, N.Y.: Doubleday, 1959), p. 245.

6 See, for example, Marx and Engels, *The German Ideology.*

7 For a more complete discussion of Marx's theories of capitalist development and class struggle, see Anthony Giddens, *Capitalism and Modern Social Theory* (Cambridge, England: Cambridge University Press, 1971).

8 Quoted in Anthony Giddens, *Capitalism and Modern Social Theory* (Cambridge, England: Cambridge University Press, 1971), p. 49.

9 The relationship between Marx and other sociological theorists has received considerable attention. See especially, Alvin W. Gouldner, *The Coming Crisis of Western Sociology* (New York: Basic Books, 1970); also see Irving M. Zeitlin, *Marxism: A Re-examination* (Princeton, N.J.: Van Nostrand, 1967).

10 C. Wright Mills, *The Sociological Imagination* (New York: Oxford University Press, 1959).

11 Ibid., p. 3.

12 Ibid., p. 128.

13 Ibid., pp. 6–7

14 C. Wright Mills, *White Collar* (New York: Oxford University Press, 1951).

15 Ibid. p. xvi.

16 Anthony Giddens, *The Class Structure of the Advanced Societies* (New York: Harper, 1973).

17 E. P. Thompson, *The Making of the English Working Class* (New York: Random House, Pantheon Books, 1963), p. 9.

18 Ibid., p. 9.

19 George P. Rawick, *The American Slave: A Composite Autobiography,* Vol 1, From Sundown to Sunup: The Making of the Black Community (Westport Conn.: Greenwood Publishing Co., 1972), p. xiii. Used with the permission of Greenwood Press, the original publishers.

20 Ibid., p. xiv.

21 Eugene D. Genovese, *Roll, Jordan, Roll* (New York: Random House, Pantheon Books, 1974).

22 For a comprehensive account of this controversy and the text of the Moynihan report itself, *see* Lee Rainwater and William L. Yancy, *The Moynihan Report and the Politics of Controversy* (Cambridge, Mass.: M.I.T. Press, 1967).

23 See Genovese, *Roll, Jordan Roll,* p. 145.

24 Ibid., pp. 452–57.

25 Ibid., p. 455.

26 Rawick, *The American Slave,* Vol. 2, *Arkansas Narratives,* Part 7, and *Missouri Narratives,* pp.111–12. Used with the permission of Greenwood Press, the original publishers.

27 Rawick, *The American Slave,* Vol. 18, *Unwritten History of Slavery* (Nashville, Tenn.: Fisk University), p. 228. Used with the permission of Greenwood Press, the original publishers.

28 Christopher Jencks, et al., *Inequality: A Reassessment of the Effect of Family and Schooling in America* (New York: Harper, 1972).

29 Ibid., p. 7.

30 Samuel Bowles and Herbert Gintis, *Schooling in Capitalist America: Educational Reform and the Contradictions of Economic Life* (New York: Basic Books, 1975).

31 See, Samuel Bowles, Herbert Gintis, and Peter Meyer, "The Long Shadow of Work: Education, the Family, and the Reproduction of the Social Division of Labor," *The Insurgent Sociologist* 5 (Summer 1975): 7.

32 George R. Vickers, *The Formation of the New Left: The Early Years* (Lexington, Mass.: D. C. Heath & Co., 1975).

33 Paul A. Baran, and Paul M. Sweezy, *Monopoly Capital* (New York: Monthly Review Press, 1966).

34 Ibid., p. 287.

part
two

"Method" has to do, first of all, with how to ask and answer questions with some assurance that the answers are more or less durable. "Theory" has to do, above all, with paying close attention to the words one is using, especially their degree of generality and their logical relations. The primary purpose of both is clarity of conception and economy of procedure . . . . To have mastered "method" and "theory" is to have become a self-conscious thinker, a man at work and aware of the assumptions and the implications of whatever he is about. To be mastered by "method" or "theory" is simply to be kept from working . . . .

For the classical social scientists, neither method nor theory is an autonomous domain; methods are methods for some range of problems; theories are theories of some range of phenomena. They are like the language of the country you live in: it is nothing to brag about that you can speak it, but it is a disgrace and an inconvenience if you cannot.[1]

Who will win the next presidential election? Will it make any difference who wins the next presidential election? If X wins rather than Y, what implications does that have for the kind of society we will live in? Do the campaign issues have anything to do with what is important for our society? What is important?

We all, of course, may have opinions about the answers to these questions, but what is a scientific answer? What can we know about human society and how can we know it? The most obvious answer is that we can know facts; but what are facts? Facts are real; but what is reality?

To study any problem, sociologists must first decide what questions to ask, how to ask them, and how to understand the answers. Suppose, for example, that we want to know who will win the next presidential election. We could ask all potential voters how they will vote, but it might be practically impossible to do so. We could ask a representative sample of potential voters how they will vote, but how would we decide what was a representative sample? Even if we solved this problem, how would we know that those interviewed will actually vote according to their response? Moreover, how would we know which potential voters will actually vote? How would we know if respondents were lying? Finally, how would we know that someone else asking the same questions would not get totally different answers?

As the example suggests, studying sociological problems is a difficult task that requires us to make some complicated decisions. Since sociologists study human behavior, at least part of the time, we must discover the relevant characteristics of human beings that may affect behavior. Since we cannot study all human beings or all situations, we must decide how to choose the ones we will study. Since we must choose among people and situations for our studies, we must determine the extent to which our findings can be applied to other people or other situations.

The decisions we make result in our following certain procedures rather than others. For example, if survey researchers decide that sex is not a relevant characteristic affecting behavior, they may disregard the sex of the people selected for study. If they decide that the people and situations studied are typical of the people and situations in Chicago, they may generalize their findings to all of Chicago, but not to Phoenix or San Francisco. The procedures and techniques used to study a sociological problem are usually referred to as methods. A sociological method includes the range of procedures and techniques employed to answer a certain type of question.[2]

Methods provide us with facts. Once we have decided that a particular set of procedures and techniques can be employed to answer a certain type of question, we have also implicitly decided to accept the results of those procedures and techniques as real. If we decide that a sample of people is representative of the voting population, and that certain questions asked in a certain way will tell us how they would vote if the next presidential election were held today, then we have implicitly decided that their responses are facts about how the voting population would vote if the next election were held today. This is what public opinion polls do.

Because the procedures and techniques for collecting such facts are often very elaborate and complex, it is easy to forget that they are based upon decisions made by sociologists. Sociological methods represent decisions about how we can know about reality, and theories about the nature of reality. If we think that the procedures and techniques used by natural scientists to study natural phenomena are appropriate for studying human behavior in society, then we have decided that social reality is essentially the same as nature. On the other hand, if we think that sociological methods must reflect the capacity of people to make choices, then we have decided that social reality is somewhat different from nature, because human beings can control their behavior through their will.

All sociological methods implicitly take for granted some particular view about the nature of reality. It is theory that articulates our view of reality and guides our selection of method. A sociological theory attempts to classify and organize social events in some logical fashion, to explain the causes of events, and to offer an understanding of why and how events occur.[3]

Sociological theories include concepts and variables for formulating sociological problems. Concepts are abstractions formed by generalizing from specific cases. There are millions of different kinds of rocks, for example, but we use the concept "rock" to denote the abstract quality that distinguishes a rock from something else. "Society" is a concept that is abstract and often hard to define explicitly, yet we recognize what is meant when we hear the term used. A sociological theory consists of many concepts logically connected in some way.

Variables are concepts that describe differences among phenomena. Size, for example, is a variable that can help us distinguish between small rocks and large rocks. Age, weight, and sex are all variables that serve a similar purpose. Sociological theories systematically incorporate concepts and variables into a description of the real world.

Every sociological theory tries to explain how social order and social change occur. In addressing these problems, different social theorists have developed different, and often conflicting, systems of concepts and variables. In chapters 5 to 8 we examine three rather different types of social theories and the methods employed by their adherents.

Notes

1 C. Wright Mills, *The Sociological Imagination* (New York: Oxford University Press, 1959), pp. 120–121.

2 See Aaron V. Cicourel, *Method and Measurement in Sociology* (New York: Free Press, 1964).

3 See Jonathan H. Turner, *The Structure of Sociological Theory* (Homewood, Ill.: Dorsey Press, 1974).

Positivist
Theories

What is society? Is it a simple sum of its individual members, or is it something more? Are there natural laws that govern the social order and human behavior? Since earliest recorded history, people have sought answers to these questions about human existence. Religion answered by saying that man is created by God, and society is a working out of God's will on earth. Human beings, through faith, can seek to understand and obey God's will, or they can challenge it, at their own peril. Metaphysics provided another set of answers, by insisting that man is part of nature, and that society is a reflection of the underlying laws of nature. Human beings, through logic, can discover the abstract laws of nature, and seek to perfect the present flawed society according to these laws. With the rise of Science, a few centuries ago, still another set of answers was offered. According to the scientific viewpoint,[1] there is an underlying order to nature and human beings can discover and comprehend that underlying order by systematically observing, classifying, and interpreting the data of their senses.

But is society really like nature? Are there social laws analagous to natural laws? For those who treat sociology as a natural science—the positivists—the answer to these questions is a resounding yes. The positivist approach, derived from Auguste Comte, set out to free knowledge about society from religious beliefs and metaphysics by emulating the model of the natural sciences. The task of sociology, in this view, is to discover the essentially unchanging natural laws of human behavior. Although the ultimate goal of positivism is to predict and control social behavior, positivists believe that this will be possible only after the discovery of such laws. For this reason, positivism does not focus on immediate and pressing social problems, but engages in a disinterested pursuit of knowledge for its own sake.

Comte recorded the central tenets of positivism well over a century ago, and sociological research based on them continues to the present day. During the intervening century, theoretical and empirical studies have expanded, refined, and altered some of Comte's original formulations. These modifications have involved different ideas about the parts of society sociologists should study. Since contemporary sociology carried out within the pure science orientation contains two apparently conflicting notions about the nature of society, it is important to understand how both of these are logical outgrowths of a positivist orientation.

What Is Society?

By the time of the French Revolution in 1789, political philosophers no longer thought about society as something imposed on mankind by a source external to human beings, such as a deity. Instead, philosophers like Hobbes, Locke, and Rousseau considered society to be a creation of human beings.[2] According to this view, isolated individuals existed prior to society and entered into an agreement, or social contract, that established laws to regulate interpersonal relations. These laws were designed to foster cooperation and prevent the war of each against all that would result from unrestrained competition among individuals in a so-called state of nature. As a consequence of this view, philosophical studies of society increasingly focused on identifying the elements of human nature, and on examining the ways in which human beings agree to establish society. Society was seen as the sum of all its individual persons, and the problem was to explain how and why these separate individuals came together to form a whole.

Auguste Comte wanted to make the study of society truly scientific. He believed that there were two principles always at work in the world—order and progress—and he proposed that sociology be divided into two branches to study these different principles. Social statics would discover the natural laws governing the fundamental condition of the social organism; social dynamics would focus on the natural laws governing social change.[3] Because social statics was designed to focus on the eternal and unchanging basis of society, while social dynamics was to deal with its changeable and passing features, the latter tended to become a secondary concern in Comte's sociology. Order was a more important principle than progress, for Comte. He concluded that the servitude and misery of most people living in society resulted from the natural laws of social order. The task of sociologists was to show the masses of people that their predicament was necessary to the existence of society. It could be eased only within narrow limits.

During the nineteenth century, the positivist view of society was further developed and modified by Herbert Spencer, a British sociologist (1820–1903). For Spencer, society is analogous to a living organism. It is made up of parts that function very much like the parts of a human body.[4] In *Social Statics,* Spencer argued that the development of society involves two basic processes—integration and differentiation. As society grows larger in numbers of individuals, it becomes more and more integrated; individuals are more and more dependent on one another. Simultaneously, society becomes more complex and differentiated; there are more and more specialized tasks, so that individuals increasingly develop very differently. These two processes lead to the evolution of human society—a notion that Spencer seems to have arrived at independently of Darwin's theory of evolution. Indeed, Spencer came very close to formulating a theory of evolution in nature prior to Darwin. His ideas about the struggle for survival and the survival of the fittest were formulated prior to the publication of Darwin's *The Origin of Species.*

Spencer, however, was later greatly impressed by other aspects of Darwin's work. He began to alter Comte's view of human action as basically a rational activity. Instead of rational choice, he suggested, heredity and environment are the main determinants of human action. Relations among individuals in society are characterized by a struggle for existence; the existing state of genes and environmental conditions determines the survival of the fittest. For Spencer, deliberate human intervention to change society could not help much, and might even make things worse. He insisted that social organization could change only through evolution over a long period of time.[5]

For Comte, society as a whole or the social organism, determines relations among individuals. Individuals must adapt their own desires and behavior to the necessary requirements of society. In a similar vein, Spencer located the twin processes of integration and differentiation within the organism as a whole; the evolution of the whole gradually altered relations among individuals within it. This view of society as something more than the sum of individuals within it quite intentionally contradicted the view of society as a social contract, which had been developed in the seventeenth and eighteenth centuries. Comte and Spencer thought that this earlier view had served to discredit existing social institutions and governments, thus fostering revolution and anarchy. At the same time, it had failed to offer new institutions, leading to stable progress. Instead of such a critical or negative view of existing society, they argued, a "positive" view was needed to show the necessity for existing social organization.

Emile Durkheim continued the emphasis on the social whole, but his work helped shift the focus of research away from the overall structure of society and toward relations among parts within the whole. Like Comte, Durkheim was concerned about the disappearance of traditional moral codes provided by organized religion, with no new morality emerging to replace them. The task of sociology, for him, was to help develop a unifying morality based on science. As he announced in his very first work, "This book is pre-eminently an attempt to treat the facts of moral life according to the method of the positive sciences.... We do not wish to extract ethics from science, but to establish the science of ethics, which is quite different." [6]

In *The Division of Labor in Society,* Durkheim examined the historical evolution of human society. Like Spencer, he characterized this evolution in terms of both integration and differentiation. In primitive societies, he argued, individuals tend to perform similar tasks; there is relatively little specialization. As societies grow in numbers and complexity, however, tasks become more and more diverse and specialized; division of labor increases. As a consequence of this division of labor, individuals become more and more dependent on each other, rather than being self-sufficient. This growing dependency Durkheim called functional interdependence. Individuals perform different functions necessary for society as a whole, and, conversely, society depends on the smooth working together of all the functions. In the human body, for example, the heart, liver, and brain all perform functions necessary for survival of the body as an organism; conversely, the body requires that all the organs work together smoothly, if life is to be sustained.

Durkheim's primary interest in his first book was to understand the nature of the "glue" that assured the smooth functioning of all the parts of society. In small, primitive societies with little division of labor, any individual deviation from accepted practices and beliefs represents a challenge and threat to the whole society. The function of law in such societies is *repressive;* it is designed to punish violators. In large, complex societies with a complicated division of labor, on the other hand, individual deviations from accepted practices and beliefs upset the balance and smooth functioning of the parts. In such a society, the function of law is *restitutive;* it is designed to restore order among the parts. In this latter kind of society, relations between individuals are like a contract providing both rights and obligations. When the contract is violated, it is necessary to restore the loss to the injured party. The important point, for Durkheim, is that there is a moral basis to such contracts. This noncontractual element of morality really provides the "glue" that holds society together.

In his later books, Durkheim continued to explore the collective conscience of society—the integrating force that has made possible the functional interdependence of individuals, even as society has grown more and more differentiated. In *The Elementary Forms of Religious Life,* he examined a large range of societies and the forms of thought found within them.[7] He concluded that the integrating force in human society is religion. The shared understanding of the past, present, and future essential to maintain the functional interdependence of individuals in society results, he said, from their experiences in communal rites, ceremonies, and festivals provided by religion. Thus, while Durkheim continued the positivist quest for fundamental laws of society as a whole, his research focused more on the various parts of society and their relation to other parts.

A similar shift is evident in the work of William Graham Sumner (1840–1910). After reading a series of essays by Herbert Spencer, Sumner abandoned a career as an Episcopalian minister to pursue sociology, and in 1872 was appointed professor of political and social science at Yale University.

Sumner picked up on the idea of a natural struggle for existence to explain inequalities of wealth and power in modern society. The greatest step forward in the struggle for existence, he argued, is the production of capital, which increases the productivity of labor and allows civilization to advance. Primitive peoples ceased to accumulate capital and to compete with one another a long time ago. As a result, they have a backward and unenlightened way of life. Hereditary wealth is indispensable for social development, Sumner argued, since it assures the hardworking man that his children will be able to carry on what he started. If the fittest are to survive, the captains of industry must be paid for their unique organizing talents. Their large fortunes are, in effect, legitimate wages. Millionaires are the product of natural selection, and, although they get high wages and live in luxury, the bargain is a good one for society as a whole.[8]

What motivates the struggle for existence and the competition between individuals? Here Sumner diverges from the focus on society as a whole and develops an explanation of social relationships based on individual characteristics. In *Folkways*, he tells us that originally there were four motives shared by all human beings—hunger, love, vanity, and fear.[9] These motives gave rise to interests. In an attempt to satisfy these interests, individuals behave in ways that experience has shown by trial and error to be the right one. Since individuals are basically alike, what is suitable for one person is suitable for others. Behavior patterns appropriate for satisfying various interests become habitual. Sumner calls these habitual patterns *folkways*. At some point, certain folkways are defined as essential to the well-being of society as a whole. They then become *mores*, and any violation is severely punished. In other words, what the members of a society decide is useful and necessary for maintaining society determines what is moral.

Starting from individual motives leads Sumner to reverse Durkheim's analysis of the integrating force in society. For Sumner, a good person is still one who contributes to the material welfare of society, while a person who hampers such progress is bad. But the pursuit of self-interest is the basic motivation in the struggle for existence, according to Sumner. As one student of his work has characterized his thinking, "It becomes a simple step to say that the good man is he who most single-mindedly seeks to promote *his own* well-being. Selfishness is raised to the status of an absolute good." [10]

As the focus of scientific research shifted from society as a whole to individuals relationships, new problems arose. When people like Comte or Spencer compared different types of societies, they employed relatively simple distinctions, such as "simple" versus "complex," or "integration" and "differentiation." Such categories applied to whole societies, and usually were meant to describe different stages of historical development. As the focus shifted to individuals, however, it became necessary to try to categorize different types of people.

Vilfredo Pareto (1848–1923) attempted to apply the natural-scientific method to the study of human actions. As he put it, "we here venture to expound a sociology that is experimental, after the fashion of chemistry, physics, and other such sciences."[11] We have to begin by recognizing that all actions are subjective in the sense that they are motivated by our beliefs about the consequences that will follow from them. If our beliefs are wrong, then we will presumably change our actions.

Pareto thought that actions should be distinguished according to whether they are logical or nonlogical. Logical actions are those that connect means and ends, in fact as well as in belief. All other actions are nonlogical. Pareto constructed a typology containing four different types of nonlogical actions. Actions performed simply as courtesies or out of habit are one type of nonlogical action. Actions that people try to justify represent another type. Instinctive acts performed by nonhuman animals are a third type, and actions that cannot reach the desired goal through the means employed constitute the fourth type.

Pareto maintained that society is a system of forces maintaining itself in balance. Within this system are physical forces (soil, climate, and so on), external forces (relations with other societies), and internal forces. The latter category includes sentiments, feelings, and ideas. Society develops from individual actions. Since these actions tend to be illogical, society itself tends to be illogical. The relative equilibrium existing in society is maintained by residues of nonlogical actions. These residues tend to be unchanging.

He argued that human beings have a basic need to defend their actions as being logical rather than nonlogical. The actions or excuses designed to disguise the nonlogical character of residues are called derivatives. These are something like ideologies.

In addition to all these typologies of individual actions, Pareto distinguished two groups of people in society—the elite and the nonelite. The elite consists of the relatively small number of people who have achieved success in a particular area of life. It includes the governing elite (which holds political power) and the nongoverning elite (which does not hold political power). Social change in society results from a "circulation of elites," sometimes involving the use of force to replace those in power. In the long run, Pareto believed, no elite can maintain itself in power forever. As one distinguished social theorist has summarized his views:

> The lions oust the foxes. Once in power, however, it is easy for the elite, resting on residues of persistence, to maintain power by combinations of force and trickery. There is an upper and lower class in every society showing a difference in distribution of the residues. There is also a circulation of individuals from upper to lower classes and vice versa. Although the intensity of circulation varies from society to society and in a given society over a period of time, it is nonetheless inevitable that any aristocracy is destined someday to disappear. All the devices of aristocracy to maintain its position—including the elevation of dangerous leaders from the lower to the upper classes, the use of bribery, corruption, and extermination— will not prevail in the long run.[12]

Although the theorists we have mentioned so far saw themselves as scientists in the positivist tradition, their fundamental views about the nature of society often reflected religious, ethical, or political views not really subject to scientific scrutiny. Max Weber (1864–1920) has been described by Julian Freund as the "first in practice to place sociology on a strictly scientific basis."[13] Sociology, he felt, must not be based on convictions alien to the scientific postulates at its center. Moral, religious, political, and ethical considerations are simply not within the proper domain of scientific sociology. Weber believed that it was not possible for sociologists to ignore the problem of the meaning of actions, since human action usually has a purpose. It is always possible to view any action from the standpoint of different values, and he cautioned sociologists to use care to indicate clearly their own value standpoints. Only by being clear about their own values, he believed, could sociologists prevent their values from influencing their scientific research. His concern with subjective understanding has caused some observers to view Weber as an advocate of *Verstehen* sociology.

It is true that Weber believed meaning and values are part of the subject matter of sociology, but his basic approach was a comparative method of analysis. He tried to construct ideal types of social behavior based on actual behavior found in society. While the ideal types never exist in a pure form in society, Weber argued that they allow sociologists to compare fundamental patterns and trends in different societies and within societies at different points in time.

Whereas Pareto's work stemmed from a basic distinction between logical and nonlogical action, Weber distinguished four separate ideal types of human action:

1 *Rational action in pursuit of a goal (Zweckrational):* this is roughly the same as Pareto's logical action. In this type, the actor presumably has a clear idea of both the goal of action and the means of attaining it. For Pareto, however, if action taken by the actor is unsuitable because of faulty information, the action is nonlogical. For Weber, such action remains rational, because rationality is defined in terms of the actor, not the observer.

2 *Rational action in pursuit of a value (Wertrational):* this is action taken not in pursuit of a goal, but for the purpose of remaining faithful to a value. A captain going down with his ship is an example of such an action.

3 *Affective or emotional action:* when action is taken not to achieve a goal or value, but reflects the emotional state of the actor, it is affective action. The action of a parent slapping a child might be such an action.

4 *Traditional action:* this is action taken by reason of habit or custom.

The purpose of constructing these ideal types was to explore the factors tending to make one type predominant in a particular society at a particular point in time. In *The Protestant Ethic and the Spirit of Capitalism*, Weber tried to show that, for a capitalist economic system to develop, it is necessary for people to have a specific kind of motivation and personality structure.[14] They must be willing to work hard, save money, and invest it in somewhat risky economic ventures. He thought that the Protestant religion provided these motivations and that, together with appropriate economic conditions, Protestantism was a crucial factor in the emergence of capitalism.

In later studies, Weber compared the role of religion in the West and in the East, and began to investigate the reasons that Western society and culture were increasingly characterized by *Zweckrational* action.[15] He concluded that the distinctive feature of Western capitalism was the attempt to satisfy the desire for maximum profits through discipline and science rather than conquest and adventure. This effort was aided by the bureaucratic organization, which, he believed, was becoming the essential and dominant characteristic of capitalist society. The expansion of bureaucratic rationality was leading to a situation in which the means used to obtain efficiency were becoming ends that often undermined the original goals of rational action.[16]

What Is Society? A Summary

As we have seen, nineteenth- and early twentieth- century positivist theorists provided an ambivalent answer to the question, "What is society?" To the extent that society was seen as analogous to an organism or system, they treated society as something more than the sum of its individual characteristics. The overall nature of society was thought to determine relationships among individuals, groups, and institutions. These parts were to be studied and explained in terms of their functions in maintaining society as a whole. This conception is explicit in Comte, Spencer, and Durkheim and, to a lesser degree, in Pareto.

On the other hand, to the extent that positivist theorists focused on human action as the basic building blocs of society, they saw society as equivalent to the sum of its parts. In order to understand society, it is first necessary to discover the fundamental types of actions and the unchanging laws of human behavior governing such actions, it was thought. Such a conception is implicit in Sumner's notion of motives and in Pareto's and Weber's typologies of human action.

This ambivalence remained unresolved in the writing of nineteenth-century and early twentieth-century theorists. Most of them attempted to analyze the formal properties of society as a whole (its structure) and to describe the relations among its parts (their functions.) At the same time, they constructed typologies of human action rooted in the meanings, values, and subjective characteristics of human behavior. Later in the twentieth century, these two strains of positivist thinking became more sharply polarized. In contemporary sociology, the positivist tradition finds expression, on the one hand, in a theory known as *structural-functionalism* and, on the other, in *behaviorism,* (or *social exchange theory*). Despite sharp differences between the formal properties of structural-functionalism and behaviorism, advocates of both share a commitment to empirical, descriptive techniques based on natural-scientific methods.

Structural-Functionalism

Durkheim was the first sociologist to employ a systematic functionalist analysis. He asked about the function of religion in establishing values and rituals that hold society together, and he asked similar questions about other institutions. After Durkheim, the functionalist approach was further developed by cultural anthropologists like Bronislaw Malinowski and A. R. Radcliffe-Brown. They tried to understand primitive societies in terms of the functions of various aspects of social life. During the 1940s and '50s, functionalism was a major theoretical framework for American sociology.

Basic to traditional functionalism is the idea that all social structures contribute to the integration and adaptation of the system in which they operate. The continued existence of some social pattern is explained by noting its consequences for maintaining the society. Usually, functionalists try to show that a specific pattern fulfills some vital need for the system, and claim that this explains its continuation. In a sense, functionalists seem to explain a cause in terms of its effects, rather than the other way around.[17]

Traditional functionalism has concentrated primarily on identifying the functional prerequisites of society—the tasks that must be performed for the society to survive. According to one such list, in order for a society to exist, its members must achieve some control over their environment, they must divide and assign tasks, and they must communicate with one another. The fact that a society exists is taken as proof that these tasks are being performed.

Critics of traditional functionalism have noted that (1) functionalist definitions of a social system and a society are very loose and hard to apply; (2) lists of prerequisites vary and remain unsubstantiated; and (3) the reasoning is circular and ahistorical. It is ahistorical because, while existing relations among parts of a social system can be explained by a functional analysis, the emergence of new relationships, new groups, or new institutions cannot. Irving Zeitlin has summarized the major critiques of traditional functionalism as follows:

1 It exaggerates the unity, stability, and harmony of social systems.

2 It imputes a positive character to all social institutions.

3 It is ahistorical.

4 It tends to regard existing institutions as necessary and indispensable, and therefore entails a conservative bias.

5 It fails to account for social change.[18]

Talcott Parsons

A serious attempt to follow the positivist tradition by combining structural and functional analysis with a theory of human action was made by Talcott Parsons, a distinguished social theorist whose writings span three decades.[19] Parsons' major effort has been to develop a formal model or theory of the "social system." His starting point is the interaction of individual actors, whose behavior cannot be reduced to biological or physiological factors. Human action, for him, is social action that must be understood in terms of social factors, not physical, biological, or psychological ones.

The simplest system of interaction is betweeen two individuals, each of whom performs specific roles dependent, to some extent, on the roles performed by the other. As a result of this mutual dependency, each actor develops expectations regarding the behavior of the other. One of them (Ego) rewards all actions of the other (Alter) that conform to Ego's expectations, and punishes those that do not conform. Alter does the same with respect to Ego. Since this interaction involves values, goals, and motives, it cannot be fully understood without considering two other systems—culture and personality—that coexist with the social system. (See chapter 10.)

For Parsons, a social system consists of a number of individuals interacting with common cultural understandings. Within this situation, each actor seeks to maximize pleasure and avoid deprivation. There are three elements involved in social action—the actors' definition of the situation in terms of individual interest (the cognitive element), the actors' search for pleasure (the cathectic element), and the actors' choice and priorities of alternatives (the evaluative element). There is always some disparity between the actual patterns of interaction (the social system) and those prescribed by the cultural system. This is so because individuals internalize cultural ideals imperfectly, and individual motives always vary to some degree from what they are supposed to be.

After developing his theory of action, Parsons turns to the problem of analyzing the structural elements of the social system. How do we know when a social system is the same thing as a society? A social system is a society, according to Parsons, when it endures longer than the life-span of an individual, when it has mechanisms for replacing its members by biological reproduction, when it socializes the oncoming generation to the cultural system, and when it meets all its essential functional prerequisites from its own internal resources. In short, Parsons employs essentially the same formulation as traditional functionalism; he identifies four functional prerequisites for any society:

1 **Integration: it must keep itself together.**

2 **Pattern-maintenance: it must find ways to continue existing social arrangements.**

3 **Goal-attainment: it must define and achieve some set of purposes.**

4 **Adaptation: it must adjust to new conditions by obtaining resources from the environment.**

In different social systems, actors are faced with different value choices. Parsons believes that the choices correspond to certain types of societies, and he lists five alternatives, or pattern-variables that actors face:

1 **Affectivity versus affective neutrality: either the actor expresses a great deal of emotion, or very little.**

2 **Self-orientation versus collective orientation: the actor pursues private interests, or the interest of the group.**

3 **Universalism versus particularism: the actor relates to others either through criteria applicable to all, or according to unique standards.**

4 **Quality versus performance: the actor orients either toward what another person is, or toward what the other person does.**

5   Specificity versus diffuseness: the actor relates either to some par-
    ticular quality of another person, or to the person as a whole.

Societies can be compared in terms of each of these pattern variables.
Thus, Parsons would say that in the United States people employ universalistic
criteria and emphasize performance, while in India they employ particularistic
criteria and emphasize quality.

Although Parsons is not very clear about the derivation of this list or
the role of these value choices in his system of action, he is quite specific
that the entire system tends to remain in equilibrium. Existing social patterns
tend to continue and maintain themselves because social systems have a
built-in tendency to remain in balance. In his own words, "the 'tendency' to
maintain the interaction process is the *first law of social process.*"[20] What
is harder to understand, says Parsons, is why social systems ever change.

His own examination of social change focuses only on the evolution
of social systems. He attempts to define several evolutionary universals that,
when used by a social system, allow the system to adapt and progress. Parsons
argues that system needs lead to evolution. The process of social evolution
involves four main trends: (1) the increasing differentiation of the personality,
social, cultural, and organismic systems from one another; (2) increasing
differentiation within each of these subsystems; (3) growing problems of integration, and the emergence of new integrating structures; and (4) the upgrad-
ing of the survival capacity of each of the subsystems, and the system as
a whole, to its environment.

Criticisms of Parsons

What Parsons has attempted is quite different from the usual approach of
social theory. Instead of making a series of theoretical propositions aimed
at explaining events that can be observed in the real world, he has concentrated on creating a formal model that defines and systematically relates a
set of abstract concepts for eventual application to empirical studies. He
maintains that the concepts do not correspond to concrete phenomena. They
refer to elements in the real world, which can be separated from other elements for purposes of analysis. Because his theory constitutes an internally
consistent model, criticism has focused on almost *every* element within the
model.

At the most general level, critics have claimed that his theory is so
abstract that it cannot be applied to the real world. There is no actual society,
they assert, that operates in the way the theory requires. In particular, critics
have complained that his notion of equilibrium is untenable. Alvin Gouldner,
for example, points out that, if Ego continues to act in accordance with Alter's

expectations, the end result might be to weaken the relationship. Thus, if a husband consistently brings his wife gifts on certain ceremonial occasions, and only on those ooccasions, she may very well experience a diminishing pleasure and reward him less for the same conduct. If, on the other hand, he surprises her with gifts when she least expects it, the relationship may be strengthened.[21]

Other critics have maintained that Parsons' elaborate theory contains the defects of traditional functionalism. Although he claims to refute theories employing only one factor, such as economics or genes, to explain social structure and human behavior, Parsons himself uses one factor—the normative structure—in a similar way. Although he claims to analyze social change, the only kind of change his theory can account for is evolutionary change. Parsons' theory is based on the claim that there are system needs or functional prerequisites that must be met for any society to survive. He is unable, however, to provide any example of a missing prerequisite that caused a society to fail. He simply asserts that nonsurvival demonstrates the absence of functional prerequisites.[22]

Because of these recurring problems, many sociologists have, in recent years, turned away from Parsons' theory. Even those who attempt to continue the functionalist emphasis have settled for more modest goals than a completely comprehensive theory based on abstract concepts.

Robert Merton

Even as Parsons was beginning to develop his grand scheme, Robert Merton argued that such an approach was premature. He claimed that the search for

> a total system of sociological theory, in which observations about every aspect of social behavior, organization, and change promptly find their preordained place, has the same exhilarating challenge and the same small promise as those many all-encompassing philosophical systems which have fallen into deserved disuse. [23]

Instead, Merton argued, sociologists should concentrate on developing "theories of the middle range." They should be content with developing theories linking concepts with empirical observations. He felt that some sort of functional analysis was necessary for such an effort, but that it was necessary to revise three of the main postulates of traditional functionalism: (1) the claim that all activities or cultural items in a society are functional for the *entire* social or cultural system; (2) the claim that *all* such social and cultural items fulfill sociological functions; and (3) the claim that these items are therefore indispensable.

In criticizing these claims, Merton argued that the unity of a society should not be taken for granted, but should be treated as a problem for study. It is also necessary, he said, to specify the unit for which any given item is functional. It should not be taken for granted that all items fulfill functions. Finally, one must not assume that only one item or structure can fulfill a given function. "Just as the same item may have multiple functions, so may the same function be diversely fulfilled by alternative items."[24]

Merton distinguished between manifest and latent functions. Manifest functions are the intended consequences of a given action. They are intended by a specified unit such as a person, group, or social system, and contribute to the adjustment or adaptation of that unit. Latent functions, on the other hand, are unintended consequences of action. During the Vietnam War, for example, government officials tried to give the impression that the Vietcong were a tiny minority in South Vietnam and that United States armed forces were constantly winning battles. They often spoke of the "light at the end of the tunnel," as though victory were imminent. The manifest functions of these actions were to justify American involvement and to bolster the morale of Americans. As the war continued without victory, and as the Vietnamese began to achieve victories, the latent function of this official propaganda was to create a credibility gap; many citizens no longer trusted or believed official statements. This was an unintended consequence, but a real one nonetheless.

Many sociologists think that Merton's revisions have not eliminated the basic weaknesses in functional analysis. Jonathan Turner, for example, points out that Merton still confuses functions with causes and is unable to demonstrate how the needs of a system cause any particular event to occur.[25] Merton violates his own criticism of traditional functionalism by assuming that the persistence of some item of social structure is evidence that it fulfills a social need. Because of the continuing difficulties of functionalist analysis, many sociologists rooted in positivist thinking have turned to a quite different theoretical approach to society and human behavior.

Behaviorism

According to George Homans, all varieties of functionalism involve some mixture of three different kinds of statements: (1) *structural* propositions that are testable but have to be explained by other kinds of statements; (2) *psychological* propositions that are testable and are required to explain structural propositions; and (3) *functional* propositions that are neither testable nor required for explanation. After examining different functional theories, he concluded that "the ultimate explanatory principles in anthropology and sociology, and for that matter in history, [are] neither structural nor functional but psychological; they [are] propositions about the behavior of men as men." [26]

This leads Homans to argue that sociologists should give up the search for functional explanations and concentrate on the actual overt behavior of individuals. In developing what he calls social exchange theory, Homans asserts that human behavior is essentially identical to animal behavior, and he puts forth a set of propositions about human behavior based on studies of animals. These propositions are part of a more general theoretical approach called behaviorism first applied to psychology and anthropology. The common elements of this behaviorism are:

1 Human beings will, in any given situation, behave in ways that will maximize their rewards and minimize their punishment.

2 People will repeat those behaviors that have in the past proved to be rewarded.

3 Stimuli that have been associated with rewards in the past will tend to evoke behavior in the present that is similar to past behavior.

4 Behavior will be repeated only so long as it continues to lead to rewards.

5 If behavior that has previously been rewarded is no longer rewarded in similar situations, a person will display emotion.

6 The more often a person is rewarded for a specific behavior, the less rewarding it seems. In this situation, a person is likely to behave differently in order to get different rewards.

For Homans, human behavior involves exchanges between individuals. Each participant in the exchange seeks to get more out of it than is put in; the basic formula is

$$\text{Profit} = \text{Reward} - \text{Cost.}$$

He argues that no exchange continues unless both parties make a profit, although they may have different notions about what constitutes a profit. The way we know an exchange is just, he says, is by whether or not it continues. An exchange that continues is just because if it were not, the individual who was not getting a profit would withdraw. Let us suppose, for example, that there are two students in a class, one of whom is very good at studying and taking tests, while the other one is unable to keep up. Suppose, also, that the slower student asks the better one for help. Homans would say that this is an exchange in which the poorer student's cost consists of the embarrassment felt by asking for help and the thanks that must be given for such help, while the reward consists of higher grades. The costs for the better student involve sharing knowledge obtained by individual effort (and, perhaps, lowering the grading curve), while the reward involves the appreciation expressed by the poorer student. So long as each feels the reward is greater than the costs, Homans argues, the exchange is likely to continue.

Let us now look at another situation. Suppose a young child is accosted by older children on the way home from school every day. They demand that the younger child give them a quarter. The child does so. The incident is repeated every day. Is this an exchange? According to Homans, it is. The younger child's cost is a quarter a day; the reward is physical safety. The cost for the older children is the risk of arrest; their reward is money. So long as both sides feel that the reward is greater than the cost, the exchange is likely to continue. Moreover, Homans might claim, this exchange is just. Is this a reasonable way of looking at such a situation? Most of us would probably say that the younger child was coerced, intimidated, and forced to give money to the older ones, but Homans would say it was an exchange. Most of us would say the situation reeked of injustice, but Homans would say it was just because it continued. It is precisely situations of this type that lead many sociologists to reject social exchange theory. The problem, they claim, is that it does not recognize that coercion and exploitation are at the root of many exchanges. . Moreover, it is not always true that individuals have an alternative to the exchanges they are in. As a consequence unjust exchanges often continue, despite the fact that one of the participants is not receiving a profit. Even to many other behaviorists, Homans' scheme seems excessively psychologistic, and some of them have attempted to develop a more sociological version of exchange theory.

Peter Blau

The starting point for Peter Blau's version of exchange theory is a recognition that the things exchanged in a relationship may not be of equal value.[27] Thus, in our first example, the better student may feel sufficiently rewarded by expressions of gratitude to help the poorer student on a few occasions, but is unlikely to do so regularly unless some more substantial compensation is received. Blau argues that frequently there is not really an equivalent exchange, and that this imbalance leads to differences of power.

According to Blau, when one individual needs the services of another, but has no equivalent service to give in return, the person has three alternatives—coercing the other into giving assistance; obtaining assistance from another source; or, trying to get along without the service. If, however, none of these alternatives is available, the only choice left is to "subordinate himself to the other and comply with his wishes, thereby rewarding the other with power over himself as an inducement for furnishing the needed help."[28] In society as a whole, those groups having a monopoly of vital services will gain a monopoly of power, by which they can command the behavior of those who need the services but have nothing to exchange except their obedience.

The imbalances of power that develop in society are not necessarily felt to be unjust. Blau claims that norms of fairness develop—standards for what constitute fair demands by those with power. So long as those in subordinate positions view the services they receive as being in line with these norms, they do not feel exploited or oppressed. When they feel that the demands upon them are much greater than the benefits they receive, however, opposition to those in power, and even revolution are likely to develop. The problem for those in power is to withhold the full exercise of their power, so as not to seem unjust.

Blau's theory represents a considerable improvement over that of Homans, in that it focuses on the actual social relations between individuals and groups that develop in society. By recognizing the existence of domination and subordination in society, Blau is able to deal with a wider variety of situations than is Homans. At the same time, Blau has been criticized for having too subjective a view of exploitation and oppression. Irving Zeitlin has observed that Blau's explanation of exploitation depends on the norms of fairness prevailing in society. It is, therefore, these norms that determine whether or not people feel oppressed. While this subjective element is undoubtedly important in determining whether or not people act against those in power, Zeitlin maintains that exploitation exists, regardless of whether or not individuals feel exploited. The exploitation lies in the imbalance of services exchanged, and so long as one party is able to *command* the services of the other, there is a degree of exploitation.[29]

Summary

There are, as we have seen, a wide variety of disagreements among positivist theorists. It may all seem a bit confusing, and a curious student may wonder just why these theorists are all grouped under the same label. When we examine the differences between them more carefully, however, we discover primarily differences of degree, rather than substance.

All positivist theories tend to view existing social institutions as "positive." Despite their differences, both functionalists and behaviorists argue that existing social structures (or exchanges) would not continue if they did not perform some necessary task—maintaining social order, in the case of functionalism, and providing mutual profit, in the case of behaviorism. In this sense, both of these theories remain true to Auguste Comte's original vision of developing a positive science of society to counter negative or critical evaluations of existing arrangements.

Finally, all positivist theories treat society and human behavior as essentially similar to nature and the behavior of natural phenomena. They assume that the factors that shape human behavior and social structure are essentially independent of human will and volition, and thus can be studied by natural scientific methods.

But while positivist theories share a commitment to the natural-scientific method, they have had to adapt that method to the particular subject matter of sociology. In studying the sources of human behavior and the nature of social structures, positivist sociologists do not use telescopes, test tubes, or centrifuges. Instead, they have developed a variety of instruments and techniques designed to provide systematic information about human attitudes and behavior. It is with the aid of these instruments and techniques that positivist theorists seek the facts about human behavior essential to testing and refining social theory.

For Further Study

Summaries of important theoretical notions are never adequate substitutes for original sources. The works of all the social theorists we have discussed are, in general, readily available in English editions. Harriet Martineau translated Comte's *Cours de Philosophie Positive* into two English-language volumes called, *The Positive Philosophy* (London: Kegan Paul, 1893). Comte himself was so impressed with this translation that the English version was retranslated into French. For a superb modern edition of Comte's work, see Gertrude Lenzer, ed., *Auguste Comte and Positivism: The Essential Writings* (New York: Harper, 1975). Professor Lenzer has written a very insightful introduction to this volume, explaining the relevance of Comte's thought for contemporary social science and sociology.

For an excellent critique of contemporary positivist theory, see Irving M. Zeitlin, *Rethinking Sociology* (New York: Appleton-Century-Crofts, 1973). For a view of sociological theory in the context of a debate with enlightenment and Marxist thought, see Zeitlin's *Ideology and the Development of Sociological Theory* (Englewood Cliffs, N.J.: Prentice-Hall, 1968). For an analysis of the historical and social roots of contemporary sociological theory—a study in the "sociology of sociology"—see Alvin W. Gouldner, *The Coming Crisis of Western Sociology* (New York: Basic Books, 1970).

Notes

1 See, for example, Alfred North Whitehead, *Science and the Modern World* (New York: Macmillan, 1925).

2 John Locke, *Two Treatises of Government* (New York: New American Library, 1965): Jean-Jacques Rousseau, *The Social Contract and Discourses,* trans. G. D. H. Cole (New York: Dutton, 1950); also see C. B. Macpherson, *The Political Theory of Possessive Individualism: Hobbes to Locke* (London: Oxford University Press, 1962).

3 August Comte, *The Positive Philosophy,* trans. and ed. by Harriet Martineau (New York: D. Appleton & Co., 1854).

4 Herbert Spencer, *The Principles of Sociology* (New York: D. Appleton & Co., 1897); *Social Statics* (New York: D. Appleton & Co., 1892).

5 See H. Stuart Hughes, *Consciousness and Society* (New York: Knopf, 1961), pp. 38–39.

6 Emile Durkheim, *The Division of Labor in Society,* trans. George Simpson (New York: Free Press, 1933), p. 32.

7 Emile Durkheim, *The Elementary Forms of Religious Life,* trans. Joseph Ward (New York: Free Press, 1965).

8 See Richard Hofstadter, *Social Darwinism in American Thought,* rev. ed. (New York: Braziller, 1959), p. 58.

9 William Graham Sumner. *Folkways* (Boston: Ginn & Co., 1911).

10 Robert Green McCloskey, *American Conservatism in the Age of Enterprise: 1865–1910* (New York: Harper, 1964), p. 47.

11 Vilfredo Pareto, *The Mind and Society: A Treatise on General Sociology,* trans. Andrew Bongiorno and Arthur Livingston, with James Harvey Rogers; Arthur Livingston, ed. (New York: Dover, 1963), vol. 2, p. 6.

12 Don Martindale, *The Nature and Types of Sociological Theory* (Boston: Houghton-Mifflin, 1960), p. 104.

13 Julian Freund, *The Sociology of Max Weber* (New York: Random House, 1968), p. 13.

14 Max Weber, *The Protestant Ethic and the Spirit of Capitalism,* trans. Talcott Parsons (New York: Scribner's, 1958).

15 See Max Weber, *The Religion of India,* trans. and ed. Hans H. Gerth and Don Martindale (Glencoe, Ill.: Free Press, 1958); Max Weber, *The Religion of China,* trans. and ed. Hans H. Gerth (Glencoe, Ill.: Free Press, 1951); Max Weber, *Ancient Judaism,* trans. and ed. Hans H. Gerth and Don Martindale (Glencoe, Ill.: Free Press, 1952).

16 Max Weber, *From Max Weber: Essays in Sociology,* trans. and ed. H. H. Gerth and C. Wright Mills (New York: Oxford University Press, 1946).

17 See Jonathan H. Turner, *The Structure of Sociological Theory* (Homewood, Ill.: Dorsey Press, 1974), pp. 15–27; see also, Irving Zeitlin, *Rethinking Sociology* (Englewood Cliffs, N.J.: Prentice-Hall, 1973), pp. 3–15.

18 See Zeitlin, *Rethinking Sociology,* p. 15.

19 See Talcott Parsons, *The Social System* (New York and London: Free Press and Routledge & Kegan Paul, 1951).

20 Parsons, *Social System,* p. 205.

21 Alvin W. Gouldner, "Organizational Analysis," in Robert K. Merton Leonard Broom, and Leonard S. Cottrell, Jr., eds., *Sociology Today* (New York: Basic Books, 1959), p. 425.

22 See Turner, *Sociological Theory;* Zeitlin, *Rethinking Sociology.*

23 Robert K. Merton, *Social Theory and Social Structure* (New York: Free Press, 1968), p. 45.

24 Ibid. pp. 87–88.

25 See Turner, *Sociological Theory,* p. 71.

26 George C. Homans, *Social Behavior: Its Elementary Forms* (New York: Harcourt, 1961), p. 29.

27 Peter M. Blau, *Exchange and Power in Social Life* (New York: Wiley, 1964).

28 Ibid. pp. 22–23.

29 Zeitlin, *Rethinking Sociology.*

Positivist
Methods

In a sense, it is always a mistake to separate a discussion of theory from a discussion of method since any procedure for gathering information must make theoretical assumptions about the nature of data. One method may assume that people's real motivations can be discovered by asking them questions; another method may assume that it is possible to design an experiment involving human subjects in which all potentially relevant factors are controlled. These assumptions are rooted in theory. For this reason it has been more common in Europe to speak of methodology which includes both theory and technique, rather than to separate theory and method. Nevertheless, American sociology tends to separate these two elements, and this is especially true of positivism.

The development of contemporary positivist methods in sociology has been strongly influenced by a school of thought known as *logical positivism* that began in the early 1920s. This school divides all significant propositions into two groups: (1) formal propositions that are internally consistent and tautological, such as logical or mathematical propositions; and (2) factual propositions that can be verified empirically.[1] According to the principles of logical positivism, if a proposition does not express something that is either formally true or empirically verifiable, it expresses nothing at all; it is nonsense.

But what does verification mean? How do we know when a proposition has been empirically verified? Does this mean that we must be able to verify every possible prediction of a scientific law? The answer given today is that a factual proposition must be capable of being confirmed or disconfirmed by observation. A law cannot be confirmed, but it can be tested by examining individual instances of the law. If, "in the continued series of such testing experiments, no negative instance is found but the number of positive instances increases, then our confidence in the law will grow step by step." [2]

According to logical positivism then, whether or not a statement is meaningful (that is, factual) depends on whether or not it can be verified, and verification depends on whether or not it can be confirmed or disconfirmed by observation. Observation, in turn, depends on measurement. For example, is the statement, "the more intelligent you are, the more money you will make," a factual proposition? If it is, it must be capable of being verified. In order for it to be verified, we must be able to observe whether or not more intelligent people make more money than less intelligent ones. To make such observations, however, we must be able to differentiate a more intelligent person from a less intelligent one. But what is intelligence? It is almost impossible to arrive at an abstract definition of intelligence that is capable of being measured. A similar difficulty occurs with virtually all abstract concepts.

The solution offered by logical positivists is to define concepts in terms of the operations by which they are measured. In these terms, a concept *is* an operational definition. Intelligence is whatever is measured by an I.Q. test, and if people with high I.Q. scores always make more money than people with low I.Q. scores, we can claim to have verified the original proposition.[3] Positivists think that a set of measurements must satisfy two additional criteria—reliability and validity—if it is to constitute a useful operational definition.

Reliability

An investigator must be able to assume that operational definitions will yield reliable results. That is, if the operations are repeated under the same conditions, they must yield the same results each time. This assumption requires that the property being measured should not change over time. For example, a physicist who weighs a cake of ice may find, over time, that the measurements of weight change. This is because ice melts. To decide whether or not the weight scale is reliable, the physicist may have to collect the melted ice and weigh it separately. Unless the physicist has some reason to believe that ice melts under certain conditions, he may simply assume that the scale is unreliable. For social scientists, the problem of reliability is especially difficult when attempting to measure such things as attitudes and opinions, since it is hard to find measures that yield the same results over time.

Validity

If a measure has a high degree of reliability, it can be used over and over again by different researchers and still produce the same results; it is consistent. But consistency is not enough, for it is quite possible to measure consistently something that is meaningless, or not exactly what we want to be measuring. For example, most husbands may reply "no" to the question, "do you beat your wife?", whether the question is asked today, or yesterday, or tomorrow. The question is, then, a reliable measure, but is it valid? *Does it measure what we want it to measure?* If we observe the actual behavior of the husbands, we may discover that a significant percentage of those who answered "no" do, in fact, beat their wives.

In a similar vein, if we mean by the concept of intelligence the quality of being smart, there is little reason to believe that I.Q. tests are a valid measure of intelligence. They don't tell us whether or not a person is smart. If, however, intelligence is only what is measured by I.Q. tests, then the tests are completely valid. The difficulty is that what they measure may not have much to do with what we are really interested in measuring, that is, the quality of being smart.

In order to establish validity for a set of measures, we must be able to show that one set of scores predicts or correlates with other measures. Often, for example, an I.Q. test is used to predict performance in school. If we decide that performance in school is a measure of being smart, and if the I.Q. test predicts this performance, then we might decide that intelligence as measured by an I.Q. test is the quality of being smart. Before accepting such a judgment, however, we would want to know why performance in school should be equated with the concept of "smartness," and we might be interested in knowing what factors other than intelligence affect school performance.

The techniques developed by positivist sociologists for gathering data are modeled after natural-scientific techniques, adapted to the particular problems studied by sociologists. There are three main sets of techniques, or methods, that are commonly employed—survey research methods, social experiments, and simulation techniques. These are all methods designed to test factual propositions. Recently, some efforts have been made to develop a mathematical sociology through which elements of social experience can be represented in formal equations, after the fashion of physics or chemistry. These attempts are more like formal propositions, in that the primary focus is on developing internally consistent models that can later be tested against reality.

Survey Research

Survey research is probably the most common and familiar type of sociological research. Questionnaires, interviews, public opinion polls—these are all part of survey research methods. A survey is a study that "selects a sample from some larger population in order to ascertain the prevalence, incidence and interrelations of sociological ... variables." [4] A survey is like a census, except that a survey selects for study only a sample from a population, while a census includes everyone in the population under study.

Survey research has become a highly developed method in the United States, and three types of organizations have been especially important in fostering this development. The United States Bureau of the Census, while best known for the census it conducts every ten years, also conducts a series of sample surveys to collect a variety of information about the social and economic state of the American people. Commercial polling organizations, including those of George Gallup, Elmo Roper, and Louis Harris, use survey methods extensively in connection with political polling and marketing of products. University research centers, like those of the Institute of Social Research at the University of Michigan and the Survey Research Center at the University of California at Berkeley, provide students with training as research assistants and conduct many surveys under contract with government and commercial customers. There is also a professional association, the American Association for Public Opinion Research, designed specifically for social scientists working with survey research methods. The association publishes a journal called *Public Opinion Quarterly*. A survey that collects data at one point in time from a sample of persons chosen to describe some larger population is called a *cross-sectional survey*.[5] A poll designed to determine the voting preferences of people before an election is such a survey. A typical question in such a poll might be, "If the election were held today, for whom would you vote?" The results of such a survey would be reported with the preface, "If the election were held today . . ." A cross-sectional survey of the relationships between religion, occupation, salary level, and education and prejudice would report these relationships at the time of the study. A cross-sectional survey can describe relationships at a particular moment in time, but it cannot tell whether those relationships have changed, or are changing, or in what direction they are changing.

When a survey allows collection of data at different points in time, it is referred to as a *longitudinal survey*. There are three basic varieties of longitudinal surveys—trend studies, cohort studies, and panel studies. A trend study examines a set of variables at different points in time. They do this by analyzing the responses of persons in different successive samples.

Since trend studies are based on different samples from a larger population, changes found may also reflect changes in the membership of the larger population. Over a period of time, some people become eligible to vote who were not eligible in earlier surveys. Some people die. Immigrants arrive in the country, while some persons leave the country. A trend study of the national electorate, of the student body at a university, or of the total citizenry will reflect different populations as well as different samples.

A cohort study focuses on the same subpopulation or cohort each time it is conducted. For example, the cohort might be the graduating class of 1977. We might select a sample of this cohort to survey attitudes toward various professions. Several years later, another sample might be selected from the same cohort to examine changes in these attitudes. Although the sample would be different, the subpopulation would be the same. A different kind of cohort study might start with a sample of all Americans in their twenties. Ten years later we might sample all Americans in their thirties. This would constitute a cohort study of a given age group.

A third type of longitudinal survey—a panel study—focuses on the same sample at different points in time. Suppose, for example, we want to explore the relationships between life experiences (such as income, jobs, marriage, and divorce) and attitudes toward professions of the graduating class of 1977. If we draw a sample of that population, and periodically resurvey the same individuals every few years, we would be conducting a panel survey. While panel studies allow us to explore in greater depth the processes causing change in individuals, it is somewhat more difficult to generalize our results to the population from which the sample was selected. We cannot be certain how unique the experiences of individuals studied are, and there is a possibility that the very fact of being selected for study over a long period of time may cause some changes in responses.

Attitudes

As this description of survey techniques indicates, much of the focus of survey research is on the relationships between characteristics such as age, sex, race, and religion and the attitudes of individuals. For sociologists, an attitude is a more or less enduring readiness to behave in a characteristic way. It is not the actual behavior, but the predisposition to behave. Social scientists believe that there are three different components of an attitude—cognitive, emotional, and action components.[6]

The things people think they know are the cognitive components of an attitude. These may vary widely from person to person. You may think you know a great deal about your friends and think you know very little about your sociology teacher, or vice versa. Included among these things are evaluations about the good and bad qualities of the object. Information about the sex, age, voice quality, and other characteristics of your teacher, and your evaluation of these characteristics, will shape your attitude toward him or her. For example, you may dislike women (or men) or old (or young) teachers.

There are also emotions or feelings attached to an attitude. Words used to suggest this component include "love," "hate," and "dislike." The emotional component of an attitude deals with the intensity of the cognitive evaluation.

People have a readiness to act in accordance with the cognitive and emotional components of their attitudes. If a political party is believed to represent good goals and practices, and if it is liked, a person may vote to support its candidates.

Sociologists have developed several different techniques for measuring attitudes by survey research methods.[7] They include the following:

1 *Self-reports of beliefs, feelings, and behaviors:* Self-report techniques include the use of questionnaires, schedules, and interview guides. A questionnaire is a form that the respondent—the person selected by a sampling procedure—fills in. A schedule is a set of questions that are asked and recorded by an interviewer. An interview guide is a list of points to be covered during an interview, and allows the interviewer more freedom in selecting the order, manner, and language used to ask questions.

2 *Observation of overt behavior:* Observation techniques attempt to understand attitudes by making inferences from overt behavior. The prototype of this method was originally developed by R. T. LaPiere in 1934.[8] LaPiere attempted to obtain reservations at various hotels for himself and some Chinese friends. Almost invariably, his mailed requests were denied, presumably because of prejudice on the part of the hotel-keepers. Yet, when LaPiere and the Chinese couple appeared in person, their request for lodging was almost always granted. The conclusion of this and similar studies was that what a person does in a specific situation is the result of many considerations beyond a single attitude. For example, employees who do not like their supervisor tend not to say so in the supervisor's presence. While direct observation of current behavior may provide insights into discrepancies between beliefs and acts, it is difficult to infer attitudes from past behavior. Written documents and records often are incomplete accounts of behavior, and much overt behavior leaves no observable traces.

3 *Indirect tests and objective tasks.* Indirect techniques involve some deception. The respondent is led to believe that one thing is being studied or that a play-time activity like storytelling is going on, while the investigator is really studying something else. For example, in one such study, pairs of matched cards were used to investigate the attitudes of white New Zealand children toward Maoris.[9] Cards of each pair were identical, except for the crucial figure, who was either Maori or white. Stories composed by white children between the ages of eight and twelve showed a marked increase in unfavorable attitudes toward Maoris as the age of the children increased.

4 *Measurement of physiological reactions:* Techniques that measure physiological reactions are seldom used by sociologists but are more common among psychologists. Physiological actions of subjects are used to measure attitudes. Since these reactions are presumably not amenable to conscious control, it is felt that subjects will be unable to hide or change their responses. One such technique measures galvanic skin response by attaching electrodes to the skin and recording changes in electrical charge as various statements are read to the subject.[10] Other techniques measure heartbeat, dilation of the eyes, and other physiological responses. Although these techniques are useful in detecting strong emotional responses, it is difficult to determine whether the attitude is favorable or unfavorable from such measurements.

Social Experiments

Although survey research is perhaps the most common technique employed by sociologists, an experiment is often thought of as the prototype of scientific method, and sociologists working in the positivist tradition have tried to adapt experimental techniques for use in sociology. Experimentation is essentially a method for testing propositions and theories dealing with cause-and-effect relationships. John Stuart Mill described four experimental methods that continue to serve as the logical basis for contemporary experimental research.[11]

1 *The method of agreement:* Suppose that we want to study the factors that influence the decision of parents to send their children to college. If we carefully select two groups of parents who have decided to send their children to college, and who are totally different in all respects (age, sex, race, education, and so on) except one (both groups saw a film stressing the importance of a college education), we would conclude that seeing the film was the cause of their decision to send their children to college. According to the method of agreement, whenever two or more occurrences of a phenomenon under study (for example, the decision of parents to send their children to college) have only one feature in common (the film), this single feature is the cause of the phenomenon. The method of agreement is difficult to use, since it is often impossible to know that the two groups are different in all the qualities that might be important. This is certainly true of the example cited.

2 *The method of difference:* Suppose that we select two groups of parents who are identical in every respect, and we show a film stressing the importance of a college education to one group but not to the other. If the parents in the group shown the film then decide to send their children to college, and those in the other group do not, we would conclude that the film caused the decision. According to the method of difference, if an occurrence of the phenomenon under investigation (for example, deciding to send children to college) and a nonoccurrence of the phenomenon have every feature in common except one (seeing the film), this solitary feature in which the two occurrences differ is the cause, or at least an indispensable part of the cause, of the phenomenon.

3 *Method of concomitant variation:* While the first two methods are designed to discover whether a relationship exists between two variables, the method of concomitant variation is designed to measure the degree of relationship. Suppose, for example, that we want to test the notion that the longer parents are exposed to a film stressing the importance of a college education, the greater will be their willingness to send their children to college. If several groups of parents who are alike in all respects are each exposed to the film for a different length of time, and if those groups exposed for the longest time show the greatest change in attitude, we would conclude that the degree of attitude change is related to the quantity of exposure to the film. According to the method of concomitant variation, if a phenomenon varies in any way (increased willingness to send children to college) whenever another phenomenon varies in a particular way (increased exposure to film), the first phenomenon is either caused by the second or connected with it in some causal way.

4 *Method of residues:* The method of residues is used to separate the effects of two or more factors that may be influencing what we want to study. Suppose that there are two groups of parents whose only difference is that one group has seen a film stressing the importance of a college education and the other has not. Suppose that, during the course of the experiment, both groups read news stories about the greater earning capacity of college graduates. According to the method of residues, it is possible to calculate the effect of the film by subtracting the known effect of the news stories. If the total increase in favorable attitudes toward college of the group that saw the film and read the news stories is T, and if the increase in favorable attitudes of the group that only read the stories is N, then F is the increase in favorable attitudes resulting from exposure to the film. The effect of the film is calculated by $F = T-N$. If the effect of certain antecendent events (such as reading news stories) is subtracted from a resultant phenomenon, the remainder, or residue, is the effect of the remaining antecedent cause (the film). In contemporary research, the interaction effect of several such variables is analyzed in much more complicated ways than those described by Mill, but the basic logical procedure is the same.

Simulations

A simulation has been defined as an operating model of a system.[12] Other models may represent aspects of a system verbally, mathematically, or pictorially. Simulations, however, are operating models; they may be all-computer, all-people, or mixed people-computer simulations. A simulation can represent, not simply existing reality, but potential or conceivable states of social systems.

Positivist researchers, however, tend to

focus on existing conditions. To the extent that a simulation is deliberately simplified, it may be called a game or simulation game.

> Such games pluck out of social life generally . . . a circumscribed arena, and attempt to reconstruct the principal rules by which behavior in this arena is governed and the principal rewards that it holds for the participants. Such a game both in its construction and in its playing then becomes of extreme interest to the student of social organization. For from it he may learn about those problems of social relations that are his central concern. The game may provide for him that degree of abstraction from life and simplification of life that allows him to understand better certain fundamentals of social organization.[13]

All-People Simulations

All-people simulations have been used and continue to be used in connection with small-group research. Small numbers of people are placed in laboratory settings and are assigned tasks or roles. Their behavior is observed carefully and studied for a variety of purposes. A classic set of studies in this tradition was conducted in the late 1930s by Kurt Lewin, Ronald Lippitt, and Ralph White.[14] The objective of these studies was to study the effect upon groups and upon individual group members of participation in three different group atmospheres with different leadership styles—democratic, autocratic, and laissez-faire. Groups of ten- and eleven-year-old children met regularly for a period of several weeks under the leadership of an adult, who was responsible for inducing the different group atmospheres. Each adult led a group under each condition to eliminate the effect of personality differences in the leaders.

In the autocratic groups, the leader determined all policy and dictated techniques and activity steps one at a time, so that future steps were always uncertain for the group members. In addition, the leader dictated the particular work task as well as the work companion of each member. In praising or criticizing the work of each member, the leader was very personal and remained aloof from the group except when demonstrating something.

In the democratic groups, all policies were matters for group discussion and decision. This process was encouraged and aided by the group leader. During the discussion period, a perspective for future activities was obtained, and the leader suggested two or more alternative procedures from which a choice could be made. The group members were free to work with whomever they chose, and the division of tasks was left up to the group. In praising or criticizing members, the group leader tended to be objective or fact-minded and tried to be a regular group member without doing too much of the work.

In the laissez-faire groups, complete freedom was allowed for group or individual decision-making, with a minimum of participation on the part of the leader. Various materials were supplied by the leader, who would also provide information when asked. The leader took no other part in the discussion and did not participate in any decisions about who would work with whom or how the tasks would be divided. The leader made infrequent comments on the activities of the group members, unless questioned, and made no effort to evaluate or regulate the course of events.

Results of the studies included the following:

1 Laissez-faire groups were less organized, less efficient, and less satisfying to the members themselves.

2 Democratic groups were decidedly more efficient than either autocratic or laissez-faire groups. Autocratic groups achieved only work goals, and laissez-faire groups achieved (if anything) only social goals (the children played more and were more silly). When the adult leader left the room, the children in democratic groups tended to keep on working; in autocratic groups, they stopped working. In addition, a higher level of originality was demonstrated in the democratic groups than in either of the other two.

3 In the autocratic groups, there seemed to be discontent that did not appear on the surface. In addition, there was less individuality manifested in these groups and more evidence of submissive or dependent behavior.

4 The democratic groups were characterized by more group-mindedness and more friendliness than the other groups.

In this research, the various group climates were created by differences in the ways the leaders played their roles. (See chapter 7 for a discussion of roles.) This kind of technique has been extended to include a wide variety of role-playing possibilities. For example, a simulated business enterprise might be constructed by defining a goal for a group of people (such as maximizing profits), assigning roles to each member of the group (such as salesman, or production supervisor), and translating the results of the group activities into simulated monetary returns. Roles of customers, potential customers, suppliers, retailers, and so on can be simulated by additional group members or by probability tables. But this is to encroach upon the domain of mixed people-computer simulations. In the pure form of all-people simulation, activity is generated entirely by people playing roles.

Mixed People-Computer Simulations

One of the most extensively used mixed people-computer simulations is the Internation Simulation (INS) developed by Harold Guetzkow and others in the late 1950s.[15] In this simulation, people play the roles of a number of decision makers representing different nations. Each nation has at least one central decision maker (similar to a prime minister or president) and an external decision maker (similar to a foreign secretary or secretary of state), but the actual division of duties among these decision makers is not specified. The decision makers represent their nations by taking actions in relation to such concerns as basic resources, capital, consumer goods, military materials, and the extent to which their respective nations are satisfied with their performance. Changes in power can occur through either peaceful or violent means. The decision makers record their decisions on decision forms. A computer then calculates the consequences of these decisions in the light of all the other decisions that have been made and the existing state of the simulated world.

It is obviously possible to vary the structure of the simulation so that some roles are played by computers in accordance with a previously specified set of strategies. It is also possible for people to play the role of computers by doing some of the calculation of decision consequences. In each case, the simulation would be referred to as a mixed people-computer simulation.

All-Computer Simulations

A computer can compress time, allow many rapid replications of a simulation experiment, control all aspects of the study carefully, and examine the consequences of a particular set of decisions or social arrangements under a large number of different conditions. Thus, in an early attempt to build a computer simulation of the American economy, Guy Orcott and his colleagues built a model incorporating such elements as predicted changes in the population, changing trends in the composition of the labor force, and various assumptions about household behavior.[16] The model was cycled repeatedly under various conditions to produce a range of outcomes. From this, a picture of probable general trends was extrapolated. "Methodologically speaking, this approach is identical to the approach that repeatedly measures the time it takes to run a maze and expresses the results as the *mean* or *average* time, rather than as any single measurement of the running time."[17]

When computers play all the roles and perform all the calculation of consequences, we have an all-computer simulation. It is possible, in principle, to begin with an all-people simulation and convert it into an all-computer simulation. This was done by Robert Boguslaw, Robert Davis, and Edward Bernard Glick, in connection with their "PLANS" simulation.[18] In its original form, this was an all-people simulation of major interest groupings within American society (labor, business, civil rights, internationalists, military, and nationalists), based on an analysis of formal documents issued by such organizations as the major labor unions, associations of businessmen, civil rights groups, peace groups, veterans, and patriotic and military organizations. Individuals and groups of individual persons made decisions about the allocation of resources to obtain favorable legislation on behalf of the interests they represented. Since the goals for each interest were carefully defined, and the decision-making process was specified in detail, it was possible to replace all the people with computer programs. This had several interesting consequences.

In some respects, the computer was more efficient than the human players; in other respects the computer was less efficient. The researchers concluded that the problem in this study was not to make the computer more intelligent but, in a sense, to make it less intelligent. But this, they said,

> is really an incorrect way of stating the problem. The computer decision-modes took at face value the various goals stated for each interest group and then proceeded in a more or less rigorous fashion to translate the decision implications of these goals into action: The human beings entering the live [i.e., "all-people"] simulation brought with them a host of previous dispositions, interpretations, perceptions of other human beings and value orientations. These inevitably served to reduce their "efficiency" from the point of view of formal goal achievement.[19]

The point is that the human beings had an undefined mass of predispositions and values serving as informal goals. No attempt was made to incorporate these informal goals in the computer program.

> The resultant discrepancies between optimal "formal" efficiency and optimal "informal" efficiency highlight a fear which many social scientists experienced in the face of efforts to introduce computerized simulations for determining the number of hamlets controlled by allied forces in Vietnam. It is the unspoken fear that a rigorous computer program will ignore many unverbalized but nevertheless crucial informal goals and value orientations.[20]

This may point up the dangers implicit in an uncritical use of all-computer simulation. Rational decisions, it is often asserted, can best be left to the reliable judgment of a computer program. However, as Boguslaw and Davis expressed it,

> Unfortunately, people sometimes behave rationally within what are essentially irrational or outdated systems of goals and objectives. They accept and pursue, in a rational manner, goals set for them by others and perhaps even by themselves—goals which are self-defeating and inimical to their own long-range welfare and survival. . . . This capacity to change goals one would like to believe is an indispensable defining quality of human beings. Yet increasingly it is more difficult to do this in a world which is ever more insistent that they remain efficient instruments rather than unpredictable and uncontrolled elements within rigorously controlled social systems.[21]

| Statistics | Statistical analysis is often a convenient and powerful tool for understanding large quantities of data gathered through survey research methods or experimentation. In order to use statistical analysis, however, data must be in the form of statistics. Statistical methods have been described as "methods used in the collection, presentation, analysis, and interpretation of data." [22] Such a definition is really a rather narrow view of life, as seen through the |

eyes of a statistician. As we shall see in the next two chapters, there are many methods for collecting, presenting, analyzing, and interpreting data—methods that do not depend on the use of statistics. To most positivists, however, statistical methods are absolutely essential, if the most elementary claims to scientific status are to be maintained.

Descriptive Statistics

The world of statistics tends to be divided into two parts. One part is called descriptive statistics. It involves collecting measurements on each member of a given population. The measurements are called raw data. Descriptive statistics are an attempt to describe raw data in a more economical, summarized form. If a baseball player goes to bat one hundred times and gets a hit thirty times, we can describe his performance by saying that he has a batting average of .300 or 30 percent. (In this case, the population is the number of occasions the player was at bat.)

Scaling is a device used to generate descriptive statistics. It is a procedure for assigning numbers or other symbols to some property of an object in order to give this property some of the characteristics of numbers.[23] Phenomena do not exist with built-in numbers; human beings measure properties of objects and impart the characteristics of numbers to the properties. We develop scales to measure such properties as length, weight, and temperature and call them rulers, weight scales, or thermometers. If the object happens to be the human body and the property something called heat, it is possible to use a scale called a thermometer to convert our conversation about heat to a conversation about degrees of Farenheit, centigrade, or Kelvin. Degrees have some of the characteristics of numbers.

Scales vary not only with respect to the particular property with which they are concerned, but with respect to the kinds of distinctions they establish. From this perspective, there are four major kinds of scales—nominal, ordinal, interval, and ratio scales. Nominal scales provide labels for any set of characteristics that are seen as being mutually exclusive. For example, a religious affiliation scale might consist of labels such as Catholic, Protestant, Jewish, Moslem, Hindu, Buddhist, and all others. A sex scale might contain the labels, "male," and "female"; an undergraduate major field scale might contain the labels, sociology, and all others. With a nominal scale, there is no implication that the labels are ordered in any way (one label is not "higher" than another).

Ordinal scales exist when items in the scale are ranked in order. Ordinal scales are used frequently in sociological research. A person in the upper class is seen to be in a higher socioeconomic category than one in the middle or lower class, but there is no implication that upper class is two or three times higher then either of the others. A person scoring 5 on an alienation scale is presumably more alienated than a person scoring 4, but the score does not tell us how much more alienated the first person is. There is no implication that a score of 4 shows twice as much alienation as a score of 2, or that it is twice as far from 0 to 4 as it is from 0 to 2.[24]

Interval scales exist when the numbers on the scale are equally spaced from each other. For example, the centigrade and Fahrenheit thermometers are interval scales. On the centigrade scale, the freezing and boiling points of water are arbitrarily called 0 and 100 degrees. The temperature range between these two points is divided into one hundred equal intervals, each called a centigrade degree. Since the origin is arbitrary, it is not possible to say that a temperature of 20° centigrade is twice as hot as one of 10° centigrade. But it is twice as far from 0° to 20° as it is from 0° to 10°.

Ratio scales are interval scales with a zero point that is not perceived to be arbitrary. Thus the Kelvin temperature scale, based on "absolute zero degrees temperature," is a ratio scale. Two hundred degrees Kelvin is twice as hot as 100° Kelvin, although 40° Fahrenheit is not twice as hot as 20° Fahrenheit, and 40° centigrade is not twice as hot as 20° centigrade. In social research, age, height, weight, and length of residence in a given city are examples of ratio scales. For example, a twenty-year-old person is twice as old as one who is ten years old.

Sampling Statistics

A second part of the statistical world is called sampling statistics, or statistical inference. Here we do not have access to the raw scores of an entire population, but only to a sample of those scores. Sampling statistics help us make inferences about a larger population to which we do not have access, but from which the sample was drawn.

A random sample is gathered so that each member of the larger population is as likely to be included in the sample as any other member. If, for example, you want to interview a random sample of all students at a university, it would not be appropriate simply to interview the first twenty students you meet in an introductory sociology class or an advanced French class. You might get too many freshmen or seniors in your sample, or too many humanities or social science students. In order to select a random sample, you might place the names of every student at the university on cards and, after the cards were well shuffled, draw at random twenty cards. The students whose names appeared on the cards would constitute the sample. Or, if you had an accurate list of all two thousand students at the university, you might select one number at random—say, 576—and include every hundredth person after that. Thus, the students in your sample would be the ones numbered 576. 676, 776, and so on (after 1976, you would go to 76, 176, and so on, until you had obtained twenty names). In practice, many sociologists use published tables of random numbers to select a random sample from a numbered population list. Tables of this kind are often printed in statistical textbooks.

A stratified random sample is a sample collected so that it will contain the same proportions of members of different classes or groups as are contained in the larger population. For example, if one-fifth of the students are juniors, you would select enough juniors to make up one-fifth of the sample. The same procedure would be followed for other classes, and for any other characteristic you felt was important. If 10 percent of the students were sociology majors and 15 percent biology majors, your stratified random sample might include 10 percent sociology students and 15 percent biology majors. Stratified random samples are often used for surveys such as election polls, since different subpopulations (religious, occupation, and geographical groups) often show great differences in voting preferences.

Examples of Descriptive Statistics

Averages. The commonsense use of the word "average" refers to the arithmetic mean. In addition to the mean, there are two other forms of average used frequently for statistical description—the median and the mode. Suppose you want to know the average weekly income of employees in a given workroom and learn that their weekly wages are as follows:

Name	Wage per Week
Mary	$125
Jane	125
Sue	150
Jim	300
Henry	500

The mode is the term appearing most frequently. The average (modal) income of this group is $125 per week. The median is a term either equal to or larger than half of the other terms and also equal to or smaller than half of them. The average (median) income of this group is $150 per week, because $150 is larger than the term $125 and smaller than the other two terms, $300 and $500. Parenthetically, we might note that a woman was earning an average wage in this workplace. Would this be true? Yes. Would it mean that women were getting the same level of compensation as men? No.

The mean is the term obtained by adding all of the terms and dividing the sum by the number of terms. The average (mean) income of the group is $240. Note that if Jim's income were raised to $400 per week, or even to $700 a week, neither the mode nor the median income of this group would change, although the mean would increase to $260 and $320 per week, respectively. In short, the mean is more sensitive than the other two averages and reflects the value of each term in the distribution. For the same reason, however, the mean can easily be distorted by increasing the value of one term by a large amount. For example, if all the wages remained constant with the exception of Henry's, and if Henry's salary were raised from $500 a week to $1000 a week, the mean would tell us that the average income of the group had increased from $240 to $340 per week. Mary and Jane, however, would continue to earn $125, Sue $150, and Jim $300 per week.

Variability. The difficulty with the mean is that it says nothing about how the various terms differ from the mean. Some distributions are more variable than others.[25] Variability refers to the relationship of all the terms in a distribution. A change in any term changes the variability of the distribution. Different measures can be used to indicate the nature of the variability of a distribution. One such measure is the average distribution. This is relatively easy to calculate but is of limited usefulness. It is calculated by subtracting each term from the mean, ignoring the plus and minus signs, and dividing this sum by the number of terms. In our example, each term would be subtracted from the mean of $240.

Salary	Mean	Difference
$125	$240	$-115
125	240	-115
150	240	- 90
300	240	+ 60
500	240	+260
Total (ignoring signs)		$640
Average deviation		$128

To obtain a more useful measure, we square each of the differences and divide by the number of terms in the distribution. This is the variance—the mean of the squared differences from the mean of the distribution.

Difference	Squared Difference
–115	13,225
–115	13,225
– 90	8,100
+ 60	3,600
$+260	67,600
Total	105,750
Variance	21,150

Another widely used measure of variability is the standard deviation—the positive square root of the variance. If, in the previous illustration, the variance had been 16, the standard deviation would be 4; if the variance had been 25, the standard deviation would be 5. In our example, the standard deviation would be approximately 145.4 (the square root of 21,150).

Examples of Statistical Inference

The t-Test. Let us suppose that we want to determine whether or not black men in a particular profession are paid significantly lower salaries than white men having approximately the same education and training. We obtain a sample of fifty black men and fifty white men working in the same profession who have approximately the same education and training. We learn that the average salary for white men is $2,000 per month, while the average salary for black men is $1,500 per month. Are black men being discriminated against in terms of level of salary in this profession? One person says, "Not at all. You have a sample of only fifty men. Had you taken another sample of fifty, the average figures might very well be reversed." Another person says, "Clearly, black men are being discriminated against." How do we settle the argument? We use a t-test for the difference between the means.

To do this, we begin by assuming that both samples (that is, the sample of white men and the sample of black men) were drawn from the same population—in other words, we assume that discrimination is not operating. This is the null hypothesis. We assume that, if we continued to take samples, the differences between the mean salary for blacks and the mean salary for whites would, in the long run, be zero. To state this somewhat more precisely, if we subtracted the mean salary for blacks from the mean salary for whites and then used these differences as a separate distribution, in the long run, the mean of this distribution would be zero because no difference exists between black and white salaries. The t-test formula allows us to determine whether the value of t is so small that we cannot reject the null hypothesis (that the blacks and whites in the sample were derived from the same population) or, conversely, whether the value of t is so large that we must reject this hypothesis and conclude that significant differences exist—differences that could be due to discrimination. Significance is characteristically defined in terms of a .05 level or a .01 level—that is, whether the difference would occur by chance less than five times in a hundred or less than one time in a hundred.

The Pearsonian Product-Moment Coefficient (or, correlation coefficient), represented by the symbol *r*, measures the degree of relationship between two variables. Suppose that we wanted to test the hypothesis that the more formal education a person has received, the less likely he is to be prejudiced. We might have scores of an attitude test measuring degree of prejudice as follows: 0 for little or no prejudice, 1 for some prejudice, and 2 for a great deal of prejudice. Suppose that we could rate the amount of formal education of each respondent as follows: 1 for a grade-school education, 2 for a high-school education, and 3 for a college education. (This is, of course, over-simplified, but we wish to demonstrate the basic idea.) If the scores for several respondents were

Name of Respondent	Prejudice Score	Formal Education
Jones	0	1
Smith	1	2
Crawford	2	3

there would be a perfect *positive* correlation ($r = 1.00$) between prejudice and education; the higher the education, the higher the prejudice.

If the scores were

Name of Respondent	Prejudice Score	Formal Education
Jones	0	3
Smith	1	2
Crawford	2	1

there would be a perfect *negative* correlation ($r = -1.00$) between prejudice and education; the higher the education the lower the prejudice.

If there were no relationship at all between the two sets of measures, there would be zero correlation; the closer the relationship approaches -1 or $+1$, the more we can speak of a negative or positive *linear* relationship between the two variables. The following formula is used to compute *r*:

$$r = \frac{N\Sigma XY - (\Sigma X)(\Sigma Y)}{\sqrt{N\Sigma X^2 - (\Sigma X)^2}\ \sqrt{N\Sigma Y^2 - (\Sigma Y)^2}}$$

In our positive correlation example, the data would be ordered as follows:

X	Y	X Y	X²	Y²
0	1	0	0	1
1	2	2	1	4
2	3	6	4	9
$\Sigma X = 3$	$\Sigma Y = 6$	$\Sigma XY = 8$	$\Sigma X^2 = 5$	$\Sigma XY^2 = 14$

The correlation coefficient would be computed as follows:

$$r = \frac{3(8) - 3(6)}{\sqrt{(3)(5) - (3)^2}\ \sqrt{(3)(4) - (6)^2}}$$

$$r = \frac{24 - 18}{\sqrt{15-9}\ \sqrt{42-36}}$$

$$r = \frac{6}{\sqrt{6}\ \sqrt{6}}$$

$$r = \frac{6}{\sqrt{36}}$$

$$r = \frac{6}{6}$$

$$r = +1.00$$

Some Statistical Traps

One of the truly ancient clichés one still hears when the subject of statistics is mentioned is, "figures don't lie but liars figure." A little book, which was written more than two decades ago, is still useful for those who wish to avoid some of the more obvious pitfalls of statistical methods. The book, *How to Lie with Statistics*, by Darrell Huff, is filled with "pretty little instances of bumbling and chicanery."[26] It describes distortions ranging from inadequate samples to the misuse of averages, and it cautions about the limitations of specific techniques like the coefficient of correlation. Huff properly observes that if a sample is small enough, it is possible to find substantial correlations between virtually any pair of characteristics. Correlations may occur simply by chance. Sometimes it is not possible to determine which variable is the cause and which the effect. Suicide rates are at the maximum in June; so are marriages. Do suicides produce June brides, or vice-versa? Sometimes a correlation does exist, but it is assumed to continue to exist beyond the data for which it has been demonstrated. The more it rains, the greater the farm crop, but excessively heavy rainfall may ruin a crop. "Permitting statistical treatment and the hypnotic presence of numbers and decimal points to befog causal relationships is little better than superstition. And it is often seriously misleading."[27]

Summary

Separating discussions of theory from those of method is a characteristic feature of positivist thought and is almost universal in American sociology, but not in European sociology. The development of positivist methods in sociology has been strongly influenced by logical positivism. According to this view, if a proposition is neither formally true nor empirically verifiable, it expresses nothing at all and is nonsense. A statement can be verified empirically if it can be confirmed or disconfirmed by observation. This depends on the use of measurement. To avoid difficulties arising in connection with the use of abstract concepts, logical positivists use operational definitions.

For a set of measurements to constitute a useful operational definition of a concept, it must be reliable and valid. If operations are repeated and they yield the same measurements or results each time, the measures are reliable. A valid measure is one that measures what we want to measure.

Survey research is the most familiar type of sociological research. Data collected at one point in time from a sample of persons chosen to describe some larger population at that point in time are characteristic of a cross-sectional survey. A longitudinal survey collects data at different points in time. There are three basic types of longitudinal survey: (1) A trend study examines a set of variables at different points in time. (2) A cohort study focuses on the same population at different points in time. (3) A panel study focuses on the same sample at different points in time.

Among the techniques sociologists have developed to measure attitudes are the following:

1 *Self-reports of beliefs, feelings, or behaviors.* These involve the preparation of a questionnaire (to be filled out by the subject), which is distributed to a chosen sample; a schedule (a set of questions asked and recorded by the interviewer); or an interview guide (a list of points to be covered during an interview).

2 Observations of overt behavior. These involve attempts to understand attitudes by making inferences from overt behavior.

3 Indirect tests and objective tasks. These involve some deception. The respondent is led to believe that one thing is being studied, while actually the investigator is studying something else.

4 Measurement of physiological reactions. These techniques are more common among psychologists than among sociologists. They involve measuring physiological responses of respondents (like heartbeat, dilation of eyes, and so on) to understand attitudes.

Another important positivist method in sociological research is the social experiment, the basic logical procedure of which was first outlined by John Stuart Mill. Simulations are experimental models that operate. They may be all-computer, all-people or mixed people-computer simulations.

Statistical methods are methods used to collect, present, analyze, and interpret data. Positivists find statistical methods essential for their research. Measurements that are collected on each member of a population that is the subject of interest are called raw data. Descriptive statistics attempt to describe raw data in a more economical, summarized form.

Scales are used to assign numbers to some property of an object, to give the property some of the characteristics of numbers. Nominal scales provide labels for any set of characteristics seen to be mutually exclusive. Ordinal scales exist when items in a nominal scale can be placed in rank order. Interval scales exist when numbers on an ordinal scale are equally spaced from each other. Ratio scales are interval scales with a zero point perceived not to be arbitrary.

Sampling statistics help us make inferences about a larger population to which we do not have access, but from which the sample was drawn. In using sampling statistics, we do not use the raw scores of an entire population, but only a sample of these scores. A random sample is gathered so that each member of a larger population is as likely to be included as any other member. A stratified random sample is collected so that it will have the same proportions of members of different classes or subgroups as are contained in the larger population.

Examples of descriptive statistics include different kinds of averages, such as the mean (the term obtained by adding all the terms and dividing the sum by the number of terms), the mode (the term appearing most frequently), and the median (the term either equal to or larger than half the other terms, and equal to or smaller than half of them). Variability refers to the relationship of all terms in a distribution. The average deviation is calculated by subtracting each term from the mean, ignoring the plus and minus signs, and dividing this sum by the number of terms. If the sum of the squared differences is divided by the number of terms in our distribution, we have the variance—the mean of the squared differences from the mean of the distribution. The standard deviation is the positive square root of the variance.

Examples of statistical inference include the t-test (a test for determining whether two separate samples were drawn from the same or from different populations), and the Pearsonian product-moment correlation (a measure of the extent to which two variables change with respect to each other). The product-moment correlation coefficient ranges from -1 to $+1$. When the coefficient is positive, the relation between the two variables is positive (for example, as more money is spent advertising a product, its sales increase).

This chapter has described a variety of methods that employ positivist assumptions about the nature of social reality. Almost all sociologists use some of these methods some of the time. The assumptions of positivism imply a belief that the social world is essentially similar to the world of nature, and that human behavior is subject to social laws and to cause-and-effect relationships. To the extent that such assumptions seem reasonable in specific situations, positivist methods can help us to understand features of society that might otherwise remain hidden. To the extent that the social world is different from nature, and to the extent that cause-and-effect relationships are not applicable to social processes, it is necessary to employ different theories and methods of inquiry. In the next two chapters we will examine some of these.

For Further Study

There are many interesting and valuable collections of reports on research conducted by positivist methods. See M. Patricia Golden. *The Research Experience* (Itasca, Ill.: F. E. Peacock, 1976), chapters 3–6; Earl R. Babbie, *The Practice of Social Research* (Belmont, Calif.: Wadsworth, 1973); and Stephen Cole, *The Sociological Method*, 2d ed. (Chicago, Ill.: Rand McNally, 1976).

For an authoritative collection of positivist studies with an applied sociology focus, designed to be useful to the consumer of research reports, see Phillip Fellin, Tony Tripoldi, and Henry J. Meyer, *Exemplars of Social Research* (Itasca Ill.: F. E. Peacock, 1969). For a sophisticated treatment of research problems, see Paul F. Lazarsfeld et al., *The Language of Social Research*, 2nd ed. (New York: Free Press, 1972).

For interesting illustrations of the use of statistics, see Judith M. Tanur et al., eds. *Statistics: A Guide to the Unknown* (San Francisco: Holden-Day,

1972). For interesting and valuable critiques of positivist methods see Derek L. Phillips, *Knowledge from What?* (Chicago: Rand McNally, 1971), and *Abandoning Method* (San Francisco: Jossey-Bass, 1973), by the same author. For a British "starter" book in research techniques, see Peter H. Mann, *Methods of Sociological Enquiry* (Oxford, England: Basil Blackwell, 1968). For a collection of articles and editorial analyses critical of both positivist methods and the discipline of sociology itself, see Larry T. Reynolds and Janice M. Reynolds, eds., *The Sociology of Sociology* (New York: McKay, 1970).

For a critique of operationalism in research and fascinating examples of research techniques based on multiple operations, see E. J. Webb, Donald T. Campbell, Richard D. Schwartz, and Lee Sechrest, *Unobtrusive Measures* (Chicago, Ill.: Rand McNally, 1966). (The original working title of this work, according to its authors, was *The Bullfighter's Beard.* This refers to the observation that toreros' beards are longer on the day of the fight than on any other day. Does the torero's beard really grow faster that day or does he simply stand farther away from the blade as he shakes somewhat with fear?)

Notes

1 See A. J. Ayer, ed., *Logical Positivism,* (New York: Free Press, 1959), introduction.

2 Rudolf Carnap, "Testability and Meaning," in *Readings in the Philosophy of Science,* eds. Herbert Feigl and May Brodbeck (New York: Appleton-Century-Crofts, 1953), p. 48.

3 See Hubert M. Blalock and Ann B. Blalock, *Methodology in Social Research* (New York: McGraw-Hill, 1968).

4 George W. Bornstedt, "Survey," in *Encyclopedia of Sociology,* eds. Gayle Johnson et al. (Guilford, Conn.: Dushkin Publishing Group, 1975), p. 290.

5 See Earl R. Babbie, *Survey Research Methods* (Belmont, Calif.: Wadsworth, 1973), for an excellent discussion of these methods.

6 See Gene F. Summers, ed., *Attitude Measurement* (Chicago: Rand McNally, 1970), introduction.

7 See William J. Goode and Paul K. Hatt, *Methods in Social Research* (New York: McGraw-Hill, 1952).

8 R. T. LaPiere, "Attitudes vs. Action," *Social Forces* 13 (1934): 230–237.

9 Louise H. Kidder and Donald T. Campbell, "The Indirect Testing of Social Attitudes," in *Attitude Measurement,* ed. Gene F. Summers. pp. 233–383.

10 See Daniel J. Mueller, "Physiological Techniques of Attitude Measurement," in *Attitude Measurement,* ed. Gene F. Summers, pp. 534–552.

11 See Bernard S. Phillips, *Social Research* (New York: Macmillan, 1966).

12 See John R. Raser, *Simulation and Society* (Boston: Allyn & Bacon, 1969).

13 James S. Coleman, Preface to *Simulation Games in Learning*, Sarane S. Boocock and E. O. Schild, eds. (Beverly Hills, Calif.: Sage, 1968).

14 See Dorwin Cortwright and Alvin Zander, eds., *Group Dynamics*, 3d ed. (New York: Harper, 1968), pp. 17–19 and 318–335.

15 Harold Guetzkow, et al., *Simulation in International Relations,* (Englewood Cliffs, N.J.: Prentice-Hall, 1963).

16 Guy H. Orcott, Martin Greenberger, John Korbel, and Alice M. Rivlin, *Microanalysis of Socioeconomic Systems: A Simulation Study* (New York: Harper, 1961).

17 Raser, *Simulation and Society*, p. 91.

18 Robert Boguslaw, Robert H. Davis, and Edward Bernard Glick, "A Simulation Vehicle for Studying National Policy Formation in a Less Armed World," *Behavioral Science* (January 1966): pp. 43–61.

19 Robert Boguslaw and Robert H. Davis, "Social Process Modeling: A Comparison of a Live and Computerized Simulation," in *Behavioral Science* 14 (May 1969): 202.

20 Ibid., p. 202.

21 Ibid., p. 203.

22 George H. Weinberg and John A. Schumaker, *Statistics: An Intuitive Approach* (Monterey, Calif.: Brooks/Cole, 1974), p.1. This is an excellent introductory text in statistics.

23 See Bernard S. Phillips, *Social Research* (New York: Macmillan, 1966), p. 167.

24 See Earl R. Babbie, *Survey Research Methods* (Belmont, Calif.: Wadsworth, 1973), pp. 138–139.

25 See Weinberg and Schumaker, *Statistics*, pp. 26–37.

26 Darrell Huff, *How to Lie with Statistics* (New York: Norton, 1954), p. 6.

27 Ibid., p. 98.

Subjective Theories and Methods

One common theme running through a variety of positivist methods and theories is the assumption that human behavior is shaped largely by factors outside the control of individual persons. Human "action" determines the characteristics of society, but the sources of human action itself are psychological traits, genes, or human nature. Positivist theories and methods tend to assume that thoughts and meanings are determined by some other, less observable, factors. In this sense, both society and human behavior are seen as objective phenomena—phenomena that exist independently of human will or volition.

Are these assumptions valid? Are human beings really passive objects who have only a very limited influence on their own destinies? A significant number of sociologists believe, on the contrary, that human beings are prime movers—creators of history—and that the thoughts and meanings held by people are crucial in shaping human society. Society is unlike nature, they say, precisely because society is subject to human will and volition.

The implications of such a view are far-reaching. Sociologists who think that human volition shapes society do not accept the methods of the natural sciences as the principal means of understanding human behavior. Instead, they think that theories and methods are needed to discover the processes by which individuals attach meaning to events and actions and to understand the impact of such processes on behavior. As one such approach puts it,

> the basic question raised by phenomenological sociology is whether the attempt to create "a sociology" in the manner of the natural sciences is not a mistaken enterprise altogether and whether, therefore, an alternative approach to the study of social phenomena would prove to be more fruitful; notwithstanding the prestige of methods of the natural sciences as a mode of cognition about the world.
>
> Phenomenological sociology attempts to provide such an alternative by grounding itself on what it takes to be the particular characteristics of social phenomena, arguing that such characteristics require a methodology that is distinct from that of the natural sciences; in particular, it suggests a methodology

which, whilst focusing on the meaningful character of social phenomena, does not degenerate into unexamined intuition.[1]

Contemporary American sociology seems to be well established within the framework of positivism. Theories focusing upon the volitional nature of human behavior are a relatively recent development within the discipline and, as is often the case with new approaches, tend to be greeted with distrust, suspicion, and even amusement. While many positivist sociologists will admit to the suggestive nature of research into subjective meanings, and concede that such research is often useful for the purpose of generating hypotheses, few of them will reward it with the precious label of "science."

The fact is that subjective theories and methods, especially when compared with those of positivist sociology, are undeniably sloppy and often imprecise. As its own proponents readily admit, this approach "does not restrict the observer to a narrow set of methods or perspectives. There is no formula or recipe for procedures which is to be applied ready-made to the problem being studied."[2] For most sociologists, however, the more fundamental difficulty with such an approach is that "the social scientist must evolve a way of looking that is different from a positivist science approach to data. In fact he must learn to regard as data some objects, events, and activities he previously did not 'see' at all. In this respect, a new paradigm enables him to see 'facts that were there all the time.' "[3]

How Do Individuals Know About Society?

Positivist theories and methods begin with the implicit assumption that the data studied by sociologists are objective and fundamentally real. The sense impressions people receive are thought to be accurate reflections of real things. If distortions do exist, they can be corrected by making additional observations and repeating these observations with other observers. Subjective theories and methods, on the other hand, begin with the conviction that human actors make sense of the world by calling upon a store of tacit assumptions and that, in doing so, they create the meaning of data. Subjective theories and methods focus on the ways in which people give meaning to their experiences. The philosophical basis for subjective theories is an approach known as phenomenology. It will be helpful to summarize some of the major ideas of this point of view.

Edmund Husserl

Edmund Husserl (1859–1938) is usually credited with being the "father of phenomenology," although the term was actually used almost a hundred years before he was born. Husserl began his professional career as a mathematician, but he soon turned to philosophy. His first book, published in 1891, was called the *Philosophy of Arithmetic*. Although he wrote prolifically throughout the remainder of his life, little else was published before his death. Shortly after his death in 1938, his unpublished manuscripts were smuggled out of Nazi Germany and sent to Louvain, Switzerland, where the Husserl Archives were established. Some of the manuscripts have since been published.[4]

The term "phenomenology" refers to a distinction made by the philosopher, Immanuel Kant, between a *phenomenon*—how something appears in human consciousness—and a *noumenon*—a "thing-in-itself." One of Husserl's students has explained the importance of this distinction by using the symbology of Plato's allegory of the cave.[5] In this cave, men are chained and placed in a position facing the wall and turned away from the entrance. The cave is dimly lit, and the only light comes from the entrance. The men, therefore, see on the walls of the cave shadows of themselves and of other things moving in front of the cave's entrance. Since the men have never had direct experience of the "outside world," their only source of information is the shadows on the walls. Their truths are truths about shadows, but they do not know that they are seeing shadows. Under these circumstances, the shadows are seen by the men as all that there really is in this world.

If one of the prisoners in the cave could get rid of his chains and move about, the initial pain and shock might well make him want to return to his imprisoned status. If he dragged himself to the cave entrance, he would, at first, be blinded by the sun, see nothing, and long for a return to the darkness. If, however, he managed to stay long enough to see himself and others as they really are, he would never again see shadows as reality or his own shadow as his true self. He would understand the shadows by referring them back to real things. In doing so, he would not reject the knowledge of the other prisoners, but would understand its shadowy nature. But the other prisoners would not understand him. They would mistrust everything he said and resist his efforts to free them from their chains and get them to walk into the light. In short, for Husserl, the process of freeing oneself from the familiar world is not a simple theoretical or intellectual act, but is a spiritual act that involves the entire person in a fundamental experience of transformation.

From a phenomenological perspective, the cave can be compared to the constant situation in which human beings find themselves. "We are always unmovably enchained in the bind of an overpowering tradition of 'prejudices' which keeps us turned away from what-really-is and turned toward the world of 'shadows,' toward the shadows of ourselves and of things." [6] Husserl was interested in seeing the world from a radically altered perspective, and this meant a return to the things themselves. For him, anything of which a person is conscious is a phenomenon, and he insisted that each experience be considered in its own terms as it shows itself and as one becomes conscious of it.

I can, for example, be conscious of a table in a room, or of a mathematical theorem. There are obvious differences between a table and a mathematical theorem. Although they are different kinds of things, both are objects of my consciousness and have separate realities that cannot be reduced to the other. The mental activity by which I know mathematical objects like theorems and axioms is quite different from the mental acitivity by which I know material objects like a table, and it would be completely inappropriate for me to investigate material objects by the same mental activity appropriate for investigating mathematical objects.

For Husserl, experience refers not only to the sense perceptions studied by natural science, but also to values, feelings, abstractions, or anything else of which one can be conscious. All of these are, for him, phenomena, and phenomenology was intended as a procedure for systematically investigating the content of consciousness.

Now, all of this may seem unnecessarily obscure to, let us say, a farmer who plants his crops, feeds his animals, and reaps a harvest. Such a farmer may be much too busy to question the reality of the world, or to ask whether it is fundamentally rational or irrational. The farmer adopts what Husserl would call "the natural standpoint." The natural world in which our farmer lives and moves is filled with objects, people, values, and many other things, and he has many ways of relating to this world. He decides to do some things, he sometimes acts spontaneously, he observes, calculates, infers, and feels joy or pain from his experiences.

The natural standpoint is probably the most basic and common relationship of individuals to the world, but Husserl describes two others—the scientific standpoint, and the philosophical standpoint. The scientific standpoint differs from the natural attitude in the sense that it excludes all values, esthetics, and practical concerns. In the natural standpoint, an individual is involved in a wide variety of subjective relationships with the world; the scientist gives up this posture and adopts an attitude that excludes all other human relationships. Thus, in the natural standpoint,

> the scientist is related to his wife by means of a whole gamut of human emotions, values, practical concerns and obligations. But as a scientist he sees her as nothing but a swarm of molecules and a collection of physical substances. The scientific attitude narrows the range of objects of possible investigation to those of one kind—namely, material nature.[7]

The philosophical standpoint first developed when people began to question the world, rather than to take it as a given. As Husserl saw it, the philosophical standpoint was fundamentally a demand to know the rational foundations of the world, to ask about the why of the world, rather than simply asking about the what. To move from the natural standpoint to the philosophical one is a difficult task. Husserl called the process involved in making such a shift "phenomenological reduction," or "epoché," or "bracketing." [8] (The terms mean essentially the same thing for him.)

"Epoché" involves a questioning of presuppositions until they can be established on a firmer basis. A positivist, for example, begins with the presupposition that all human knowledge can be explained in terms of sense perceptions. This presupposition, Husserl would say, must be suspended to allow an exploration of the full range of different dimensions of experience. Some of these dimensions may not be based on sense perception. Only after we have considered all possible kinds of experience can we decide whether or not empiricism (a reliance on sense perception) is a sufficient basis for explaining human knowledge.

The technique for engaging in this questioning of presuppositions is referred to as "bracketing" (that is, to put in parentheses). Husserl intended this usage in the mathematical sense. In mathematics, part of an equation may be bracketed or placed in parentheses when one wishes to treat it differently from the rest of the equation. It is not eliminated from the larger context of the equation, but is held in abeyance. The mathematician may do this in order to focus on what is essential in a particular problem, while temporarily ignoring superfluous or accidental features. Similarly, the process of phenomenological reduction sets aside all existing prejudices about the world and how it works, as well as presuppositions about the way to find out how the world works.

Husserl's quarrel with positivism can be summarized as follows: Positivist science begins by making some supposedly self-evident assumptions. Actually, however these assumptions are arrived at through deduction or inference, not through direct observation. So methods of reasoning are used as instruments of positivist research, but they are not products or discoveries of positivist science. If positivism restricted itself, as it claims to do, to the world of sense perceptions, it could never derive from that world such nonsensible elements as the principle of the syllogism or modes of inference. Such elements must be drawn from another realm which, while not positivist, is a realm of experience (that is, it is not supernatural or imaginary). This realm consists of things that are known intuitively and prior to any theorizing. Without it, positivist science would be helpless.

While Husserl's approach implied an alternative way of studying the social world, his own method did not really go beyond philosophical contemplation.[9] It was a method that explored the limitations of empirical research, but did this exploration only within the mind. While Husserl criticized the positivists for not understanding that there might be realities other than empirical ones, his own method separated the world of real life from the world of thought. Before phenomenology could be adopted as a theoretical approach in sociology, some further refinements were needed.

Alfred Schutz

Alfred Schutz (1899–1959) did not conform to any of the popular stereotypes of an academician, philosopher, or sociologist.[10] Born and educated in Vienna, he served briefly in the Austrian army during World War I and was decorated for bravery. He later studied law, philosophy, and sociology, but his professional life was always somewhat segmented He worked as a lawyer, banker, and a businessman during the day, and as a scholar at night. He emigrated from Austria during the Nazi occupation in 1938 and, after a stay in Paris, moved to New York. In 1943, he began teaching at the New School for Social Research in New York, and he remained there until the end of his career. While serving as a professor of philosophy and sociology during the evening, he continued his business interests in the daytime. Thus, Schutz was neither a political radical nor a scholarly recluse. He lived what many consider a normal life and at worst might be accused of moonlighting (either in academia or business, depending on how you look at it). Given this background, it is not so surprising that Schutz focused his intellectual powers on the world of ordinary people, the world of daily life, the everyday working world into which each of us is born, within whose limits our existence unfolds, and which we transcend completely only in death.[11]

How do people learn about this commonsense world? Do we simply collect facts about it? Schutz tells us there are no such things as pure and simple facts. Everything we learn about the world, whether through the use of common sense or through scientific thought, involves the use of constructs. Constructs are abstractions we apply to select and organize facts. What we consider facts are selected from an infinity of possibilities by our minds, and, therefore, all facts are interpreted facts. Whether we examine them in their own natural setting, or in some more detached and abstract setting, the meaning of facts is determined by the interpretations we place upon them. This does not mean that we cannot understand the world as we go about our daily lives, but it does mean we always only grasp certain aspects of it. We grasp those aspects that are relevant for us as we go about our daily affairs, or we may, of course, learn to also see those aspects made visible by a particular body of rules and way of thinking known as the scientific method.[12]

Schutz tells us that the commonsense world is dominated by a pragmatic motive. We learn things that are useful—we learn a language, rules for how to behave in public places or in typical situations, how to use various tools, utensils, instruments, and so on. We usually do these things in an unthinking, unquestioning manner, and they are what Schutz calls the "stock of knowledge at hand."

But only a very small portion of our stock of knowledge at hand is learned from our personal experience. Indeed, in order for us to learn anything from personal experience it is necessary to' fit the new item into our existing stock of knowledge at hand. In a sense, nothing we learn is isolated, but must always fit into what we have previously learned, what we have been taught and what we have previously experienced. "The 'stock of knowledge at hand' forms the frame of reference, interpretation, and orientation for my life in the world of daily experience, for my dealings with things, coping with situations, coming to terms with fellow human beings." [13]

Schutz argues that none of us really sees the world of everyday life as a private world. We see other objects we do not regard as objects, but as people or persons. We take it for granted that each one of them is faced with essentially the same world as we are. When we act, we do so with regard to how we anticipate that they will act and respond, and we assume that they will do the same toward us. In short, we assume that other human beings with whom we have contact have a stock of knowledge at hand that is very much like our own. We do not analyze this assumption; we simply accept it as "an unquestioned belief and certainty, on which we act and proceed but which is not made a topic for reflection and is not even rendered explicit, unless we engage in philosophical inquiries."[14]

Living in this commonsense world, I am a person who acts. I am not a theoretician or impartial observer. I have a wide range of interests, aims, and goals I am trying to reach. I am not only a member of society in general, but I occupy a particular place within society. My position within society is a consequence of my entire life history. Some of this results from choices I have made in my life, but much of it is due to circumstances that have been thrust upon me. In Schutz's terms, I am in a "biographically" determined situation—a situation that is the "sediment of my personal past and continues to change as long as I live, developing in continuity with my past ... it is given to me, and to me alone; I do not share it with anybody." [15]

I take it for granted that every other human being has his or her own unique biographically determined situation, but I also take it for granted that we all live in the same world. I believe that other people see the same things I see, but that they do so from different perspectives. I further assume that our goals and interests cannot be identical, since we have different biographically determined situations. Nevertheless, I assume that we all have what Schutz calls an "interchangeability of standpoints." I take it for granted that I can reverse positions with other persons and see things from their perspective, and that they can do the same with respect to me. "I also believe," he says, "that differences in biographically determined situations can be treated as irrelevant for many purposes." Thus, I believe that it is possible for us to agree upon a common world made up of identical objects having qualities sufficiently identical for the practical purpose of living together with others in the same society. But my knowledge about everyday life is really quite limited. What I know "has the quality of an instrument that cuts a path through a forest and, as it does so, projects a narrow cone of light on what lies just ahead and immediately around; on all sides of the path there continues to be darkness." [16]

What any of us know about the world, in short, is shaped by what we find to be relevant. Some of what we know is determined by our own practical interests, while the rest depends on our general situation in society. What an airline must do to schedule its flights, arrange for maintenance, and train pilots, may be completely uninteresting to me so long as the plane is available to take me where I want to go when I want to go. I may be completely uninterested in how coffee beans are grown, processed, and transported, so long as I have a cup of hot coffee available in the morning.

At the same time, my own personal structures of relevance intersect with those of other people at many points, and this makes it possible for me to communicate with others in practical ways. A very important part of my knowledge of everyday life consists of what I know about the relevancy structures of others. I don't discuss legal problems with my physician; I don't talk to my lawyer about an upset stomach; I don't analyze my religious concerns with my accountant. Beyond this, the common stock of knowledge at hand in a society has its own relevancy structures. For example, in contemporary American society it is "irrelevant to study the movements of the stars to predict the stock market, but it is relevant to study an individual's slips of the tongue to find out about his sex life, and so on. Conversely, in other societies astrology may be highly relevant for economics, speech analysis quite irrelevant for erotic curiosity, and so on."[17]

Positivism Versus Phenomenology

The essential point of disagreement between positivism and phenomenology concerns the nature of reality. Positivism assumes that the world of sense perceptions is real, and that knowledge obtained about the world by the natural-science method is, therefore, true. Phenomenology assumes that there are multiple realities and that the world seen through the eyes of the scientist is only one reality. It may be very different from the reality seen by people living out their everyday lives. Since the meanings people hold are crucial in shaping their actions, according to phenomenologists, we must develop methods for investigating how ordinary people formulate reality. It is not enough to say, on the basis of positivist methods of research, that the world really is a certain way; we must discover what people think the world really is.

There is, however, a crucial difference between the thinking of Husserl and Schutz on this issue. Husserl says that we should suspend our belief that the world is as it appears to us, in order to investigate the sources of our belief. Thus, Husserl calls for a critical attitude toward existing reality and for considering the possiblity that things are not as they seem. Schutz, on the other hand, argues that in their everyday life, human beings suspend their *disbelief* and assume that the world is as it appears. For Schutz, the task of sociology is to discover the procedures by which people convince themselves that things *are* as they seem. Both Husserl and Schutz have suggested procedures for investigating structures of meaning, but both have left the actual application and development of such procedures to others. As we shall see, the adaptation of phenomenology to sociological purposes has followed the formulations of Schutz, rather than the more critical approach of Husserl.

Ethno-Methodology

The term "ethnomethodology" was invented by Harold Garfinkel in the 1960s to refer to the sociological study of the methods by which people make sense of the world. Garfinkel's *Studies in Ethnomethodology*, published in 1967, contained reports of several studies conducted by him and his associates.[18] Ethnomethodology is essentially the study of commonsense knowledge and activities. Instead of taking for granted the techniques and implicit assumptions by which people in a given society manage their affairs, ethnomethodology treats them as a problem to be studied. Ethnomethodologists undertake "to treat practical activities, practical circumstances, and practical sociological reasoning as topics of empirical study, and by paying to the most commonplace activities of daily life the attention usually accorded extraordinary events, seek to learn about them as phenomena in their own right."[19]

Ethnomethodology—despite the name—is not so much a method of study, as it is a study of method. There is no single technique of research, and Garfinkel reports a wide variety of techniques he has employed in order to discover the methods by which people construct meaning. For example, he once asked students to report actual conversations they had participated in by writing on the left side of a sheet of paper the actual words spoken, and on the right side the student's understanding of what was being talked about. One such conversation between a student and his wife started out as follows:

Actual Conversation	Unspoken Conversation
Husband: Dana succeeded in putting a penny in a parking meter today without being picked up.	This afternoon as I was bringing Dana, our four-year-old son, home from the nursery school, he succeeded in reaching high enough to put a penny in a parking meter when we parked in a parking meter zone, whereas before he has always had to be picked up to reach that high.
Wife: Did you take him to the record store?	Since he put a penny in a meter that means that you stopped while he was with you. I know that you stopped at the record store either on the way to get him or on the way back. Was it on the way back, so that he was with you or did you stop there on the way to get him and somewhere else on the way back?
Husband: No, to the shoe repair shop.	No, I stopped at the record store on the way to get him and stopped at the shoe repair shop on the way home when he was with me.
Wife: What for?	I know of one reason you might have stopped at the shoe repair shop. Why did you in fact?
Husband: I got some new shoelaces for my shoes.	As you will remember I broke a shoelace on one of my brown oxfords the other day so I stopped to get some new laces.
Wife: Your loafers need new heels badly.	Something else you could have gotten that I was thinking of. You could have taken in your black loafers which need heels badly. You'd better get them taken care of pretty soon.[20]

Now this is clearly not the kind of conversation one expects to see headlined in the daily newspapers. It is not news. It is not even the kind of conversation calculated to produce a best-selling novel. It is humdrum, somewhat boring, and evocative of little more than a stifled yawn or, at best, a *sotto voce* "so what!"

To an ethnomethodologist like Garfinkel, however, the dialogue suggests ideas like the following: (1) There were many things the husband and wife understood as they were talking that they did not mention. (2) Many things both husband and wife understood in the conversation were known, not simply on the basis of what was said, but were derived from many things that were left unspoken. (3) Many things were understood through a process of paying attention to the sequence in which statements were made, rather than because of the invariant meaning of these statements. (4) The meanings to each speaker came, not only from what had just been said, but from a whole set of larger shared understandings.[21]

Many words in the conversation were simply shorthand references or signs for these previous understandings. Therefore, this conversation cannot be understood solely from the words used. It is necessary to know something about the biographies of both speakers, their purposes, the circumstances of each utterance, the previous course of the conversation, and the particular relationship between the speakers. The words and phrases do not have a meaning that remains unchanged in changed contexts. Some statements can be understood immediately in the conversation, but the meaning of others depends upon their position in a sequence.

Garfinkel suggests that everyone expects others to understand that speech patterns are vague. For example, one must often agree implicitly to wait before the meaning of a statement becomes clear. These unspoken agreements, he says, provide an unnoticed background that allows understandable plain talk to occur. He has tried to demonstrate this with another technique, in which he asks students to engage in an ordinary conversation with an acquaintance. He instructs the students to insist, during the course of the conversation, that the acquaintance clarify the meaning of all expressions used. For example, an acquaintance told a student that she had a flat tire the previous day. The student asked, "What do you mean, you had a flat tire?" The acquaintance appeared to be stunned for a moment, then answered with hostility, "What do you mean, 'What do you mean?' A flat tire is a flat tire. That's what I meant. Nothing special. What a crazy question!"[22] Similar reactions were produced in comparable situations. For example,

> "How are your med school applications coming?"
> "What do you mean 'How are they coming?'" or

> "I'm sick of him . . ."
> "Please explain your ailment."[23]

Another technique employed by Garfinkel was to have his students spend a period of time in their own homes viewing activities there and acting as though they were strangers. The reports submitted by students, who described persons, relationships, and activities as though they had no history, are very strange documents, indeed. For example, one reported, "A short stout man entered the house, kissed me on the cheek and asked, 'How was school?'"[24] More serious difficulties arose when Garfinkel asked students to behave as boarders in their own homes—to use formal address, to speak only when spoken to, and to act in a circumspect, polite fashion. In the majority of cases, family members became quite disturbed.

> They vigorously sought to make the strange actions intelligible and to restore the situation to normal appearances. Reports were filled with accounts of astonishment, bewilderment, shock, anxiety, embarrassment, and anger, and with charges by various family members that the student was mean, inconsiderate, selfish, nasty, or impolite. Family members demanded explanations: What's the matter? What's gotten into you? Did you get fired? Are you sick? What are you being so superior about? Why are you mad? Are you out of your mind or are you just stupid? . . .[25]

Because of such techniques. Garfinkel has sometimes been accused of enjoying the discomfort of others. These criticisms betray a lack of understanding of what Garfinkel and his associates are trying to do. Ethnomethodological techniques are designed "to discover the 'methods' that persons use in their everyday life in society in constructing social reality and also to discover the nature of the realities they have constructed."[26] The hope is that, as the naive subjects involved in these experiments are shocked, bewildered, or angered when their expectations are violated, they will reveal the nature of unstated assumptions they hold in everyday life. Getting people to reveal these unstated assumptions is at least a "major part of the general program of ethnomethodology."[27]

This program is so unlike the methods used in conventional American positivist research that some sociologists have concluded that "ethnomethodology is *not* a new methodology, but rather a theoretical perspective."[28] Ethnomethodology, in this view, is a theory, because it rests upon an interrelated set of untested assumptions about the relationship between individuals and society. Jonathan Turner has tried to summarize these assumptions in his book, *The Structure of Sociological Theory.*[29]

In Turner's view, ethnomethodology is a theory. It assumes that human beings try to agree about the important features of an interaction situation—features like attitudes, opinions, or beliefs. People do various things to make it appear that they agree about these features. As a result, they see the setting in which they are located as having an orderly and understandable structure. They can do so because they obey a set of rules and procedures for constructing their perceptions. But in each interaction situation the rules for constructing perception are in some respects unique, and cannot be generalized to other settings. People must therefore use interpersonal methods that allow them to agree about the rules for constructing perception. By developing these rules, parties to an interaction are able to see an orderly and connected world "out there." This leads them to perceive everything in a characteristic way and act in a characteristic fashion.

At the beginning of this chapter, we said that phenomenology began as a strong critique of positivism, and there is certainly no love lost between positivist sociologists and ethnomethodologists. In one very important sense, however, the two theories may be more complementary to one another than their adherents would like to believe. Positivists assume that human behavior is largely shaped by external, objective factors over which individuals have little control, and they seek to discover the causal relationship between such factors and human behavior. Ethnomethodologists assume that people "believe" their behavior to be compelled by objective factors. They study the subjective processes by which individuals convince themselves that there is an objective reality. While a positivist like Talcott Parsons concentrated on specifying the system needs and functional prerequisites of society as a whole, the ethnomethodologists have attempted to specify the fundamental rules and procedures by which individuals construct the appearance of and belief in an ongoing social order. As a result, both tend to view existing social institutions and relationships as necessary or normal, and view efforts to change those institutions or relationships in any fundamental way as dysfunctional or deviant. In this sense, ethnomethodology, like functionalism, has been criticized for having a built-in, conservative bias.[30]

Symbolic Interaction

Ethnomethodology is a relatively recent arrival on the sociological scene. An older and more well-established subjective approach is symbolic interaction, which can be traced back at least to 1937, when Herbert Blumer coined the term "symbolic interactionism" to characterize the orientation of George Herbert Mead and other American thinkers, including John Dewey, W. I. Thomas, Robert E. Park, William James, Charles Horton Cooley, Florian Znaniecki, James Mark Baldwin, Robert Redfield, and Louis Wirth.[31]

Sociologists who use a symbolic interactionist approach do not see themselves as being bound by any orthodoxy, but they do seem to make a similar set of assumptions:

1 Valid principles of human behavior cannot be obtained from the study of nonhuman forms. People are qualitatively different from other

animal forms, and principles obtained from studying other forms cannot completely account for human behavior. (In this sense, symbolic interaction is "antireductionist.")

2 The basic unit of observation is interaction among human beings in society.

3 A newborn human infant is asocial. It is an active organism and has various kinds of impulses, but these are not directed toward any specific ends.

4 The human being is not an organism that simply responds to external stimuli. In addition to reacting, it acts. Something can become a stimulus for a human being only to the extent that it relates to the person's concerns. (This leads to a fundamental methodological principle of symbolic interaction: the researcher must see the world through the eyes of the person being studied.)[32]

For George Herbert Mead, who is generally credited with developing the fundamental ideas of symbolic interactionism, the important thing about the human mind is its ability to use symbols to represent objects. Symbols are gestures representing something other than the gesture itself. Thus, infants initially engage in a wide range of gestures. The range of these gestures is gradually narrowed as some of them bring forth favorable reactions from those upon whom the infant is dependent for survival. For example, crying is a gesture that may come to symbolize hunger or fright, and it may bring forth either food or reassurance. (See chapter 11 of this book.) Gestures come to have common meanings, both to the infant and to other humans in the infant's environment. Eventually, the infant learns to understand the gestures of others. For Mead, it is only after the biological organism has developed a capacity to understand gestures, to use them to "take the role" of others, and to consider and evaluate different possible courses of action, that the organism possesses a mind.

Unlike the behaviorists,who have tended to focus on innate physiological or psychological characteristics of individuals as the fundamental causes of human action, Mead argued that the essential features of individuals and society are created through social interaction. He reasoned that the biological weakness of human beings (as compared with other species) compels them to cooperate with each other in order to survive; they retain those actions that facilitate cooperation and survival.[33]

After the human being develops a mind, it can designate others symbolically, and it can also designate itself as an object. By placing itself in the role of others, it can look at itself through the eyes of others. This process is crucial, Mead felt, in the development of the self. Society, for Mead, emerges from the continual interaction of individuals, who are constantly acting on the basis of their image of *self* and modifying that image as a result of the actions of others toward them. An individual considers various courses on the basis of his or her symbolic understanding of how others are likely to respond, selects an action likely to foster cooperation and survival, and continues to modify that action, depending on the actual response of others in an interacting situation. Thus, society is constantly changing and is shaped by the meanings people attach to situations and actions.

Mead did not believe that human interaction and social structure could be completely predicted if we knew enough about the various images of self relevant to a given interaction. Human behavior, he maintained, is not only based on the "me" part of the self, which is shaped through interaction with others, but also on the "I." The "I" is a second part of the self, based on biological impulses such as hunger, fear, sex, and so on. The "me" is always shaped by my understanding of how others respond to the "I," and this understanding may lead me to change my behavior. However, human behavior is always unpredictable to some extent because of the "I." As a consequence, Mead viewed change in society not only as inevitable, but also as somewhat unpredictable.

Building on Mead's theoretical work, contemporary symbolic interactionists explain human interaction as follows. Each participant picks up clues from the behavior of the other and adjusts his or her behavior to steer the interaction toward some desired end. This is a continual process, with each participant constantly giving off clues, responding to clues, initiating clues, altering behavior, and so on. These clues are both verbal and nonverbal, and the only real substance to an interaction is the manipulation of symbols to reach desired ends.

The analogy of human interaction to game-playing is most vividly illustrated in the writings of one of the best-known contemporary symbolic interactionists, Erving Goffman. Although Goffman refers to his approach as "dramaturgy," his writings have increasingly used the vocabulary of games to describe human interaction.[34] He begins with the premise that, in each interaction, people try to control the impressions they convey of themselves, while they are at the same time attempting to penetrate the impressions conveyed by others and to discover the true feelings and intentions of others. Usually, he says, people do not express their true feelings in such situations, but project an image they believe the other will find acceptable. Typically, they project both an image of themselves and a "definition of the situation."

Each interaction is, for Goffman, a kind of performance, with different actors performing different roles. The purpose that motivates our performance in each situation is "impression management." We attempt to hide those characteristics we do not wish others to see and pretend to qualities that are not ours. In his later books, Goffman further develops the notion of impression management by referring to "expression games," "information contests," and "assessment contests."

It is frequently thought that Goffman, and symbolic interactionists in general, believe that there is no objective reality in society, but only the constantly changing manipulation of symbols. Concepts like "exploitation," "oppression," and "inequality" have no independent existence in this view, but are merely symbolic understandings of situations growing out of human interaction. They can be altered or eliminated by more effective manipulation of symbols.

Symbolic interaction helps the sociologist focus upon the positions people occupy in society and the behaviors that are connected with these positions. In this context, symbolic interactionists are very much concerned with roles and role theory.

Role Theory

Individuals occupy many different positions within a society. An individual may occupy one position in the family, another on the job, another with close friends, and still another in school. For each position, there exists a set of expectations on the part of members of society about the way an occupant of the position should behave. Thus, the occupant of the position of father in a family is expected to behave in a characteristic fashion, and the occupant of the position of supervisor in a factory is expected to behave in a different way. These positions, together with the set of behavioral expectations connected with them, are what sociologists call roles.

Role theory views society as a network of interconnected roles. The focus is on the factors that influence the role behavior of individuals in different settings. In general, three major factors are thought to influence role behavior—formal norms, interactional norms, and imaginary norms. For many positions, there are formal guidelines, or norms, that specify how an individual ought to behave. For example, there are often formally defined job descriptions telling a worker in a factory how to behave. In addition to formally defined norms, there are also expectations and demands of other players in any interaction setting. In a family setting, for example, the role behavior of a parent is affected by the demands and expectations of a child. Finally, an individual acting out a role may behave according to certain assumptions about the expectations of the audience for such behavior. Thus, elected legislators may vote on the basis of their understanding of the wishes of their constituents, rather than according to their own judgments about an issue.

Although many sociologists have written extensively about the theoretical aspects of roles, most of the techniques developed for examining actual role behavior were originally developed by one man—J. L. Moreno. He saw these techniques as part of what he called "sociometry"—an orientation to life, a theory of society, and a method of research.[35]

Sociometry and J. L. Moreno

It is somewhat ironic that Moreno was originally viewed by positivists as one of their own.[36] George Lundberg reviewed the first edition of Moreno's book, *Who Shall Survive? A New Approach to the Problem of Human Interrelations,* and was very impressed with Moreno's "sociometric test." Moreno wanted to discover the networks of influence among the six hundred girls who lived in cottages at a closed community (the State Training School for Girls at Hudson, New York). Each girl was asked to choose, in order of desirability, the other girls with whom she would like to occupy the same house. The choices were to be kept confidential, but each girl understood that her choices would insofar as possible, be the basis for actual assignments. On the basis of this sociometric test, Moreno prepared "sociograms" that diagrammed the nature and strengths of relationships among the girls. Lundberg saw great possibilities in using similar techniques to chart relationships in local communities, and felt that the technique had essentially "the same relation to readily observable overt social behavior as the atomic structure of matter" had to "the more obvious physical universe."

To be received so warmly by the positivists must have come as a bit of a shock to Moreno who, when once asked what he thought of American sociology, replied, "The only American sociologist I can think of is Walt Whitman." In fact, a central element in Moreno's methodology was the belief that society and social relationships can be understood only when the researcher is not a detached observer, but a genuine participant. People being studied must be considered not simply as research objects, he maintained, but also as *"research actors,* not only as objects of observation and manipulation but as *co-scientists* and *co-producers* in the experimental design."[37] There were three primary methods of research that Moreno developed to implement this belief—psychodrama, sociodrama, and role-playing.

Psychodrama. Moreno defined psychodrama as "the science which explores the 'truth' by dramatic means. It deals with interpersonal relations and private worlds."[38] There are five basic elements involved in psychodrama: (1) a circular, three-level stage; (2) the subjects, who are asked to be themselves on the stage and to portray their own private world; (3) the psychodramatic director, who is responsible for the whole "production"; (4) a staff of auxiliary egos, who act out the roles of various persons in the subject's private world; and (5) the audience, which may help subjects by serving as a sounding board or simply by being willing to understand and accept the subject. Just as the director, auxiliary egos, and audience may help the subjects to better understand themselves, provide them with themes with which they can identify and thus improve their own self-understanding.

Sociodrama. Although similar to psychodrama, sociodrama differs in terms of its dramatic focus. Moreno defined it as "a deep action method dealing with inter-group relations and collective ideologies."[39]In psychodrama, the focus of all attention is on the individual and the private world of the individual. In sociodrama, the focus is on the group. It is a method designed to understand the extra-individual factors that influence group behavior and group beliefs.

Role-Playing. Role-playing is essentially a method for learning to perform roles more adequately; it has been widely applied as a teaching method in schools, industry, and in other settings. It has been defined as "a procedure whereby various real-life situations are created and participants have an opportunity to practice specific human relations skills in a safe laboratory environment."[40] It is different from acting, in that the role players are required to remain themselves, although they may be given new names, jobs, and personal histories for the purposes of the exercise. Role players do not simply read lines written by somebody else, but retain their own personal characteristics in situations that are structured in varying degrees.

In one common role-playing exercise, a person is asked to portray a salesman selling a product to different types of buyers. The purpose is to discover the most effective sales pitch for different types of buyers, and to test the adaptive ability of the potential salesman. A similar procedure is sometimes used in mental hospitals to prepare patients for the variety of situations they will confront outside the hospital, and to test their ability to deal with such situations.

While psychodrama and sociodrama have been used by psychologists as an aid in therapy, role-playing has been used in a wide variety of social settings. It is especially useful as a training technique, since it prepares people in advance for situations they are likely to confront. All of these techniques, however, are at least as much therapeutic in purpose as they are designed to gather scientific data about human behavior.

Symbolic interactionists, ethnomethodologists, and others interested in subjective theories and methods have used role-playing and variants of psychodrama and sociodrama widely in their work. In general, a commitment to a subjective approach in sociological work seems to imply that social scientists cannot be effective if they insist upon remaining outside observers. To see the world through the eyes of one's research subjects it is necessary, it is felt, to be a participant in the interaction being studied. Another important technique developed in this connection and extensively used by contemporary sociologists is called participant observation.

Participant Observation

In 1943, the first edition of what was to be a sociological classic was published. William Whyte's book, *Street Corner Society* does not look very much like a work of science.[41] It contains virtually no numbers, has no experimental design, and appears to be a short story or perhaps some version of an autobiography. It is, in point of fact, a participant observation study.

Upon graduating from Swarthmore in 1936, Whyte received a fellowship from Harvard providing him with the opportunity to pursue any line of research he chose. He tells us that he decided to study a slum district in "Eastern City." He finally chose "Cornerville," because it most closely corresponded to what he thought a slum district looked like.

After a few false starts, the head of girls' work at the Norton Street Settlement House arranged for Whyte to meet Doc, the head of one of the local youth gangs. Doc volunteered to help Whyte learn about the community by escorting him around the district and introducing him as a friend. Whyte observed events, conversations, and relationships, and drew conclusions on the basis of these observations. In his book, these conclusions are summarized under three headings—"The Gang and the Individual," "The Social Structure," and "The Problem of Cornerville."

Whyte discusses the origin and growth of the corner gang and tells us that the gang structure arose from habitual associations of the members over a long period of time. The core of the gang is traced to early childhood, when members lived close to each other and had many opportunities to meet and have social contacts with one another. The gang persisted until the members reached their late twenties or early thirties. Home played a small part in group activities. It was typically a place where the gang member appeared only to eat, sleep, and recover from an illness. Even after marriage, the corner boy could be found on his corner virtually every night of the week. This long and close association led, says Whyte, to a system of mutual obligations fundamental to group cohesion. The members did favors for each other, helped one another, and refrained from harming fellow members.

Cornerville people see society as a structure of "big" and "little" people, with intermediaries who bridge the gap. Since the masses are "little people," they must establish connections with an intermediary person and make him obligated to them. Intermediaries perform similar functions for the "big people." Corner gangs, like the Nortons, and cliques, like the Cornerville Social and Athletic Club, fit at the bottom of the hierarchy. Corner boy leaders serve as intermediaries to represent the interests of their members to higher-ups.

Whyte tells us that the problem of Cornerville is not a lack of organization, but the failure of the organization to mesh with the structure of the society in which it is located. It is very difficult to get ahead in Cornerville because there are few avenues for upward mobility. One path is the world of business and Republican politics; the other is the world of rackets and Democratic politics. In effect, the larger society puts a premium on disloyalty to Cornerville and penalizes those who are best adjusted to the life of the district. It rewards those who discard their distinctively Italian characteristics and penalizes those who are not fully Americanized. Even if Cornerville residents should want to forget their Italian origins, the surrounding society refuses to allow this. Cornerville residents are marked as inferior persons, "like all other Italians."

Like ethnomethodology, participant observation is not characterized by one single procedure, and there is a good deal of diversity in the studies of different sociologists. Nevertheless, there are some general rules that guide participant observation research.

1 The participant observer must share the life activities and sentiments of people in face-to-face relationships. The role requires both "detachment and personal involvement."[42] The participant observer must be truly interested in the events and people being observed, and at the same time refrain from judging or moralizing about the actions of those being studied. The investigator must also find a role that makes sense to the people being studied.

2 Whatever role the participant observer adopts, it must be a "normal part of the culture and the life of the people under observation."[43] Inevitably, however, there arises a tension between the scientific role of the observer and the social role within the culture being observed. This usually raises problems about how to become a natural part of the culture, or how to maintain scientific integrity while becoming emotionally involved in everyday events. There may develop strong tensions between scientific responsibilities to report all findings and ethical problems involving personal obligations and commitments developed during the research process.

3 The work of the participant observer becomes increasingly effective and valuable when the observer can see some universal character and relevance in the particular culture being studied. Studying even one family may help to illuminate the meaning and consequences of political and economic changes occurring in a country over an extended period of time. Similarly, research conducted in only one factory may provide useful insights into the nature of corporate organization in an entire society.

What does the participant observer do? Suppose that a researcher is interested in studying a particular organization or facility like a school or hospital. The researcher goes to the facility regularly over a long period of time, gets to know the staff and other participants by interacting with them and watching them interact with others, and keeps detailed notes on what has been observed. These notes are recorded after each observation, out of sight of those being observed.[44]

The participant observer finds a way of being at the facility every day, or at least at regular intervals, in some capacity that seems reasonable to the others who are there. The researcher speaks with the other people, jokes with them if this is appropriate, shares their worries and ambitions. "His goal is to see the world as the subjects conceive it. He enters the experience of his subjects by sharing experiences with them."[45]

It has been suggested that in many ways participant observers are very much like thoughtful persons going about their daily affairs. All try to understand the world from the perspective of other persons, as well as from their own. But typical, thoughtful persons are so deeply involved in the setting in which they live that it is very difficult to see things impartially. People's careers, statuses, friendships and love relations, and fundamental life chances are deeply involved in the setting in which they live. For the participant observers, however, things are usually quite different. They earn their living somewhere completely removed from the research setting. Their friends, family, and dating relationships exist primarily in another place. Their work performance is evaluated by someone outside the research setting, so the material stakes they have in their roles in the setting being studied are considerably less than those of a regular occupant of that world. Accordingly, it is possible for the observers to devote much more time and energy to observing, recording observations, and thinking about what they observe than can the ordinary, thoughtful person in the actual situation.

The matter of selecting an appropriate role is always a difficult one for the participant observer. One basic decision is whether to work as a hidden observer, whose research interests are not known to the subjects, or as an overt researcher. Quite apart from the implications this decision has for the kind of information that can be collected, there are serious ethical problems raised in connection with being a hidden researcher. In extreme cases, this role seems quite analagous to that of an intelligence agent or government investigator. These problems are exacerbated when the research is sponsored by a government agency, business firm, or labor union, where there is a possibility, however remote, that information collected might be used for purposes other than pure science, or might be used to the detriment of the subjects.

Since the practice of participant observation varies widely with different researchers, any attempt to list an invariant set of procedures would be misleading. The strength of the method is derived largely from its flexibility and from the researcher's willingness and ability to adjust to unforeseen situations. We can, however, review some useful suggestions.

How does the participant observer select a research site? Some sociologists are interested in a particular group of people or social setting; others in some theoretical problem. Some are interested in a particular ethnic, racial, or religious group, while others are interested in various forms of deviant behavior, ranging from drug addiction to homosexuality. Still others are interested in management techniques or in a particular profession or occupation. In all cases, there tend to be geographical and other practical considerations that limit the search for a research site. In many cases, the problem is the simple but fundamental one of obtaining access to a particular site. Many organizations have gatekeepers, who can grant either formal or informal permission to work in the setting. Gatekeepers characteristically wish to insure confidentiality with respect to the name, location, and even the activities of the setting that can easily identify it. It is the researcher's responsibility to insure that privacy is respected and that the data collected will not be used in a way that might be harmful to the subjects.

What does the participant observer do in the field? The best participant observers seem to be very quiet, unassuming persons, with whom many different kinds of people can develop a trusting relationship They are seen as having no special interest in the outcome of whatever conflicts exist in the research setting and as being nonthreatening people. To begin, it may be necessary for the researcher to develop a special relationship with one or more persons, but it is important that the researcher not be seen as an extension or agent of that person. In all cases, the particular sets of relationships developed will very much depend upon the researcher's own personality and ability to relate to others. The researcher must learn the special language of the setting in order to hear and understand the fine nuances of what is being said. Field notes should be recorded after every observation period. This may be once a day or more frequently, if the opportunity presents itself. Participant observers should record everything they can remember about the observation period, including actual conversations when possible, the context in which everything proceeded, and their own reactions, opinions, and developing hypotheses.

How does the participant observer analyze data? Here again, there is no rigid or invariant process to be recommended. It is usually suggested that researchers read over all the field notes they have collected to test the hypotheses they have developed, to generate new ideas, and to uncover various forms of relationships among the research subjects. These concepts can then become coding categories for use in sorting the data in various folders. Coding categories can provide useful topic headings for the subsequent research report. The research report should give a clear description of the setting, the researchers' relationship to it, the events observed, and the ideas they and others have about what was observed. It may also deal with questions emerging from the phenomenological perspective adopted in this form of research. Attempts may be made to answer questions like the following: How do each or most of the research subjects define their organizational or social world? Is it possible to group some or all of these persons into an appropriate category based on common definitions? How do the various definitions develop and change? How do these definitions compare with the definitions of other persons related to the group? For example, if it is a deviant group, how do the definitions of group members compare with those of "straight" persons? If it is a group of working people, how do their definitions compare with those of their employers?

Summary

Sociologists who use subjective theories and methods question the attempt of positivists to create a sociology in the manner of the natural sciences. The philosophical basis for subjective theories is phenomenology, first developed by Edmund Husserl. Husserl attacked positivism for its use of assumptions about things that cannot be observed empirically. These assumptions are actually derived, he claimed, through deduction or inference, rather than through direct observation.

Alfred Schutz provided a more sociological framework for phenomenology. He focused on the world of ordinary people and everyday life. He concluded that everything people learn about the world, either through science or by common sense, involves the use of constructs. These are abstractions used to select and organize facts. Thus, all facts are interpreted facts.

Positivism assumes that the world of sense perception is real and that knowledge obtained about the world by the natural-scientific method is true. Phenomenology assumes that there are multiple realities, and that the world seen through the eyes of scientists may be different from the reality seen by people living out their everyday lives.

Ethnomethodology is a term introduced by Harold Garfinkel in the 1960s. Ethnomethodology addresses itself to the ways in which people make sense of the world. Instead of taking for granted the techniques and implicit assumptions by which people manage their affairs in everyday life, ethnomethodology tries to make them problematic so that they can be studied.

A subjective approach that is older and more widely accepted than ethnomethodology is symbolic interaction, which owes much to the theory of George Herbert Mead. It refers to the distinctive character of human interaction. Human beings do not simply react to each other's actions. They can look at themselves as well as other people symbolically, interpret these symbols, and then act on the basis of their interpretation.

Role theory views society as networks of interconnected roles. Roles are the positions people have within society, together with the behavior expected in connection with these positions. Techniques for examining actual role behavior were originally developed by J. L. Moreno, whose sociometry embraced not only sociometric tests, but psychodrama, sociodrama, and role-playing as well. Participant observation, a research technique used extensively by sociologists who work within a subjective frame of reference, was introduced by William Foote Whyte in his book, *Street Corner Society*.

For Further Study

Most of the available literature on subjective theories and methods tends to be very difficult for American undergraduate students. For many years, the clearest and most comprehensive discussion of phenomenology in relation to sociology has been *The Social Construction of Reality*, by Peter L. Berger and Thomas Luckmann (Garden City, N.Y.: Doubleday, 1967). Peter Berger has also written a useful little introductory text presented from this perspective—*Invitation to Sociology* (Garden City, N.Y.: Doubleday, 1963). An excellent, more recent treatment of phenomenology, by David Stewart and Algis Mickunas is *Exploring Phenomenology* (Chicago: American Library Association, 1974). See also Michael Phillipson Filmer, David Silverman, and David Walsh, *New Directions in Sociological Theory* (Cambridge, Mass.: M.I.T. Press, 1973); and Joseph J. Kockelmans, ed., *Phenomenology* (Garden City, N.Y.: Doubleday, 1967).

A comparison of subjective and positivist theories can be found in Jonathan Turner, *The Structure of Sociological Theory* (Homewood, Ill.: Dorsey Press, 1974). Irving Zeitlin presents an excellent analysis of subjective theories from the perspective of a critical sociologist in his book, *Rethinking Sociology* (Englewood Cliffs, N.J.: Prentice-Hall, 1973). Some excellent articles reflecting subjective research and theorizing can be found in George Psathas, ed., *Phenomenological Sociology: Issues and Applications* (New York: Wiley, 1973). For a serious and authoritative effort to explicate and defend ethnomethodology, see Hugh Mehan, and Houston Wood, *The Reality of Ethnomethodology* (New York: Wiley, 1975). For an attack on ethnomethodology by a recent president of the American Sociological Association, see Lewis A. Coser, "Presidential Address: Two Methods in Search of Substance," *American Sociological Review* 40 (December, 1975): 691–700. For a review of the Mehan and

Wood volume from the perspective of a philosophically sophisticated, critical sociologist, who is sympathetic to phenomenology but troubled by ethnomethodology, see Paul Piccone, "Review of Mehan and Wood: The Reality of Ethnomethodology," *Telos* 26 (Winter, 1975–76): 195–205.

Participant observation continues to provide some of the most readable reports of sociological study. For discussions of the method itself, see Severyn T. Bruyn, *The Human Perspective in Sociology: The Methodology of Participant Observation* (Englewood Cliffs, N.J.: Prentice-Hall, 1966); Robert Bogdan and Steven Taylor, *Introduction to Qualitative Research Methods* (New York: Wiley, 1975); Rosalie Wax, *Doing Fieldwork: Warnings and Advice* (Chicago: University of Chicago Press, 1971); William Filstead, ed., *Qualitative Methodology: Firsthand Involvement with the Social World* (Chicago: Markham, 1967).

Examples of participant observation studies include Elliot Liebow, *Talley's Corner* (Boston: Little, Brown & Co., 1967); Harvey A. Farberman, "A Criminogenic Market Structure: The Automobile Industry," *Sociological Quarterly* 16 (Autumn, 1975); Barry Glassner, "Kid Society," *Urban Education* 11 (April, 1976), pp. 5–21; Laud Humphreys, *Tearoom Trade: Impersonal Sex in Public Places,* rev. ed. (Chicago: Aldine, 1975); William B. Helmreich, *The Black Crusaders* (New York: Harper, 1973); Howard S. Becker, et al., *Boys in White: Student Culture in Medical School* (Chicago: University of Chicago Press, 1961).

A useful collection of articles and bibliography on the role of subjectivity in science will be found in Marcello Truzzi, ed., *Verstehen: Subjective Understanding in the Social Sciences* (Reading, Mass.: Addison-Wesley, 1974). For an excellent discussion of some psychodramatic, sociometric, and role-playing techniques, see Martin R. Haskell, *Socioanalysis: Self Direction via Sociometry and Psychodrama* (Long Beach, Calif.: Role-Training Association of California, 1975).

Notes

1 Michael Phillipson Filmer, David Silverman, and David Walsh, *New Directions in Sociological Theory* (Cambridge, Mass.: M.I.T. Press, 1973), p. 14.

2 George Psathas, *Phenomenological Sociology: Issues and Applications,* (New York: Wiley, 1973), introduction, p. 16.

3 Ibid., p. 17.

4 See, for example, Edmund Husserl, *Ideas: General Introduction to Pure Phenomenology* (New York: College Books, 1962); *The Phenomenology of Internal Time Consciousness* (Bloomington, Ind.: Indiana University Press, 1964); *Formal and Transcendantal Logic* (The Hague, Netherlands: Martinus

Nijhoff, 1969); *The Crisis of European Sciences and Transcendental Phenomenology,* (Evanston, Ill.: Northwestern University Press, 1970).

5   See Eugene Fink, "What Does the Phenomenology of Edmund Husserl Want to Accomplish?" trans. Arthur Grugan, in *Research in Phenomenology,* vol. 2 (1972): pp. 7–9.

6   Ibid., p. 7.

7   David Stewart and Algis Mickunas, *Exploring Phenomenology* (Chicago: American Library Association, 1974), pp. 22–23.

8   Ibid., pp. 25–26.

9   See Irving Zeitlin, *Rethinking Sociology* (Englewood Cliffs, N.J.: Prentice-Hall, 1973).

10   See Maurice Natanson, ed. *Phenomenology and Social Reality: Essays in Memory of Alfred Schutz,* (The Hague, Netherlands: Martinus Nijhoff, 1970), introduction, pp. ix–xi.

11   Maurice Natanson, ed. *Alfred Schutz: Collected Papers,* vol. 1, (The Hague, Netherlands: Martinus Nijhoff, 1962), introduction, p. xxv.

12   See Alfred Schutz, "Common-sense and Scientific Interpretations of Human Action," in *Alfred Schutz: Collected Papers,* vol. 1.Maurice Natanson, ed.

13   Aron Gurwitsch, *Alfred Schutz: Collected Papers,* vol. 3, ed. Ilse Schutz (The Hague, Neterlands: Martinus Nijhoff, 1966), introduction, pp. xvi–xviii.

14   Ibid., p. xviii.

15   Ibid., pp. xix–xx.

16   Peter L. Berger, and Thomas Luckmann, *The Social Construction of Reality* (Garden City, N.Y.: Doubleday, 1967), p. 45. According to the authors, chapter 1 of this book is based on Alfred Schutz's work, especially *Die Strukturen des Lebenwelt,* which has since been completed from fragmentary materials by Thomas Luckmann and published in English as *The Structure of the Life World,* by Alfred Schutz and Thomas Luckmann, trans. Richard M. Zaner and H. Tristam Engelhardt, Jr. (Evanston, Ill.: Northwestern University Press, 1973).

17   See Berger and Luckmann, *Social Construction of Reality,* pp. 45–46.

18   Harold Garfinkel, *Studies in Ethnomethodology* (Englewood Cliffs, N.J.: Prentice-Hall, 1967).

19   Ibid., p. 1.

20   Ibid., pp. 38–39.

21   Ibid., pp. 39–40.

22 Ibid., p. 42.

23 Ibid., pp. 42–44.

24 Ibid., p. 45.

25 Ibid., p. 47.

26 George Psathas, "Ethnomethods and Phenomenology," *Social Research* 35 (Autumn, 1968): 509.

27 James S. Coleman, "Review Symposium," *American Sociological Review* 33 (February, 1968): 126.

28 Lindsey Churchill, "Ethnomethodology and Measurement," *Social Forces* 50 (December, 1971): 185.

29 Jonathan H. Turner, *The Structure of Sociological Theory* (Homewood, Ill.: Dorsey Press, 1974), pp. 324–325.

30 See Zeitlin, *Rethinking Sociology;* also see Alvin W. Gouldner, *The Coming Crisis of Western Sociology* (New York: Basic Books, 1970).

31 Herbert Blumer, *Symbolic Interactionism: Perspective and Method* (Englewood Cliffs, N.J.: Prentice-Hall, 1969), p. 1.

32 See Sheldon Stryker, "Symbolic Interaction as an Approach to Family Research" in *Symbolic Interaction: A Reader in Social Psychology,* ed. Jerome G. Manis and Bernard M. Meltzer (Boston: Allyn & Bacon, 1967), pp. 373–374.

33 See George Herbert Mead, *Mind, Self and Society,* ed., Charles W. Morris (Chicago: University of Chicago Press, 1934).

34 See Erving Goffman *The Presentation of Self in Everyday Life* (Garden City, N.Y.: Doubleday Anchor, 1959); *Asylums* (Garden City, N.Y.: Doubleday Anchor, 1961); *Stigma* (Englewood Cliffs, N.J.: Prentice-Hall, 1963); *Strategic Interaction* (Philadelphia: University of Pennsylvania Press, 1969).

35 See Robert Boguslaw, "J. L. Moreno—Obituary," *Footnotes, American Sociological Association* (November, 1974): 6 and Henry J. Meyer, "The Sociometries of Dr. Moreno" *Sociometry,* vol. 15, nos. 3–4 (1952): 354–363.

36 For three articles on "The Work of J. L. Moreno" written from different perspectives see Edgar F. Borgatta, "Three Contributions of Jacob L. Moreno"; Robert Boguslaw, "Moreno, Sociometric Methodology and the Redesign of Society"; Martin Haskell, "Moreno's Image of Man" in *Sociometry,* 38 March, 1975): 148–161.

37 J. L. Moreno, *Who Shall Survive?* 2d ed. (Beacon, N.Y.: Beacon House, 1953), p. 64.

38 Ibid., p. 81.

39 Ibid., p. 87.

40 Norman R. F. Maier, *Psychology in Industrial Organizations,* 4th ed. (Boston: Houghton-Mifflin, 1973), p. 65.

41 William F. Whyte, *Street Corner Society: The Social Structure of an Italian Slum* (Chicago: University of Chicago Press, 1955).

42 Severyn T. Bruyn, *The Human Perspective in Sociology: The Methodology of Participant Observation* (Englewood Cliffs, N.J.: Prentice-Hall, 1966), p. 12.

43 Ibid., p. 15.

44 See Robert Bogdan, *Participant Observation in Organizational Settings* (Syracuse, N.Y.: Syracuse University Press, 1972).

45 Ibid., pp. 3–4.

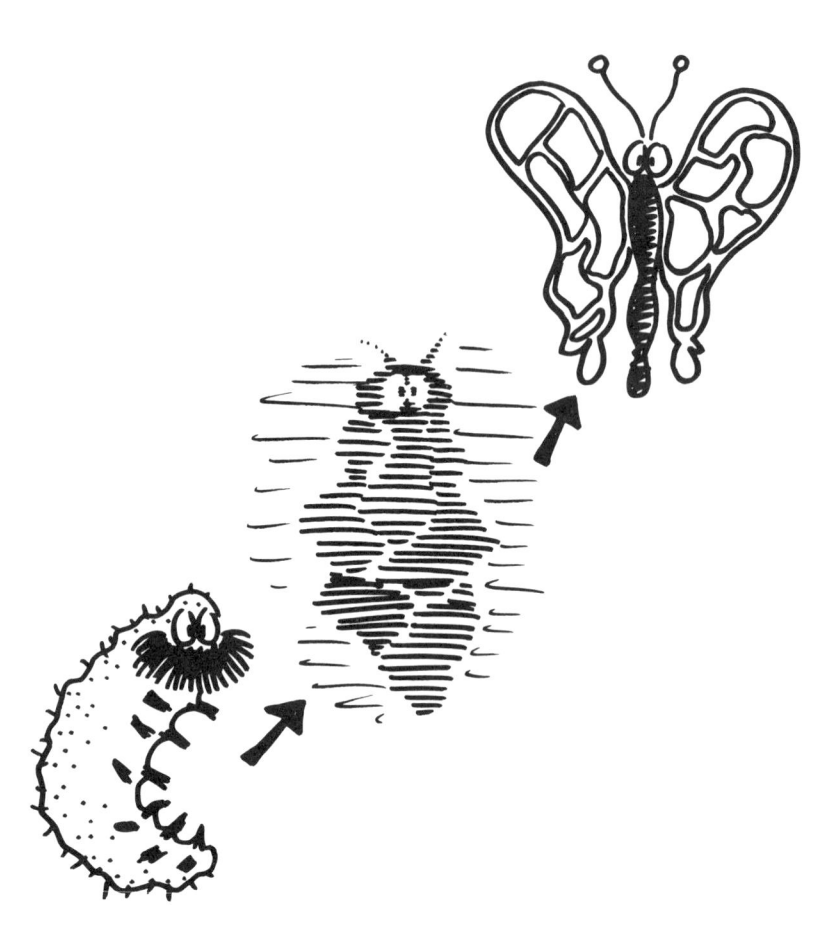

Dialectical Theories and Methods

Can we assume that the social institutions, power relations, and laws of contemporary American society will remain basically unchanged in the future? Of course not. We take it for granted that changes in all these features will occur over time. But will these changes be simply matters of detail, or will they be fundamental transformations? What do we really mean when we speak of social change?

The central conflict between positivist and dialectical approaches concerns the existence of unchanging laws of human behavior that operate in all societies at all times. In the positivist view, it is possible to treat society as a relatively static phenomenon. The laws of society are thought to be general ones, not unique to time and place. In the dialectical view, on the other hand, laws governing human behavior in specific societies at particular times are subject to change. From this perspective, social laws can be understood only in terms of a process of change.

The subjective or phenomenological theories also question the validity of general laws of human behavior. Ethnomethodologists like Harold Garfinkel talk about basic rules that individuals apply to different situations in order to maintain their image of reality. Symbolic interactionists like Herbert Blumer seek to identify the basic elements of symbolic communication. Individuals use symbolic communication to shape the nature of interaction, it is thought. While these rules or elements are thought to be unchanging, subjective theories emphasize the fact that the result or effect of these rules is different in different kinds of interactions. For phenomenologists, a key task of sociological research is to describe the different kinds of events that occur in interactions and to identify the rules that are applicable to each event.

This approach may make many of us uncomfortable. We are accustomed to the principles of common sense or simple logic, and we believe that things do not just "happen." If something occurs, it is because something else caused it to happen. We also believe that the world is made up of things that are different from each other. Acorns are acorns, and oak trees are oak trees. Acorns are *not* oak trees. These commonsense ideas are derived from the basic principles of formal logic. A thing can be only what it is (A is A); a thing cannot be what it is not (A is not –A); a thing must be either itself or something different, but cannot be both itself *and* something different, especially at the same time (any X is either A or –A, but not both at once.)[1]

These principles help us identify distinct properties of different things, and describe the relations between these things. Thus, they help us distinguish between beliefs and behavior, identify components of beliefs and characteristics of behavior, and explore the relationship between beliefs and behavior.

It is often forgotten, however that formal logic (sometimes called Aristotelian logic, since it was Aristotle who suggested these principles) represents only one way of looking at the world. Another way is to view the world as a process rather than as a collection of things. It can be said that everything is in constant motion and is undergoing a process of development. All of us recognize, and occasionally use, this way of thinking, but we probably are unaware that it implies principles different from those of formal logic. For example, we know that acorns and oak trees are different things, but an acorn can become an oak tree. A river and an ocean are different things, but a river may flow into an ocean. A human fetus and a person are different things, but a fetus can become a person. At what point does an acorn become a tree? At what point does a river become an ocean? At what point does a fetus become a person?

These examples illustrate how dialectical theories and methods begin to answer the question "What is social change?" Where positivism and formal logic focus on what a thing is, dialectical methods focus on the process of becoming.[2] Dialectical theorists believe that the changes occurring in society are not simply changes of detail or form, but changes in kind—not merely quantitative changes, but qualitative ones. The difference between acorns and oak trees is not only a difference in size, form, and so on, but a qualitative difference between a nut and a tree.

Similarly, differences between slave society and feudal society, or between feudal society and modern capitalism, are not simply quantitative differences. The institutions, power relations, and laws characterizing feudal society were not simply larger versions of those typical of slave society, nor are the institutions, power relations, and laws characteristic of modern capitalist societies simply larger versions of those typical of feudalism. Relations between masters and slaves are different from relations between nobles and serfs, and the latter are different from relations between owners and workers.

According to dialectical theories, we cannot assume that the laws governing human behavior and social structure in a particular society at a particular moment in time can be applied to society in general or to human behavior in general. Instead, we must assume that the present structure represents a qualitative change from the past, and that it will undergo qualitative change in the future. The task for sociologists is to discover how the present structure grew out of earlier structures, the nature of changes taking place within the present structure, and the possible kinds of future structure that may result from such changes. Social change is seen as a historical process. Dialectical theories treat the laws governing society at any moment as unique to that historical period.

Dialectical theories assume that the history of human society reflects qualitative changes resulting from contradictions within earlier societies and that contradictions will continue to be found in the future. These theories attempt to explain contradictions as processes of change. There are, however, different approaches and emphases within the broad framework of dialectical theories.

What Is Social Change?

Dialectical thinking can be traced back at least as far as the ancient Greeks. Socrates supposedly employed dialectical methods in his debates. The word "dialectic" derives from the Greek word for "dialogue" or "debate." In a dialogue, A's views about a subject may be directly opposite to those of B. The views of both persons may change as a result of their discussion. Dialectical thinking begins with the assumption that all people view the world from their own special perspectives. These, in turn, are shaped by their personal backgrounds and life circumstances. The truth as seen by an individual is, therefore, a partial or one-sided truth. It contains elements that anyone can agree with, but at the same time it is biased by the unique characteristics of the individual. To discover a more general or complete truth, it is necessary to counterpose each one-sided truth with its opposite, so that the common elements can be ascertained. The result of this process, however, may also be a one-sided truth with respect to someone else, so the process must continue until some indisputable version of truth is arrived at. This ongoing process is sometimes described as follows: a thesis (one person's ideas) is opposed by an antithesis (someone else's opposing views), and as a result of the struggle between thesis and antithesis, a synthesis (a new view that both people accept) emerges.

The dialectical truth emerging from this process is one that has overcome many theses, antitheses, and syntheses. The partial, one-sided truths existing at the beginning are affected in three different ways by the dialectical process: (1) they are *overcome* or annulled with respect to what is fragmentary, partial, or one-sided (that is, what an individual takes to be the truth is shown to be an opinion); (2) they are *preserved* with respect to whatever is essential or universal in them; and (3) they are *sublimated* (that is, they are raised to a higher level of knowledge and reality).

A German philosopher, George Wilhelm Friedrich Hegel (1770–1831), first systematically gathered together the previous history of dialectics and showed that dialectical thinking had played a role in the thought of most great philosophers. In his book, *The Science of Logic,* Hegel spelled out an entire system of logic based upon dialectical principles and argued that human history itself was a dialectical process.[3] He claimed that human logic moves through different stages. In the first stage, the principles of formal logic apply, and it is useful to think of things as separate and unchanging. An acorn is an acorn, and an oak tree is an oak tree. In the second stage of logic, however, there is a recognition that things are not separate and unchanging. Acorns are not entirely distinct from oak trees. In the third stage, there is a synthesis of the two previous stages based upon the recognition that apparently separate and unchanging things are really involved in a process of change. Acorns become oak trees.

Hegel began with a concept he considered to be at the highest possible level of abstraction, and from this concept he proceeded to deduce concepts that were less abstract. This most abstract concept he called *being.* Objects, persons, and events may do many different things or have different things done to them, but in the first instance they *are.* If we remove all conceivable descriptions of quality, quantity, and so on, the feature that remains is a certain "isness"—the characteristic shared with every other element in the universe. This is the category of being.

In dialectical logic, the second concept is deduced from the first and is its opposite (or negation). The opposite of being is the negation of being, or *not* being. Hegel calls this concept *nothing.* How is it possible for something to both be and not-be at the same time? Hegel answers that this is possible when it *becomes.* The concept of becoming resolves the opposition (or contradiction), between being and nothing and provides a fresh basis for the search for concepts at a lower level of abstraction.

When Hegel applied his dialectical method to the study of political problems, he did so within a framework of *idealism.* All philosophy deals with the relationship between the material world (the world of nature, of objective reality) and the ideal world (the world of ideas, of thought, of subjective reality). Idealism is the view that the material world depends upon the ideal world—that ideas and thoughts come first, and the material world is a reflection of the ideal world.

Human history is, for Hegel, a process involving the gradual unfolding of "Reason." In his view, reason is not only a faculty possessed by individuals, but is the force that determines the structure and development of the universe.

At times, he refers to reason as the Spirit, the Absolute, or even God. At any given moment, individuals possess some partial understanding of this absolute reason, and they create governments and other social institutions based on this understanding. Because they possess only a partial understanding, however, social institutions are imperfect reflections of ideal forms. Hegel refers to such imperfections as contradictions. As a result of these contradictions, there is conflict in society, and this conflict gets resolved by creating new institutions that more perfectly reflect the ideal. Despite the improvement, these institutions are still imperfect, and therefore new contradictions are generated, which lead to new conflict, which leads to the creation of new institutions.

Hegel argued that the nation is the highest human form through which reason develops. The nation is the highest and most perfect embodiment of reason, and therefore individuals must be subservient to the nation. He even went so far as to claim that the German culture and Prussian state of his day represented the highest possible expression of reason, and thus the dialectical process was ended, and no further change was likely or desirable. In short, Hegel used the dialectical methodology to justify a conservative theory about the desirability and necessity of existing society.[4]

Materialism and Dialectics

Hegel's dialectical method deeply influenced a number of young social theorists at the beginning of the nineteenth century, particularly in Germany and France. At the same time, many of these theorists were troubled by the idealist framework within which Hegel located the dialectical method. The first systematic attempt to free the dialectical method from this framework was by a young German named Ludwig Feuerbach.

Feuerbach argued that Hegel was wrong in believing that social institutions and conditions were a reflection of human ideas and thoughts. Such a belief, he said, was a metaphysical way of thinking that separated human beings from nature. Feuerbach maintained that human beings are part of nature, and that ideas and thoughts are only a reflection of the conditions and experiences of people. What is ultimately real is not some abstract idea called reason, but those sense perceptions that can be confirmed by observation and reason. That is, what is real is matter. Feuerbach claimed that the dialectical process occurs, not in the world of ideas, but in the world of matter, and that *materialism* rather than idealism is the proper framework for using the dialectical method.[5]

It was Karl Marx who first went beyond the mere substitution of materialism for idealism and argued that such a change also required changes in the dialectical method. Hegel had begun his dialectical analysis with pure being, the abstract category he believed to be the most elementary reality. Marx argued that, in a materialist dialectic, the proper place to begin is with the category that is predominant within a particular type of society. Under capitalism, for example, he said the category to begin with was that of *commodity*.[6] (See chapter 4.) In doing this he was trying to bring the discussion down to earth—to make it practical.

In dealing with contradictions in society, Hegel had claimed that the struggle between opposites is immediate and unconditional, and that contradictions are a unity of opposites. Thus, the acorn is a unity of opposites in which the seed and the oak tree are in contradiction. Marx claimed that, in society, the unity of opposites is not always immediate and unconditional, but rather it develops over time and may be affected by changing circumstances. In short, the unity of opposites is a historical process that is mediated by other factors. Not all acorns become oak trees; some get eaten; others do not get planted, and so on. Although it is true that all acorns have the potential to become oak trees, to do so, the process must be mediated by other factors.[7]

As we have noted in chapter 4 of this book, Marx began his analysis of society by saying that human beings produce the things they need to survive. They do not merely take directly what they find in nature. In the process of production, people are limited by the available forces of production. These include the natural sources, such as land, and mineral resources as well as the tools, instruments, techniques, and skills that humans have created to supplement their own labor. As people use these forces of production, they enter into relationships of authority, ownership, and control, or "social relations of production" typical of the current level of the forces of production. In slave societies, the principal social relations are between master and slave; in feudal society, between lord and serf; and in capitalist society, the principal ones are between employer and employee.[8]

Marx said that the forces of production and the social relations of production together constitute the "mode of production" and represent the "base" of society on which the "superstructure" is constructed. The superstructure consists of systems of law, government, religion, arts and so on. It is through these superstructures that human beings express the rules and principles they accept, the image they hold of themselves, and the goals they have established.

Marx's view of historical development, then, begins with the view that the built-in need of people to supply themselves with goods necessary for survival creates a constant pressure for improvement in the forces of production. Changes in the environment also cause changes in these forces. Changes in the forces of production require changes in the social relations of production, and these, in turn, lead to less visible changes in law, politics, religion, and so on.

The Marxist View of Social Change

In human society, according to Marx, the relationships between forces of production, social relations of production, and superstructures, are manifest in class struggle.[9] The term "class" refers to a group that has a common relationship to the forces of production, a relationship that brings the group into conflict with another group having a different relationship to the same forces of production. The common relationship of slaves to the forces of production is that they can be legally compelled to work upon them, even though they do not own them. Slaves are among the forces of production that can legally be owned by others. The common relationship of masters to the forces of production is that they own at least some of the forces and can sell them if they wish. Obviously, the interests of these two groups are in conflict, since slaves want to own themselves and their own labor, while masters profit from owning slaves.

Under capitalism, the main relationships are between wage-workers and owners. The common relationship of wage-workers to the forces of production is that they work upon them for wages but do not own or control them. The common relationship of owners (or capitalists) to the forces of production is that they own them and realize profits but do not necessarily work upon them. Again, there is a conflict of interests. It is to the advantage of wage-workers to get higher salaries, while it is to the advantage of owners to get higher profits, but both salaries and profits must come from the same source.

Because there are built-in conflicts of interest between social classes, different social classes tend to struggle for power against other classes, and the legal, political, and other superstructures of a society tend to reflect the social relations of production. Thus, in a slave society, the law declares slavery to be legally permissible and physically enforceable by the power of government. A slave society does not have antislavery laws or an antislavery government. Similarly, the prevailing religion in a slave society cannot be expected to condemn slavery. Capitalist societies do not have laws making private ownership of property illegal, and they do not have governments that oppose private ownership. Religion in capitalist societies does not say that private ownership of property is immoral.

Marx argued that profound changes in the legal, political, and religious position of classes in society reflect changes in the relations of authority, control, and ownership. These, in turn, reflect changes in the forces of production. Marx claimed that such a process of change is a dialectical one, and he tried to show this by examining the change from feudalism to capitalism.

In feudal society, the principal forces of production were agricultural. They were based on the land and on simple tools and techniques for using the land. Manufacturing was not highly developed nor very efficient, and trade and commerce had not reached an advanced stage. As the population grew and contact with other societies increased, pressure mounted for greater productivity and for trade and commerce with other countries. The dominant class in feudal society was that of the landed nobles, who were not equipped to meet these pressures. New occupations therefore emerged—merchants, bankers, manufacturers, and shipbuilders. These groups made up what would later be called the bourgeoisie in capitalist society. Under feudalism, they did not have the legal or political power of the landed nobles. The laws of feudal society not only gave special privileges to nobles, but also hindered more efficient uses of the land and industrial development. Industrial development required the removal of restrictions on commerce, land use, and serf-noble obligations. The only way in which this could be brought about, however, was for the bourgeoisie to replace the nobles as the dominant class.

The nobles resisted the efforts of the bourgeoisie, and social revolutions occurred in England, France, and elsewhere before social change was accomplished. It was possible for the new and relatively weaker class to win out over the established ruling class only because the basic development of the forces and relations of production favored the new class by adding to its strength and by diminishing the strength of the opposition. The whole growth of science, technology, trade, and commerce added strength to the bourgeoisie, while the landed nobles found their power steadily eroding because of these changes.

Marx did not say that all revolutions are caused by tension or contradictions between forces and relations of production. He did say that contradictions between forces and relations of production lead to revolutions and that, in order for revolutions to be of lasting historical significance, they must spring from such contradictions. There were many peasant rebellions, wars among nobles, and other social conflicts between groups in feudal England and France, and these often resulted in changes in the individuals holding office or in specific laws. It was not until the struggle between nobility and bourgeoisie, however, that the feudal mode of production itself was overturned and replaced by capitalism.

The differences between the idealist dialectic of Hegel and the materialist dialectic of Marx seem quite striking. Where Hegel focused on ideas and thoughts as the main source of change in society, Marx focused on the actual conditions of existence of social groups as the main source of change. The method employed by both to investigate change was, however, very similar.

This dialectical method continues to be used by contemporary sociologists to investigate the nature of social change.

Dialectical Methods In Sociology

The dialectical method developed by Hegel and Marx differs from positivist methodology in a number of important respects, and these differences tend to reflect the fact that dialectical methods grow out of the study of social change:

1 Contrary to the assumptions of positivist methodology, dialectical methodology does not allow us to treat things as independent of one another, but requires that we treat things as connected with, dependent on, and determined by each other. The laws of formal logic require us to treat different ideas, values, and objects as separate things. While we may move from one idea to another, each idea is fixed and unchanging. This is essentially the same view that was taken of biological species before Darwin's work. Different species were thought to exist alongside each other; they were not seen as growing out of one another. Dialectical methodology focuses on where a thing has been and where it is going or, perhaps more accurately, what will become of it.

2 Contrary to the assumptions of positivist methodology, dialectical methodology assumes that society is in a constant state of movement and change. Some features are always in the process of arising and developing; other features are disintegrating and dying away. Not only does each thing have a history, it also has a future. According to dialectical methodology, it is better to think of the change from one idea to another as a process of growth and evolution, rather than as a change from one thing to another thing.

3 Contrary to the assumptions of positivist methodology, dialectical methodology does not view the process of development as a simple process of growth, but as a process involving initial quantitative changes that become qualitative in character. All change is, first and foremost, a change of degree or quantity, but at a certain point, the accumulation of quantitative changes leads to the emergence of new qualities. According to dialectical methodology, the only way in which new qualities emerge is from quantitative changes. But new qualities cannot be seen simply as increased or decreased amounts of old qualities. The emergence of *Homo sapiens* as a species resulted from quantitative changes in apes, but human beings are not simply bigger and better apes.

---

4 Contrary to assumptions of positivist methodology, dialectical methodology views the present as a moment in a continuum from past to future. According to formal logic, a thing is itself and cannot be other than itself, but according to dialectical methodology, a thing is both itself and not itself at the same moment. A thing is not only what it is changing from, but also what it is changing into. An acorn is not only a seed, but also an oak tree. Change does not result from one thing acting on another thing, but from contradictions within a thing.[10]

If we were to summarize briefly the implications of these differences, we might say that dialectical methodology makes three assumptions: (1) that everything has a history; (2) that the history is qualitative as well as quantitative; and (3) that this kind of history does not stop.[11] Some of these assumptions may seem little more than common sense. The insistence that we must always consider things in the context of their connection to other things rather than in isolation seems obvious, but positivist methodology maintains that, for many purposes, we can isolate phenomena for study. What is at issue, fundamentally, between positivist methodology and dialectical methodology is not whether social change occurs, but whether we can legitimately ignore it while studying social order. Since some of the assumptions of dialectics in this regard are less obvious that those of positivism, they deserve a bit more explanation.

The Transition from Quantity to Quality

When we increase the temperature of a pan of water, a quantitative change takes place. The water becomes hotter. It remains a liquid, however. If we continue to change the water temperature, at some point, the water undergoes a transition from a liquid state to a gas. Steam is not simply a liquid of high temperature, but possesses qualities that are not present in the liquid state. Similarly, if we steadily decrease the temperature of water, we will witness a transition from a liquid state to a solid. Ice is not simply a cold liquid, but possesses properties that are not present in a liquid.

According to dialectical theories, a similar process takes place in society. In feudal society, the predominant forces of production were agricultural, and the vast majority of people were either nobles or serfs whose place in society was largely determined by their relationship to the land. The growth in scientific knowledge, technology, industry, and commerce led to a growth in the numbers of people whose place in society was determined by their relationship to commercial and industrial forces of production, rather than to the land. The struggle between the classes related to the land and the classes related to industry led to social revolutions in which a qualitative change from feudalism to capitalism occurred. Capitalism is not simply a quantitatively different type of society from feudalism; it contains fundamentally different qualities. Relations between owners and wage-workers are qualitatively different from those between nobles and serfs.

The transition from quantitative to qualitative change has occurred in the past, and it is also going on at this very moment. Accordingly, to understand any aspect of contemporary society, we must examine the history of quantitative changes of that aspect. A dialectical analysis of education in contemporary America, for example, could not stop with a description of types of education, numbers of students enrolled at different levels, opportunities for getting an education, relationships between educational and other institutions, and so on. A dialectical analysis would examine the historical changes in each of these areas to discover the types and direction of change. Where a structural-functionalist explanation of education would describe either the function of education in society in general, or the function of education in this society at this moment in time, a dialectical explanation would describe the changing function of education in American capitalism. Ultimately, a dialectical explanation would seek to determine whether or not there has been a qualitative change in the function of education, and how any changes that have occurred are related to other changes in the society.[12] Many dialectical theorists would insist that, to the extent that American capitalism retains its characteristic identity, only quantitative changes and no qualitative changes in education can occur. A study of American schools under these circumstances can be nothing more than a study of schools that are possible under American capitalism. Thus, qualitative changes in education are not possible without qualitative changes in the larger economic, political, and social system. Social change is thus not seen as an event or an occurrence, but as a process of development. It is a process involving not only quantitative change, but qualitative change as well. Not all quantitative changes lead to qualitative ones, however. What causes the transition from quantity to quality?

Development through Contradictions

According to dialectical theory, we should look for the primary source of change within a process rather than outside of it. We should search for opposing tendencies within processes of quantitative change. Opposing tendencies that lead to social conflict are called contradictions. A contradiction must be more than just two different tendencies. It must arise from the very nature of the process within which the tendencies are located. For example, Marx spoke of the contradiction between feudal relations of production and the developing industrial forces of production. As a result of this contradiction, social conflict between the nobility and the emerging bourgeoisie developed and eventually led to the qualitative change from feudalism to capitalism. The key conception of dialectical methodology is the notion of contradiction—that the motive force of qualitative change lies in the contradictions contained within social processes.

A real contradiction is a unity of opposites. We speak of a contradiction within a process when opposite tendencies are combined in such a way that neither can exist without the other. When Marx spoke of the class struggle between workers and capitalists, he was describing an inherent contradiction in capitalist society between workers and capitalists, and arguing that this struggle will exist so long as capitalism exists because the very nature of capitalism requires the existence of both workers and capitalists whose interests are opposed to one another.

Change in any aspect of society, or in society as a whole, is seen as resulting primarily from internal sources. A process that contained no contradictions would simply go on in the same way until some external force modified or changed it (this would be very much like Talcott Parsons' explanation of change). If a society contained no contradictions, people would be able to satisfy all their needs by continuing to do the same things in the same ways (George Homans views society essentially in this way). There would be movement and process in society, but the movement and process would be repetitive. Only by gradual evolution, or by war, would society change in significant ways.

It is important to stress that dialectical methodology requires that all contradictions be observable phenomena. It asserts that everything contains contradictions. It does not claim that all contradictory propositions can be true. Dialectical methodology does not try to apply some preconceived scheme to any particular situation. Each social process must be studied concretely. We cannot learn about a particular society by deducing its characteristics from the general notion of contradiction. We can only learn about it by investigating the actual social processes taking place within the society.

Rules for Inquiry

How is dialectical methodology applied to the study of actual problems? There are no set formulas that can be applied to all situations, but there are a number of rules to guide investigation and explanation:

1 Do not assume that any problem can be studied as though it were unchanging and isolated from other problems. Only if concrete investigation shows that the amount and rate of change taking place is insignificant

for the problem studied, can the rules of formal logic be used. Otherwise, dialectical logic should be used.

2 In dealing with change, study a problem in terms of its evolutionary development. Where has the problem come from, and where is it going? What was the origin of its present form? In what ways is it now changing?

3 In order to understand the evolutionary development of a problem, try to discover opposing elements and tendencies representing contradictions within it. Investigate the nature of internal conflict and the direction in which opposing tendencies are developing, and determine which tendencies are weaker and which stronger.

4 Look for changes that are not only quantitative but also qualitative.

5 In dealing with change and development, examine the connections and interrelations between elements of the process of change. Do not treat developments in isolation from one another.

6 Do not treat ideas or theories as eternal and unchanging. The meaning of ideas changes with time, place, and circumstance. Meaning is determined by context, and context changes.[13]

The use of dialectical methodology is not restricted to political or economic subject areas. The following illustration is taken from the work of Wilhelm Reich (1897–1957), one of Sigmund Freud's disciples, who tried to use dialectic methods in his psychoanalytic work. Reich considers the case of a married woman who has a neurotic fear of burglars and imagines that they are about to attack her with knives.[14] She cannot remain in a room alone; she suspects that there are burglars in every corner.

Reich deals with the relevant history of the woman in three phases. In the first phase, she meets a man who pursues her and suggests arrangements she would like to accept if she were not inhibited morally. She defers the resolution of this conflict by thinking about eventually getting married. The man discontinues his efforts, and she marries someone else. She does not, however, forget the first man, and the memory of him continues to disturb her. She meets him again subsequent to her marriage and experiences a conflict between her desire for him and the demands of conjugal fidelity. The conflict is intensified, and she begins to avoid him and finally seems to forget him. This, however, says Reich, is not a true forgetting but a repression of the conflict.

In phase two, there occurs a breakthrough of the repression. The woman has a violent quarrel with her husband because he has apparently been flirting with another woman. She thinks, "If you can do this, I am a fool to keep from doing the same." The thought of her first lover is too dangerous, so she represses it immediately. That night, however, she is overcome by fear. She has the notion that a strange man is creeping toward her bedside wanting to rape her. This, says Reich, is the instinct reentering her conscious in a disguised form as its own direct opposite. Desire has been replaced by fear of the stranger. This disguise opens up phase three, in which the actual neurotic symptoms appear.

This case illustrates a problem that is in a continual state of change. The history of the problem is discussed, but we know less about the prognosis. Presumably the subsequent course of the problem will be altered by the insight made available to the patient in the course of psychoanalytic therapy. The initial sexuality, the moral inhibition, the state of fear containing both of these, and the subsequent emergence of neurotic symptoms all reflect qualitative changes in the condition of the woman. A more complete description of the case would include the relation of her moral inhibition to the education and training she received in her home and by the larger society. These and related matters must be dealt with, if any meaningful therapy is to occur.

Dialectics, History, and Science

We have stressed the point that dialectical theory is historical. Everything has a history, that history involves qualitative as well as quantitative change, and the history does not stop. Not all positivist sociologists would deny the first of these principles. One of the classical positivist studies for example, criticizes the tendency of many sociologists to ignore the historical background of problems.

Sociology has largely taken over from functional anthropology its tendency to account for the existence and persistence of institutions or patterns of behavior by the way in which they are related to other parts of a functioning social system .... The sociologist directs himself rather to the question of why given patterns persist rather than how they come to be in the first place, a problem he leaves to the historian.[15]

These sociologists were interested in understanding why one type of trade union (the typographers' union) had a high degree of internal democracy, while most unions had become undemocratic. They argued that it was necessary to "consider both the historical conditions which gave rise to this social structure and the factors which support and maintain it as a going system." [16] In other words, history may help us to understand how a problem or pattern was born, but not what causes the problem or pattern to continue in the present.

Their explanation was the typographers' union had a history quite different from that of most unions. This unique history resulted in practices insuring the continuation of internal democracy. "Democracy in the ITU was thus no necessary consequence of a particular set of static factors, but rather was favored as time went on and numerous events added to the system's stability."[17]

Positivist methodology, then, may recognize the need to examine the historical origin of a social pattern, but it continues to treat the present character of a pattern as a stable or unchanging reality. Dialectical methodology studies present patterns as phenomena continually in a process of change. From a dialectical perspective, two major criticisms can be made of the study cited. First, democracy is defined operationally as a two-party system within the union. This definition does not deal with what is central to the idea of democracy—the extent to which a majority of members are able to select policies, programs, and leaders they desire. Second, and more important, to assert that the internal democracy of the typographers' union is a stable system is no more valid than to assert that the undemocratic character of the other unions is stable. What should be investigated is the way in which changes in technology, the division of labor, and the organization of work affect the nature and form of union organizations. These are historical questions that require us to look at trends of change that continue to develop in the present. Since the study of the typographers' union was published in 1956, for example, changes in technology and work organization have drastically reduced the size, power, and character of internal democracy in the typographer's union.

To think of dialectical method as a mechanical movement from thesis to antithesis and synthesis represents a serious distortion of an orientation addressing itself to the concrete analysis of concrete conditions. To deal with concrete conditions, it is necessary to study the way things are interconnected in the real world—how they are interdependent, how they change, how they come into being and pass away. To think dialectically is to think less abstractly. Consider for example, a commercial greenhouse. A customer enters and wishes to buy a dozen roses. The proprietor of the greenhouse thinks of his roses as completed products or commodities ready for sale. He sees his beds of roses as containers for X amount of roses at V amount of cents or dollars per rose. In going over his books that evening, he continues to think in a similar fashion about the number of roses, the price of each rose, the cost of each rose calculated in terms of prorated operating costs, and so on. This is an appropriate way to think of his enterprise, so long as his interest in roses is restricted to their value as commodities. But the proprietor cannot always think in this abstract fashion. He must grow the roses and, in doing so, must think of them not as a complex of things but rather as a complex of processes. The apparently stable roses go through a continual process of coming into being and passing away. When the proprietor's interest is broadened to extend beyond the view of roses as commodities, this view is seen to be an inadequate abstraction from a larger reality.[18]

From a more general perspective,

> If you accept existing economic relations and existing political power structures as unchangeable, then abstract and limited generalizations about economic phenomena and state institutions are all that you practically require, and you will have no use for dialectics. If, on the other hand, you are practically interested in changing economic relations and the political power structure, you are compelled to replace such abstract generalizations by a more concrete analysis of the concrete conditions in which you live. You have to resort to dialectics.[19]

Some dialectical theorists might well criticize our examples, presented earlier in this chapter, of the acorn-tree, river-ocean, and fetus-person, since they do not illustrate the reversibility of change. The examples appear to be one-directional. The acorn produces a tree, but it is not so obvious that a tree can also revert to an acorn. Chinese and other Marxist critics insist that the socialist revolution in the Soviet Union did not proceed with due attention to the problem of reversibility which, they assert, has in fact occurred. They believe that state capitalism has replaced what initially began as a move toward socialism. Chinese theorists use this experience as an example of dialectic reversibility. They insist upon the necessity for a permanent revolution to overcome this problem. But this is a theoretical as well as a political problem.

Karl Marx's *magnum opus, Capital,* provides a centrally important illustration of dialectical thought in operation. The dialectical nature of this work has been analyzed very perceptively by Karl Kosik.[20] Kosik points out that Marx introduces the work with an analysis of a commodity—apparently a simple, trivial, even a banal object. However, Marx demonstrates that the object can be viewed as something mysterious and even mystical. Marx knows that commodities are the cells of capitalism. They can, however, become the point of departure for a scientific explication of capitalism only because Marx knew capitalism as a whole. In dialectical methodology, this is the procedure of showing the connections between an element and a totality—between an undeveloped germ and a fully developed and operating system.

Marx's analysis, beginning with the focus on commodities, proceeds to explain capitalism as a system whose central character, hero, or subject is a commodity rather than a human being. It is a mechanism through which dead labor (contained in a commodity) holds sway over human beings—a system in which objects dominate over persons, products are more important than the producer, the object is more important than the subject. This dialectical analysis thus reveals capitalism as a system that changes by alternately expanding and contracting. Capitalism is a complete abstraction, but people acting behind what are essentially character masks serve as its elements or components. The entire analysis proceeds by identifying and examining the implications of these and other contradictions within the system.

Marx uses the literary device of an odyssey to accomplish his purpose, much as Hegel did in his book, *Phenomenology of the Spirit*. The subject of this device may be anything from a person, or a person's consciousness, to a human collectivity. In any case, the subject must journey through the world before it can know itself. Knowledge about the subject can be obtained only on the basis of the subject's own activity in the world. The subject learns about the world only by actively interfering or attempting to change it. The subject at the end of the odyssey is different from the one who started out. The world through which the subject has passed is a changed world. It has been changed by the subject, but it also appears to be different to the subject, since the odyssey has changed the way in which things are seen by the subject. Thus, Marx begins by dealing with a social product of capitalism. His analysis deals with the rules or laws describing its coming into being and its movement through the system. The analysis ends by finding that these laws express the social relations of people who make the product and the things they do. Thus, in order to describe the laws of economic behavior under capitalism, one must deal with them independently of human consciousness and at the same time examine people's awareness of the economic process and their position within it. Marx's *Capital* is not simply a description of what exists. It is a critique of what exists. It is also an inquiry into the ways in which a subject is formed—a subject that can make revolutionary changes in this system.

Marx's use of dialectics aims at understanding society as a whole, rather than any individual part. As Georg Lukacs has expressed it, "Bourgeois thought concerns itself with objects that arise either from the process of studying phenomena in isolation, or from the division of labour and specialization in the different disciplines," while "Marxism . . . simultaneously raises and reduces all specialisations to the level of aspects in a dialectical process."[21]

Thus, in the last analysis, "Marxism does not acknowledge the existence of independent sciences of law, economics or history, etc.: there is nothing but a single unified, dialectical and historical science of the evolution of society as a totality."[22] From this perspective, however, the value of abstractions is not denied, nor is the usefulness of isolating elements and concepts in special disciplines for scientific purposes. The decisive consideration is whether or not knowledge about an isolated fragment retains its autonomy and becomes an end in itself.

In a strange sort of way, dialectical thinking leads to what appears to be inconsistency. The distinguished dialectician, Leszek Kolakowski, has observed that humanity owes its very survival to the principle of inconsistency.[23] For example, he asks. What is required of a soldier who is about to go off to war? He must, of course, be consistent in his duty to defend his country. But complete consistency would require that battles fought by consistent soldiers would end only when the last man on one of the sides had died. Similarly, consistent loyalty to a government would require that a citizen always cooperate with the secret police, since the secret police are an indispensable part of the government. Any citizen who hesitated to inform on his neighbors by writing to the secret police would be inconsistent. Or, if we assume that a particular idea, such as a universal obligation to wear a top hat, is the most important thing in the world, to be consistent we must not object to any steps taken to insure that the idea is imposed on the world, whether these steps are war, blackmail, assassination, terror, murder, or torture. In practice, total consistency is equivalent to fanaticism. Inconsistency can be the source of tolerance. Thus, says Kolakowski, inconsistency is simply a secret awareness of the contradictions existing in this world.

> Inconsistency is a constant effort to cheat life, which incessantly tries to place us before alternative doors, each of which is an entrance, but through neither of which can we return. Once we have entered we are compelled to fight to the end, to the last bullet, for life or death, with him who entered through the other door . . .[24]

Is there any sphere of human events in which we can insist upon total consistency? Here the answer, inconsistently enough, is yes. This sphere is one that Kolakowski calls "elementary situations"—human situations in which our moral attitude remains unchanged, despite the ultimate consequences. For example, if a person is dying of hunger and it is possible for me to feed him or her, there is no set of circumstances in which it would be right to say, "Tactically speaking, it is better to let the person die." Neither can it be right to say, "It is better, all things considered, for me to conceal the fact that the person died of hunger." Elementary situations include such things as open aggression, genocide, torture, and mistreatment of the defenseless. In short, the consistent dialectician is shown to be inconsistent even in his inconsistency, thereby becoming, to some extent, consistent. But this is necessary since, if he were absolutely inconsistent, he would, of course, be consistent.

> To this extent therefore, we propose to preserve the principle of consistency as a value, by practicing the principle of inconsistency inconsistently. To this extent we mold our praise of inconsistency to a perfect form, protesting against the practice of inconsistency in its perfect form.

So much for praise of inconsistency. The rest cannot be verbalized. The rest must be done.[25]

Summary

To be consistent, we should provide a brief summary of this short chapter, which many will feel has already been abbreviated too much. We omit the customary summary, thereby demonstrating our inconsistency, and ask that the reader reread the chapter and examine some of the sources to which we have referred. This will, we hope, illustrate the contradiction that the shortest road to knowledge is sometimes the longest.

For Further Study

The clearest explanation of Marx's dialectical methodology is in John Somerville, *The Philosophy of Marxism: An Exposition* (New York: Random House, 1967). Unlike most second-hand accounts, Somerville retains the sophisticated nature of Marx's analysis, yet renders it easily understandable. Another simple, though more dogmatic, presentation is by Maurice Cornforth, *Materialism and the Dialectical Method* (New York: International Publishers, 1971). The student who wishes to examine Marx in the original should read *Grundrisse,* translated with a foreword by Martin Nicolaus (Middlesex, England: Penguin Books, 1973).

The most recent, sophisticated application of dialectical methodology to a specific problem is by Samuel Bowles and Herbert Gintis, *Schooling in Capitalist America: Educational Reform and the Contradictions of Economic Life* (New York: Basic Books, 1975). One of the classic dialectical studies of recent times is by E. P. Thompson, *The Making of the English Working Class* (New York: Vintage Books, 1963).

The best explanation of the relationship between historical and dialectical methods is E. H. Carr's, *What Is History?* (New York: Vintage Books, 1961). The best-known attack on these methods is Karl Popper, *The Poverty of Historicism* (New York: Harper, 1964). Other positivist criticisms can be found in May Brodbeck, ed., *Readings in the Philosophy of the Social Sciences* (New York: Macmillan, 1968). There have been some attempts to merge functional and dialectical perspectives. A good source on these attempts is N. J. Demerath III and Richard A. Peterson, eds., *System, Change, and Conflict* (New York: Free Press, 1967).

The People's Republic of China has vigorously encouraged the use of dialectic methods in political and social life. Recent history revolving about the "cultural revolution" and the doctrine of "permanent revolution" is literally incomprehensible without some understanding of dialectical thought. For an excellent explication of these ideas, see Mao Tse-tung, *Four Essays on Philosophy* (San Francisco: China Books, 1968). This volume contains the essays, "On Contradition," "On Practice," "On the Correct Handling of Contradictions among the People," and "Where Do Correct Ideas Come From?"

Notes

1 Karl R. Popper, *The Logic of Scientific Discovery* (New York: Science Editions, 1961).

2 Irving M. Zeitlin, *Marxism: A Re-examination* (Princeton, N.J.: Van Nostrand, 1967); also see John Somerville, *The Philosophy of Marxism: An Exposition* (New York: Random House, 1967).

3 G. W. F. Hegel, "The Logic of Hegel," trans. William Wallace, in *Encyclopedia of the Philosophical Sciences,* 2d ed., ed. G. W. F. Hegel (Oxford, England: Clarendon Press, 1892).

4 G. W. F. Hegel, "Philosophy of Right and Law, or Natural Law and Political Science Outlined," excerpts trans. J. M. Sterrett and Carl J. Friedrich, in *The Philosophy of Hegel,* ed. Carl J. Friedrich (New York: Modern Library, 1953).

5 For discussion, see Shlomo Avineri, *The Social and Political Thought of Karl Marx* (Cambridge, England: Cambridge University Press, 1968).

6 Karl Marx, *Capital,* Vol. 1 (New York: International Publishers, 1967).

7 Karl Marx, *Grundrisse,* trans. Martin Nicolaus (Middlesex, England: Penguin Books, 1973).

8 Karl Marx and Friedrich Engels, *The German Ideology* (New York: International Publishers, 1970).

9 For a discussion, see John Somerville, *The Philosophy of Marxism: An Exposition* (New York: Random House, 1967); also see Irving Zeitlin, *Marxism.*

10 See Maurice Cornforth, *Marterialism and the Dialectical Method* (New York: International Publishers, 1971); also see Louis Schneider, "Dialectic in Sociology," *American Sociological Review* 36 (August, 1971): 667–678.

11 See John Somerville, *Philosophy of Marxism,* pp. 67–71.

12 Samuel Bowles and Herbert Gintis, *Schooling in Capitalist America: Educational Reform and the Contradictions of Economic Life* (New York: Basic Books, 1975).

13 See John Somerville, *Philosophy of Marxism*, pp. 69–71.

14 See Wilhelm Reich, "Dialectical Materialism and Psychoanalysis," *Studies on the Left*, 6 (July–August, 1966): pp. 5–46.

15 Seymour Martin Lipset, Martin Trow, and James Coleman, *Union Democracy* (Garden City, N.Y. Doubleday Anchor, 1956), p. 17.

16 Ibid., p. 18.

17 Ibid., p. 441.

18 See Maurice Cornforth, *The Open Philosophy and the Open Society* (New York: International Publishers, 1968), pp. 74–75.

19 Ibid., p. 81.

20 Karl Kosik, *Dialektik des Konkreten,* trans. into German from the original Czech (Frankfurt, Germany: Suhrkamp, 1966), unpublished English translation by Karel Kovanda. (We are indebted to Professor Paul Piccone for calling our attention to this manuscript and making it available to us.)

21 Georg Lukacs, *History and Class Consciousness: Studies in Marxist Dialectics* (Cambridge, Mass.: M.I.T Press, 1968), p. 28.

22 Ibid., p. 28.

23 See Leszek Kolakowski, *Toward a Marxist Humanism* (New York: Grove Press, 1968), pp. 212 ff.

24 Ibid., pp. 214–215.

25 Ibid., p. 220.

part
three

The fundamental fact of human existence is neither the individual as such nor the aggregate as such. Each, considered by itself, is a mighty abstraction. The individual is a fact of existence insofar as he steps into a living relation with other individuals. The aggregate is a fact of existence insofar as it is built up of living units of relation. . . . What is peculiarly characteristic of the human world is above all that something takes place between one being and another, the like of which can be found nowhere in nature.[1]

Why does society exist? Is it because someone once recognized the need for an umpire to formalize, legitimate, and regulate a set of rules for the games people play with one another? Is it because, without this umpire, people would constantly fight and try to dominate one another? Are human beings basically selfish, competitive, ruthless, and concerned only with themselves? Or are they fundamentally cooperative, and does society exist to facilitate this cooperation and help them do more effectively what they would try to do in any case?

Questions like these have occupied philosophers, political theorists, and theologians for centuries. They involve debates about original sin and the perfectability of human beings, as well as about the actual and ideal political and social life of human beings.

For sociologists, the basic area of disagreement has concerned the purpose of society. To ask, "Why does society exist?" is to suggest that society has a purpose. Many sociologists, and especially functionalists, have tried to define this purpose, whether it be survival, self-maintenance, growth, or some other goal that is supposed to shape the development of social relationships.[2] If society has a purpose, then that purpose has been around as long as society itself. It must, therefore, have come from outside society. Thus, sociologists who argue that society has a purpose are forced to rely on theological or metaphysical explanations of the source of the purpose of society.

Many other sociologists reject the notion that society has a purpose. Only people, they argue, can have purposes. Critical sociologists claim that we should study people in a society and the relationships among them without attributing to society the characteristics of people. When we do this, we find that social structures have developed to benefit some people at the expense of others, and thus the structure of society generates potential conflicts between those who are greatly benefited and those who are not.[3]

As we have noted previously, different conceptions of the nature of society lead to different ways of studying social reality. Sociology focuses on social relationships. Does society create social relationships, or do individuals create them?[4] In one view, society is an objective reality; it exists prior to the birth of individuals and confronts them as a given. The social relationships making up society seem to exist independently of human actions. Sociologists use the concept of social structure to organize and explain their observations of society viewed as an objective reality.

In another view, society seems to be a human product. Individuals understand the social structure and consciously decide to act in ways that reinforce or undermine the social relationships making up social structure. In this view, society seems to be under the control of human beings, who are capable of altering social relationships and the problem is one of explaining how individuals learn to behave in ways that reinforce existing social relationships. Sociologists use the concept of culture to organize and explain their observations about the nature of the mental map people use to guide their actions in society.

Although human beings are capable of acting to change relationships, very often their choices seem limited and controlled by their circumstances. Human beings seem to be shaped and molded by society. We do not face each situation completely free to do anything we want, since from the moment of birth we have been taught what to want, how to act, and what is expected of us. To an important degree, our conceptions of ourselves as unique individuals have been shaped by others. Sociologists use the concept of socialization to organize and explain their observations about the ways in which understandings and expectations are transmitted from one generation to another, and among different members of a society.

The different basic orientations to sociology described in previous chapters strongly influence a sociologist's conception of social structure, culture, and socialization, and these, in turn, strongly influence sociological explanations of the workings of society. In the next three chapters, we examine each of these concepts to see how different orientations employ their theories and methods to arrive at descriptions of social relationships. The basic description of each concept is drawn from the critical orientation. We then look at points of disagreement from the pure-science and applied-science orientations. We have not, however, followed this procedure rigidly. Where it seemed more appropriate to describe the concept first from a pure or applied orientation, we have done so. Throughout, we have tried to show how the concepts are utilized within varying theoretical and methodological orientations.

Notes

1 Martin Buber, *Between Man and Man* (Boston: Beacon Press, 1955), pp. 202–203.

2 See Marion J. Levy, Jr., *The Structure of Society* (Princeton, N.J.: Princeton University Press, 1952).

3 See Margaret A. Coulson and David S. Riddell, *Approaching Sociology* (London: Routledge & Kegan Paul, 1970).

4 See Peter L. Berger and Thomas Luckmann, *The Social Construction of Reality* (Garden City, N.Y.: Doubleday, 1967).

Social
Structure

The sociological theories and methods described in previous chapters guide the thought and actions of sociologists as they go about their work. In teaching sociology to students, however, the crucial role of theories and methods is too often hidden from view. Most textbooks begin by presenting facts about society, concepts that organize those facts, and theories that explain the facts. But these facts are always selective and one-sided. They are the facts as seen from one or another theoretical perspective. In this book, we have reversed the normal order of presentation, focusing first on the problems of philosophy and logic that underlie our selection of facts. We want to close by turning to some basic concepts of sociological inquiry, in order to show how the formulation and use of these concepts is shaped by basic orientations.

Society as a Human Product

Human beings, like other animals, have needs. At the very minimum, these include material objects necessary for survival, such as food and shelter, sexual relations with members of the opposite sex to perpetuate the species and, of course, simple human contact with members of both sexes (see chapter 11). The objects capable of satisfying human needs must be obtained from the natural and social environment. Food must be hunted, gathered, grown, or otherwise produced; shelter must be found or created; sexual relationships must be established. *Social structure* is the name we use for the patterns and types of relationships human beings form with each other as they attempt to satisfy their needs. Thus, social structure is not fixed and absolute, but emerges out of a process of social interaction between people.

A number of fundamental problems of social structure confront members of any society. They must organize to produce the material necessities of life, to reproduce the species, to develop and improve their knowledge about and mastery over nature, and to transmit knowledge and customs from one generation to the next. Many patterns of relationships emerge from the attempts to solve these problems. Marriage and family relationships, for example, represent an attempt to provide for and regulate the production of the species; various forms of education and learning represent attempts to produce and improve knowledge; religion, education, and even the family are concerned with transmitting knowledge and customs.

Throughout most of human history the most difficult problem has been how to produce enough of the material necessities of life to insure the survival and growth of the species.[1] The resources available for dealing with this problem are of three types: (1) the available natural resources, such as land, animals, and mineral resources; (2) technological resources, including the tools, instruments, methods, techniques, and skills, available in a specific society at a given moment; and, (3) the resources of human labor. The initial problem for any society is to combine these various resources to insure survival for at least some of its members. In preliterate societies, people gather plants, fruits, and berries, using crude weapons to hunt fish and game. As knowledge about nature increases, agriculture may supplant gathering as a principal means of producing food.

Preliterate societies are often nomadic. People in them move from place to place until the local plants and game are exhausted. Within these societies, males characteristically are responsible for hunting, while females provide most of the food by gathering fruits and berries. These societies tend to be small and relatively constant in population, since their numbers cannot grow beyond the available food supply. Authority tends to be rather loose in hunting-and-gathering societies, with no tight coordination of activities.

With the end of the last ice age and a gradual change in climate, a slight surplus of food became available for the first time. Increased technical knowledge made possible the domestication of animals, and agriculture developed as people used some of the surplus food to plant edible crops. The human population began to grow, and problems of regulating relationships became more important. Specialized positions such as chiefs and priests were established, and for several thousand years a relatively simple form of social organization based on agriculture developed and took root. Artisans who manufactured artifacts for processing and storing food began to emerge as another kind of specialist.

As food began to be produced in surplus, it became possible to use a portion of the surplus as exchange for other goods. As agriculture replaced hunting and gathering as the principal means of food production, the division of labor and relationships of authority and control also gradually changed. Villages no longer moved from place to place, but formed concentric circles, with homes in the center and farmlands extending outward in all directions. Contact between villages grew and exchange increased, all creating a demand for additional artisans and for new specialists in government.

In the 7,000 years following the emergence of agricultural society in

Europe, some villages became marketplaces where farmers from many villages came to exchange their surplus food for artifacts and other goods. As these cities grew and became powerful, they often brought the surrounding villages into submission by armed force, requiring them to provide food and support for the city dwellers. This is the type of society known as feudalism.

Since land was the key to agricultural production, control of the land was the key to relationships of authority and control under feudalism. As these feudal cities conquered surrounding villages, the powerful city families divided up conquered lands among themselves. Ownership of the land passed to these feudal lords, and those who lived on the land became serfs, who used the land at the pleasure of the lord and were required to turn over a portion of their produce to him. That, at least, was the pattern in Europe. As these relationships were established and persisted, they were also formalized by laws, protected by government, and sanctioned by morality. Laws established the right to private ownership of land and the right to pass on such ownership to children, the right of owners to tax the land, and so on. Owners had the right to call on the military power of government to protect their land. Priests told the serfs that their plight was God's will, and that the rights of the lords were divine rights.

Thus, in the process of trying to produce objects to satisfy their needs, people entered into relationships with one another that established patterns of authority and control. These patterns then became formalized and sanctioned in law, government, and morality. Patterns of social structure emerging out of social interaction became more rigid and developed an existence somewhat separate from the interaction that created them. Relationships created by human activity came to seem natural or predetermined.

Society as an Objective Reality

Social structure can be viewed as a creative process, in which individuals establish patterns of relationships to satisfy their needs. Subjective sociological theories emphasize this creative aspect by treating social structure largely as a product of human interaction, and this is a useful view, so long as these patterns remain fluid and flexible. The problem, of course, is that individuals born into society do not start building relationships from "scratch."

We learn we are already members of a family and are expected to behave in certain ways. We discover we are expected to do certain jobs in certain ways, and we learn that some things are legal or moral, while others are not. In short, we find that society is already there when we arrive on the scene. There are existing patterns and expectations of behavior, existing relationships of authority and control, and existing laws and morality. Social structure appears to us, not as a product of our own activity, but as a thing with a life of its own that requires us to behave in certain ways.

This sense of separation between the individual and society does not present major problems so long as the existing expectations, relationships of authority and control, laws, and morality all correspond to our sense of what is necessary, as we struggle to satisfy our needs. So long as hunting and gathering were the principal means of producing food, the relationships of authority and control, laws, and morality of primitive societies seemed natural to people and corresponded to the situations they encountered. The same was true for simple agricultural societies and, later, for feudalism.

But human history does not stop at any particular level of ability to satisfy human needs. The desire of human beings to supply themselves with objects necessary for survival and enjoyment creates a constant pressure for improvement in the means of satisfying needs. As natural resources evolve and change, and as technology improves, new relationships of authority and control and a new division of labor are required to exploit their potential efficiently.

As feudal society continued to develop, for example, population grew, as did the demand for necessities and luxuries. The slow growth of commerce and trade led to an awareness of the possiblities for exploiting foreign markets by conquest or commerce. This led to a constant pressure to improve tools and production techniques, to voyage farther, and to solve the scientific problems connected with geography, navigation, metallurgy, and so on. Commerce, industry, and trade occupied increasingly important places in the productive life of society.

These new opportunities and demands were best met by people associated with industry and trade—shipbuilders, craftsmen, merchants, and bankers. The hereditary lords of feudal society had neither the training nor the incentive to take advantage of these opportunities. At the same time, however, the laws, traditions, and customs of feudal society all granted privileges and power to these nobles and restricted the uses of land and natural resources in ways that helped the hereditary lords, but hindered industrial and commercial development.

Industrial development required the removal of restrictions on land sales on the open market, and required a wide variety of goods to be manufactured and freely transported from one place to another. It also required the ability of workers to move from one place to another in response to market demands, and the authority to hire or fire workers according to prevalent conditions of the market.

Since the interests of the feudal lords were protected and advanced by existing restrictive laws, industry and commerce could not begin to develop freely until the industrialists, bankers, and merchants successfully challenged the power of these lords. The English revolution in the seventeenth century, and the French and American revolutions at the end of the eighteenth century, were among such successful challenges. They brought about the end of feudalism by breaking the power of hereditary lords and reorganizing the laws and government of their societies. Under this reorganization, the burghers of feudal society (the merchants, bankers, and so on) became the bourgeoisie of a new type of society, whose laws, customs, and government favored the unrestricted expansion of industry and commerce. This new type of social organization is given the name of capitalism.

One consequence of the change from hunting-and-gathering societies to simple agricultural societies, from agricultural society to feudalism, and from feudalism to capitalism, was that different segments of the population gained or lost power. Those who owned and controlled land held most power in feudal society, but under capitalism the power of hereditary lords declined relative to the power of industrialists, merchants, and bankers. These changes, it must be stressed, were neither planned nor inevitable. People did not, for the most part, analyze changes in technology, resources, or the division of labor, in order to plan how to take power from others. They simply did what they felt to be necessary to fulfill the basic needs and possibilities of their way of life. The landed nobles did what they thought was necessary, as did the new bourgeoisie. Changes in resources, technology, and the division of labor added impetus and strength to the actions of the bourgeoisie. They were the ones in the best position to solve the emerging problems of social structure, while the landed nobles were no longer needed, and thus the bourgeoisie could rally other sections of society behind them.

At the same time, the defeat of the landed nobles was not inevitable. The changing resources, technology, and division of labor did not defeat them; other people did. These changes provided the ammunition available to the bourgeoisie, but the ammunition still had to be used effectively by human beings. Defeat was inevitable in somewhat the same sense as the certainty of defeat of a group armed only with crossbows, trying to hold out in a castle besieged by another group that is growing in numbers and finds it increasingly profitable to use firearms.

Elements of Social Structure

Population and social structure are clearly not identical. Society is more than the sum of people in it. It is the people and the way they are related to one another. Since many people in society share common relationships binding them together and setting them apart from others, it is possible to subdivide society into groups. And within larger groups there are smaller groups, until one gets back to single individuals.

Sociologists try to explain the actions of individuals, at least in part, by examining the groups to which they belong. In turn, group behavior can be at least partly understood by understanding the organization of the socie-ty—the social structure. Sociologists do not claim that all individual actions can be explained in terms of social structure; they insist, however, that social structure strongly influences individual actions. Moreover, since individuals belong to many different groups, explanation is never a simple matter.

Some sociologists like to compare society to an organism. They argue that societies have regulative systems, digestive systems, and so on, analagous to the systems of a human body.[2] Others have compared society to a watch, made up of assemblies of individual parts.[3] While such analogies can help us imagine what society is like, they can also be very misleading. It cannot be shown, for example, that any particular biological system has an equivalent in society. A watch is designed for a specific purpose—to tell time. There is little room for variation in the parts of a watch, since if they do not do what they are made to do, they are faulty, and we say that the watch is wrong. But there is no externally defined purpose for society, not even survival. Societies are created by people interacting with one another. Since there is no external purpose, it is quite possible that different groups of people within the structure may have conflicting views about the purposes of society. In trying to study the ways in which social interaction shapes social structure, sociologists usually focus on three main elements of structure—groups, roles, and institutions.

Groups

From the moment we are born, we are involved in relationships with other people. Our first relationships are with members of our family, who have special rights and obligations toward us, not shared by other people. Although family relationships may vary widely from one society to another, and are formally defined by law and custom, we experience these relationships as natural. If we were asked why we are members of our particular family, or why we behave in certain ways within the family, we would probably respond, "Because that's the way it is, and I was born into this family."

Sociologists use the concept of social group to refer to any collection of two or more people conscious of a distinctive set of relationships that bind them together and set them apart from others.[4] As we grow up, we participate in a steadily increasing number of groups. We participate in peer groups of people our own age with similar backgrounds; we participate in work groups comprised of people doing similar or related jobs where we work; we may even join a political group of people trying to implement some program or elect a candidate. All of these involve distinctive sets of relationships that bind members together and distinguish them from other groups. Thus, we do not confuse our family group with our work group, or our work group with our peer group.

Most of the time, our awareness of being part of a group does not result from a conscious decision to join a group, but instead just seems to happen. We occupy positions in an already existing social structure. This places us in a relationship to specific other positions. When we become students, for example, we are placed in relationships with other students and in different relationships with teachers. When we take a job, we find that the tasks we must perform establish relationships between us and specific others. We do not create these positions, we merely occupy them.

Although we belong to many groups, not all groups are equally important to us. In some groups we meet on an intimate, face-to-face basis with others, and tend to involve our whole personalities in the relationships. In groups such as the family, for example, we tend to relate to other family members as ends in themselves rather than as means to an end. Charles Horton Cooley called such groups *primary groups*.[5] There are many studies indicating the importance of primary group relationships to personal happiness and positive feelings about life. Primary groups also exert a strong influence on the attitudes and behavior of members.

Groups in which such ties are weaker, where we may be dealing with others as means to an end, are often called *secondary groups*. A nineteenth-century German sociologist, Ferdinand Toennies, argued that most of the relationships in society tend to cluster either around primary-group ties or secondary-group ties. He referred to these as *Gemeinschaft* and *Gesellschaft* relationships.[6] *Gemeinschaft* relationships are intimate, based on sentiment, and involve other people as ends in themselves rather than as means to an end. They are the relationships found between a loving mother and her daughter, between husbands and wives, and between very close friends. They can involve anger, but the anger is based on intimacy and sentiment rather than on conflicts of interest.

Gesellschaft relationships involve calculations of rational self-interest. Implicitly or explicitly, they involve contracts. Nothing is done for another person, unless we receive some equivalent in exchange. Obligations are limited to very specific situations, and relationships with others extend only to clearly defined areas of mutual concern. Other people are treated as means to reach one's own goals. Relationships of customers with clerks in a store are typically like this. A customer might not even notice a change in the particular person acting as clerk, so long as someone was available to help with the transaction.

Toennies tried to demonstrate that societies tend to be characterized predominantly either by *Gemeinschaft* or by *Gesellschaft* relationships. Of course, both types of relationships exist in any society, but he argued that, as societies become larger and more complex, *Gesellschaft* relationships become more typical. When we look at relationships within a particular society, it is probably more helpful to speak of primary-group and secondary-group relationships.

Group Relationships

Since social groups involve relationships that bind people together and set them apart from others, it is possible for different groups to have different interests in a specific situation. They may desire different outcomes. When this occurs, we say that *competition* exists between them. If there is a limited amount of food available, for example, different groups may compete for the same items. When competition reaches a point at which groups consciously seek to satisfy their interests at the expense of other groups, *conflict* exists.

Often, however, different groups have similar interests in a specific situation, and *cooperation* results. Different groups may cooperate with one another because of a common conflict with other groups, and there may even be cooperation between groups that would otherwise be in conflict in order for both of them to gain a particular result. Any group depends on cooperation among its members in order to achieve shared objectives.

While we usually think of conflict as breaking off or destroying relationships, this is not always the case. Conflict between groups, for example, tends to bind the members of each group more tightly together; it fosters group solidarity in the face of an outside threat. Conflict within groups, on the other hand, tends to destroy group solidarity and weakens the ties among group members. Similarly, cooperation between groups can weaken the ties between members of each group, since it may blur the distinctive character of the relationships among the group members and make them aware of other interests.

Conflict and cooperation grow out of the differing interests of social groups. Interests have to do with the desired outcomes of social interaction and, more particularly, with the desire to obtain resources that can satisfy group objectives. There are many different types of resources that may be sought. Money is a resource that can be exchanged for a wide variety of other resources. Authority and influence—the ability to control the actions of others—may also be a resource. People may even be a resource, as in political campaigns, where a large corps of dedicated volunteers can offset the financial resources of the opposition.

There would be no basis for conflict if all social groups could always obtain sufficient resources to accomplish their objectives. In fact, however, resources are not distributed equally in society. Some groups have more money than others; some groups have more authority and influence than others. Conflict and cooperation arise out of the efforts of groups to control the resources they need to accomplish their objectives in specific situations.

Sociologists use the concept of *power* to refer to control over resources.[7] Those groups that can control more resources to accomplish their objectives in particular situations are said to have more power than other groups. At an auction, for example, money is the key resource for accomplishing objectives, and wealthy people have more power than poor people. In business, owners and executives have more authority than clerks or factory workers, but their power may be partly offset by the ability of workers to exert influence through a union.

To a certain extent, we experience power in the same way as we experience other aspects of social interaction. In some situations, we feel powerless because we do not see any way to satisfy our desires with the resources available to us. In an election, for example, we may feel powerless because none of the candidates represent our interests, or because we sense that our candidate has no chance of winning.

But power is more than a personal experience. Power is associated with social positions and social groups, rather than with individuals. Resources are allocated unequally to social positions, and those positions confer power upon the individual occupants of the positions. Some jobs pay more than others; some positions have more authority than others; some positions have more influence than others. The study of social stratification is, in large part, the study of how resources are allocated to positions and groups in society, and the impact of such unequal distribution on people.

Social Roles

When we occupy social positions or join social groups, we discover an already existing pattern of social relationships. The immediate problem confronting us is to know what we are supposed to do in those relationships. W. I. Thomas first spelled out an essential feature of all social interaction when he said, "If men define situations as real they are real in their consequences."[8] In other words, the process of social interaction requires that we have a definition of the situation that tells us how to act and how to expect others to act in specific contexts. Such a definition can be factually wrong, but it still shapes our actions and expectations.

When we enter a classroom on the first day of class and find a number of people sitting in chairs facing a blackboard, we assume that they are students taking the course. When another, usually older, person walks in, faces the people sitting in the chairs, and begins to discuss the subject matter of the course, we assume that this person is a teacher. It does not occur to us that the students might really be teachers, or that the teacher may be an imposter. We have a definition of the situation telling us what to expect in a classroom and what kinds of people belong there.

Much of the information on which a definition of the situation is based does not come from any intimate or direct knowledge about the specific individuals with whom we interact. Instead, we base our definition on expectations about the behavior of people in certain positions. We may expect different kinds of behavior from people in different social positions. Social roles include all the behavior required or expected in a particular position. Individuals learn social roles by becoming aware of what people occupying a certain social position must do and be, and what others expect them to do and be.[9] The role of a student may include going to class, asking questions, studying, taking tests, and similar behavior. The role of a teacher may include going to class, presenting information, answering students' questions, giving tests, and so on. Teachers expect students to perform the role of student, and students expect teachers to perform the role of teacher.

As this language suggests, the term "role" comes from acting. Actors performing a role in a theater are performing a part whose outline has been drawn by the author of the play, not by themselves. By using the term "role," sociologists are drawing an analogy between social behavior and acting. The implication is that our behavior in social positions follows a script. But who is the author of the script? Who determines the role appropriate to a given social position? If we assume that there is a general consensus about appropriate role behavior, we are forced into the vague assertion that society defines the content of social roles. This is precisely the position taken by most positivists.[10]

The problem with such a formulation becomes evident when we examine the performance of an actor on-stage. While it is true that the author of a play defines the roles of different parts, this is not the only source of role definition. The director of the play may interpret roles differently than the author and may require the actors to emphasize different characteristics; the audience may expect different behavior from the characters than does the author; the actors, in responding to these different expectations, may actually perform the roles differently.

Similar problems exist with respect to social roles. We can distinguish at least three different aspects of any social role: the normative role, as specified by the general culture; the perceived role, as interpreted by the individual; and the enacted role, as performed by specific individuals.[11] The perceived role may differ from the normative role, and the enacted role may differ from both of these, since individuals involved in social interaction may be forced to respond to pressures that prevent them from exactly enacting the perceived role.

There is seldom any general consensus about a particular social role. Instead, different groups have different expectations about the behavior of people in certain positions. The actual behavior of people depends upon the outcome of an interaction between their own learned expectations and the pressures put upon them by others, who may have different expectations. The enacted role behavior will depend, in part, on the power of others over the situation.

Roles are reciprocal in the sense that every role assumes the existence of another role or group of roles, and this is one source of pressure on enacted roles. The role of teacher, for example, has no meaning without the role of student. The expectations of students about their own role, as well as their actual behavior, can change the perception of their teacher about the expected role behavior of a teacher.

Another source of pressure is challenges to the normative role. In recent years, for example, many women have challenged the normative role of woman in American society and have deliberately enacted the role differently from the cultural norm. Since the role of men is bound up with the role of women, men have been forced to alter their perception and behavior in situations where they interact with women. These challenges may lead to long-term changes in the normative roles of men and women in this society.

Institutions and the Individual

A variety of social positions, groups, and roles are characteristically required to satisfy any specific human need. Within a social structure, these positions, groups, and roles tend to cluster together and channel behavior. Sociologists refer to such clusters as *institutions*. The cluster of positions, groups, and roles involved with satisfying material needs such as food, clothing, and shelter, for example, is called the economic institution. The cluster of positions, groups, and roles involved with sexual and reproductive needs is called the family. The cluster involved with creating and transmitting knowledge is called education. The cluster involved with maintaining relations of authority and control is called government.

Individuals create institutions by establishing relationships with one another as they attempt to satisfy needs. Over time, however, many of these relationships become reified—that is, they exist by law or custom but no longer correspond to the actual activities they were established to facilitate. As a result, individuals find themselves confronted with already existing relationships that pressure them to behave and believe in certain ways.

Since this process is historical, it is often difficult to isolate the impact of social structure on individual behavior. There are certain types of settings, however, in which this process is illustrated in intensified form. Erving Goffman found one such setting in a mental hospital.

The advantage of studying an institution like a mental hospital or a prison is, according to Goffman, that it is a "total institution"—"a place of residence and work where a large number of like situated individuals, cut off from the wider society for an appreciable period of time, together lead an enclosed, formally administered round of life." [12] The number of social positions and groups in such a setting is limited, as are the number of people with whom social interaction occurs. All of these features make it easier to examine the processes of social interaction without the constant introduction of new factors.

Total institutions also have a stratified character. In mental hospitals, there is a basic division between inmates and staff, and relationships between these two groups tend to be formalized and restricted. The staff clearly has more power than the inmates, and both groups are aware that the hospital is ruled in the interests of the staff. Upon entering the hospital, inmates are systematically deprived of previous identities and forced into relationships designed to influence their beliefs and behavior.

Goffman observes that the staff members in a mental hospital find sharp contradictions between their normative roles and the roles they perceive and enact. The public image of the mental hospital is that of a rational and effective mechanism for humanely treating people who are ill. As the staff members go about daily tasks, however, the principal role they find themselves performing is that of "keeping" a bunch of inmates. In order for the hospital to function properly, the inmates must obey the rules and orders of the staff, and staff have the responsibility of coercing such obedience. One of the first effects of this dilemma, according to Goffman, is that staff perceive all inmates as being ill.

For the inmate, the very fact of being institutionalized fosters illness. Most mental patients enter the hospital unwillingly, and in the process, they lose all ties to friends on the outside. Their lives are totally controlled by others, and every word and deed is interpreted by staff in ways reinforcing the diagnosis that the inmate is sick. The inmate is denied the customary means available to members of the outside world for expressing anger and alienation. The inmate must turn to unauthorized means for obtaining personal ends.

One of the chief ways in which inmates resist the power of the staff is by seeking to create spaces which they control. Goffman identified three main types of spaces: (1) "free places," which an inmate shares with other inmates; (2) "group territories," which an inmate shares with a select few; and (3) "personal territory," which no one but the particular inmate controls. Obviously, physical coercion is an important element in controlling private spaces, and in mental hospitals the rule of strong inmates over weak ones is highly visible. Human beings, Goffman argues, continue to desire what they are denied by repressive controls. To realize their desires, inmates manipulate authorities and dominate and exploit their fellow patients.

But, while inmates continually attempt to resist controls, every act of resistance is treated by the staff as further evidence that the patient is sick. The two worlds—staff and inmates—are fundamentally at odds with one another and constantly threaten to explode in conflict. One way hospital authorities try to lessen the danger of such explosion is through what Goffman calls "institutional ceremonies." By allowing an inmate newspapers, or occasional parties and events where normal restrictive rules are relaxed, authorities allow a slight lessening of the gulf separating the two worlds. They do not give up any power by such ceremonies, but rather attempt to blur some of the harsh enormity of their power, and thus weaken the desire of inmates to resist.

Goffman's analysis of total institutions illustrates the dynamic nature of social interaction. By starting with the various interest groups existing in a mental hospital, Goffman shows how every stage of a patient's career is determined by relationships with others who are more powerful. Some people become inmates by offending the interests and values of other people. Once they become inmates, they are subjugated to those who control the institution. The relationships of authority and control characterizing the social structure of the mental hospital exist before the individual arrives on the scene, and they have a profound effect on the daily life of inmates. Inmates are forced to behave in specified ways, even though they may seek subtle ways to resist the power massed against them. All of this, of course, raises important questions about the nature of insanity and about the use of diagnostic labels as instruments of social power and control.

Social Structure and Society

Different types of social structure can create very different possibilites for people to satisfy their needs. In *Class Inequality and Political Order*, British sociologist Frank Parkin examines the possibilities for using government as an instrument for equalizing the distribution of rewards and privileges among different social classes.[13] Parkin begins by distinguishing three types of social structure: (1) those with capitalist economies in which liberal or conservative political parties have controlled government for a long period of time; (2) those with capitalist economies in which political parties espousing some form of socialism have achieved control of government; and (3) those with socialist economies in which political parties espousing socialism control the government.

The most obvious measure of an unequal distribution of rewards and privileges is the existence of widely varying salaries for different occupations. Parkin notes that the main criterion for determining whether or not an unequal distribution of rewards represents systematic class inequality is the extent of social mobility—whether or not members of one social class have equal access to the same occupations as do other classes. Most Western countries that have had conservative or liberal political parties in power for long periods of time have great inequality both in the actual distribution of rewards, and in social mobility. Since education is often seen as a tool for increasing social mobility, Parkin examines access to education, and he finds little equality of access. Higher classes have greater access to higher education, while lower classes have relatively little access to higher education.

When he examines countries with capitalist economies where socialist political parties control government, Parkin discovers that there is little difference in the actual distribution of rewards and privileges from societies with liberal or conservative political parties. In such countries as Sweden, there is increased access to education and somewhat greater mobility, but greater equality of opportunity is not matched by greater equality of distribution. Parkin argues that part of the reason for this lies in the character and programs of the socialist parties in these countries. Increasingly, he shows, the socialist parties have become controlled by upper-class and middle-class people rather than by the working class, and therefore the ideological emphasis has shifted from equality of distribution toward equality of opportunity. At the same time, the formal separation of powers in these countries limits the extent to which socialist political parties can affect equality of distribution, even if they want to.

In the socialist countries of Eastern Europe, on the other hand, Parkin finds much greater equality of distribution as well as greater equality of opportunity. He notes that this pattern has not been uniform but has fluctuated—in certain periods there has been increasing inequality and in others increasing equality. At all times however, the extent of inequality has been much less than in the other two types of societies. As for the future, Parkin observes that the class composition of many communist parties seems to be following a pattern similar to that of the socialist parties of the West, where an elite of intellectuals and bureaucrats represents an increasing proportion of the membership. Since control of the parties provides greater access to opportunity, he foresees the possibility that inequality may grow in the socialist countries.

This comparison of different types of social structure leads Parkin to conclude that, in capitalist countries, control of the government is not sufficient to bring about equality of distribution, whereas in socialist countries, such control is sufficient. He also draws the rather startling conclusion, at least in terms of traditional Marxist theory, that class consciousness is likely to be greater in socialist countries than in capitalist ones. He thinks that, in capitalist countries, the very pluralism of power that helps to maintain the system also blurs the source of inequality. It is hard to know whom to blame. In socialist countries, on the other hand, it is quite clear that control of the party provides control of the government, and control of the government provides control of the economy, and control of the economy provides control over inequality. If there is inequality, then the party is to blame.

This seems to further document the position held by many western Marxists that eastern European "socialist" countries have not maintained a consistently dialectical approach to the solution of social problems. To the extent that party doctrine hardens into formulae prescribing rigid patterns of political or social action, it begins to take on the undesirable qualities of positivism. When this occurs, the doctrine is often referred to as "vulgar Marxism." Some Marxist critics insist that the modes of social organization that have emerged in East European countries are based on such a doctrine.

Positivism and Social Structure

So far, we have adopted the viewpoint of critical sociologists in examining social structure. Accordingly, we have looked at the development of social structure as a process by which, over time, groups with different interests appear and compete with one another for power. By such an analysis, we can learn the principles by which the society is organized, its social structure, and the pressures for and resistance to change.

Positivist sociologists understand social structure very differently. Starting from the belief that there are underlying, unchanging laws of human behavior, positivists seek to discover those characteristics and relationships common to all societies. The main concept they employ is that of social systems.

Social Systems and Social Structure

A system consists of two or more units related to each other in some sort of logical, purposive fashion. An automobile is a kind of system. The engine, chassis, tires and other parts are component units related in such a way that they form an automobile. In the solar system, the sun and the various planets and moons are related to each other in definable ways.

Interestingly enough, the concept of a system has much in common with dialectics. The focus is the whole rather than the component parts, and the emphasis is on the relationships among various system elements, as well as the relationship of all the elements to the total system. But when the concept of a system is applied to the physical world, there is a tendency to think of each component as a relatively unchanging, invariant item. Such items can be listed as inventory and ordered when necessary through a stockroom. The relationships among items can be calculated by using mathematical models that assume that specified behaviors are characteristic of each item. The items are thought to be causally related to each other; a change in one part produces change in other parts.

When positivists apply systems theory to social systems, individual human beings playing social roles tend to be thought of as system components in precisely the same terms. They are seen as "operating units" having durable characteristics that are specifiable in "personnel requisitions," and they are expected to perform within specified limits. All of this creates some difficulties, not only in terms of analysis, but in terms of ethical considerations as well.[14]

Since roles do not exist in isolation, but are related to one another, any role implies a set of related units. Within a social system, roles may be related either by their similarity or by their differences. Thus, the behavior of friends toward one another is based on the similarity of their expectations. Positivists use the term "role reciprocity" to refer to such relationships.[15] When relationships are based on the differences between roles, the term "role complementarity" is used. In the family, for example, the role of parent involves very different expectations and behavior than the role of child, but the roles are complementary to each other in the sense that both must be performed in order to maintain the family as a system.

It is often very difficult to determine the boundaries of a system. Functionalists attempt to solve this problem by arguing that systems include only those relationships that are patterned and predictable. Any random or unpredictable elements fall outside the boundaries of the system. According to this approach, the natural environment, heredity, technology, and population are all elements that influence social systems but are not within their boundaries.

To continue in operation, systems must keep their internal patterns free from outside interference, and at the same time maintain necessary relationships with their external environment. This means that social systems must accommodate their internal processes to changes in human biology and the natural environment. Ideally, then, social systems are largely self-sufficient. As one contemporary textbook puts it,

Society is simply the name which is given to the largest and most nearly in-dependent social system. Ideally, societies are substantial collections of people living in near isolation from other such collections, operating with their own distinctive social patterns, and without being affected much by human agents outside their own geographical boundaries.[16]

If societies are social systems, and social systems are purposive, what is the purpose of society? Talcott Parsons and some other functionalists have maintained that the purpose of society is the maintenance of social order and social stability, and that the function of social structure is to maintain this stability.[17] Parsons argues that the common values shared by the vast majority of people in society hold this social structure together. Some posi-tivists, wary of the conservative implications of Parsons' formulation, have argued that society cannot possess a consciousness of purpose, but they too claim that "it is still possible to say that systems must maintain some pattern, some integrity if they are to be systems. Such order is implied in the definition of system where regularity and pattern are emphasized." [18]

Thus, positivists claim that societies are social systems, and that social systems must maintain their underlying order if they are to survive. They see two principle sources of change in social systems. Changes in the external environment require adjustments within the social system. If, for example, the key industries of a town decide to move, life in the town will deteriorate, unless new industries can be attracted to replace those that leave. A second source of change is evolution within the system. As the component parts of a system adjust to changes in the external environment, other parts of the system must adjust so that the basic character of the system remains stable. As new industries are attracted to a town, for example, new laws, housing patterns, and so on may be required to keep the town operating smoothly.

Behaviorists tend to focus on the behavior of individuals and to use the notion of systems of human action rather than the functionalist notion of social systems. Like the functionalists, however, behaviorists treat social structure as a kind of fundamental, unchanging reality that holds true for all societies at all points in time. For all positivists, the groups, roles, and institutions making up a social structure are essentially independent elements related to one another by processes such as cooperation, conflict, and power. Social structure is viewed as a kind of subsystem of society, logically indepen-dent of culture and socialization which are viewed as other subsystems. Each of these subsystems has its own unique features and is related to the others through some sort of social processes.

While critical sociologists tend to view social structure as the most impor-tant sociological concept, positivists tend to view culture as the most important concept. For them, culture is the glue that holds together a social structure.

Phenome-nology and Social Structure

Subjective sociologists argue that the most important fact about social structure is that it is based on interaction. They maintain that social organization is more of a process than a structure, and that the real focus of sociological study should be the rules or laws that govern human interaction. Since interaction requires behavior, and behavior is meaningful, subjective approaches emphasize the need to understand how meaning is formed and how meanings influence overt behavior.

One consequence of the subjective viewpoint is that social structure appears to be a defining rather than a determining influence on individuals. Certain social contexts call forth appropriate behavioral responses from individuals; these responses then influence the actions of others. Goffman's study of a mental institution reflects this view. He shows how human interactions are shaped by social conditions, while at the same time, they influence the social conditions.

Summary

Social structure is the name we use for the patterns of relationships human beings form with each other as they attempt to satisfy their needs. These relationships become formalized by law, government, and morality. Although social structure originally emerged from the interactions of human beings, it tends to become rigid and to develop an independent existence. This rigidity is usually maintained by those who have reason to benefit from it.

Sociologists usually focus on three elements of structure—groups; roles; and institutions. Any collection of two or more people conscious of a distinctive set of relationships that bind them together and set them apart from others is a group. Primary groups, such as families or play groups, meet on an intimate basis. Members relate to each other as ends in themselves rather than as means to an end. In secondary groups, such as trade associations, relationships are more contractual in nature.

The behavior required or expected of a particular position is called a social role. A normative role is one that is specified by the general culture. A perceived role is one that is interpreted by an individual. An enacted role is one that is performed by specific individuals.

Institutions consist of clusters of roles and groups that channel behavior to satisfy a given social need. There are economic institutions, religious institutions, family, educational, and government institutions—to name only a few.

Critical sociologists view social structure as a process of social interaction based on power differentials between different groups in society. Positivists view social structure as one part of a social system. A system consists of two or more units related to each other in some purposive fashion. Positivists treat the various elements of social structure as independent. The elements are thought to be held together by the underlying purpose of society, but positivists do not agree on what that purpose is. Subjective sociologists argue that social structure emerges out of the interaction between individuals. The focus of sociology, they argue, should be the rules and laws governing interaction.

While critical sociologists tend to see social structure as the most important sociological concept, positivists tend to see culture as the most important, and subjective sociologists emphasize socialization.

For Further Study

The critical sociologist's view of social structure grows out of Marx's analysis of capitalism. A classic statement is Karl Marx and Friedrich Engels, *The German Ideology* (New York: International Publishers, 1947). A more detailed and sophisticated presentation is Karl Marx, *Grundrisse,* translated with a foreward by Martin Nicolaus (Middlesex, England: Penguin Books, 1973). A modern sociological presentation of the critical view of social structure is Anthony Giddens, *The Class Structure of the Advanced Societies* (New York: Harper, 1973). Two texts that also present a critical view of social structure are by the Frankfurt Institute for Social Research, *Aspects of Sociology* (Boston: Beacon Press, 1972), and by Margaret A. Coulson and David S. Riddell, *Approaching Sociology* (London: Routledge & Kegan Paul, 1970). The latter book also contains a critique of the functionalist view of social structure.

The positivist view of the social system is most clearly spelled out by Talcott Parsons, in *The Social System* (New York: Free Press, 1951). Many of Parsons' positions have been criticized by other positivists, and their current view of social systems and social structure builds on the work of Robert Merton, *Social Theory and Social Structure* (New York: Free Press, 1949). While Parsons and Merton both represent functionalist interpretations, the behaviorist formulation is best expressed by George C. Homans, *Social Behavior* (New York: Harcourt, 1961); and Peter M. Blau, *Exchange and Power in Social Life* (New York: Wiley, 1964). Two contemporary texts also present the positivist view at an introductory level. The functionalist approach is reflected in Leonard Broom and Philip Selznick, *Sociology* (New York: Harper, 1973), while the behaviorist approach is best presented in Gerald R. Leslie, Richard F. Larson, and Benjamin L. Gorman, *Order and Change* (New York: Oxford University Press, 1973).

A somewhat dated presentation of phenomenological views of social structure is by Peter Berger and Thomas Luckmann, *The Social Construction of Reality* (Garden City, N.Y.: Doubleday, 1967). A more recent attempt to apply phenomenology to the study of social structure is found in George Psathas, *Phenomenological Sociology: Issues and Applications* (New York: Wiley, 1973). For a critical view of the subjective approach, see Irving Zeitlin, *Rethinking Sociology* (Englewood Cliffs, N.J.: Prentice-Hall, 1973).

For a more detailed treatment of systems and systems theory, *see* C. West Churchman, *The Systems Approach* (New York: Dell, 1968); Kenyon B. Greene, *Sociotechnical Systems: Factors in Analysis, Design, and Management* (Englewood Cliffs, N.J.: Prentice-Hall, 1973); Ludwig von Bertalanffy, *General Systems Theory: Foundations, Development, Applications* (New York: Braziller, 1968). For critical assessments of systems theory and practice, see Robert Boguslaw, *The New Utopians: A Study of System Design and Social Change* (Englewood Cliffs, N.J.: Prentice-Hall, 1965); Ida Hoos, *Systems Analysis in Public Policy: A Critique* (Berkeley, Calif.: University of California Press, 1972).

Notes

1 See Karl Marx, *Grundrisse*, trans. Martin Nicolaus (Middlesex, England: Penguin Books, 1973); Immanuel M. Wallerstein, *The Modern World System: Capitalist Agriculture and the Origins of the European World Economy in the Sixteenth Century.* (New York: Academic Press, 1974); Fernand Braudel, *Capitalism and Material Life:1400–1800* (New York: Harper, 1967).

2 Herbert Spencer, *Principles of Sociology* (New York: D. Appleton & Co., 1897).

3 See Margaret A. Coulson and David S. Riddell, *Approaching Sociology* (London: Routledge and Kegan Paul, 1970).

4 See Charles Horton Cooley, *Social Organization* (New York: Schocken Books, 1962).

5 Ibid.

6 Ferdinand Toennies, *Community and Society*, trans. Charles P. Loomis (East Lansing, Mich.: Michigan State University Press, 1974).

7 See Charles H. Anderson, *Toward a New Sociology* (Homewood, Ill.: Dorsey Press, 1974).

8 W. I. Thomas, *The Child in America* (New York: Knopf, 1928).

9 See Tullio Seppilli and Grazietta Guaitini Abbozzo, *Conceptual Scheme of a Theory of Culture* (Perugia, Italy: Institute of Ethnology and Cultural Anthropology, 1974). Also see Erving Goffman, *The Presentation of Self in Everyday Life* (Garden City, N.Y.: Doubleday, 1959).

10 See Talcott Parsons, *The Social System* (New York: Free Press, 1951). Also see *Toward a General Theory of Action*, eds. Talcott Parsons and Edward A. Shils (Cambridge, Mass.: Harvard University Press, 1951).

11 See Anderson, *Toward a New Sociology.*

12 Erving Goffman, *Asylums* (Garden City, N.Y.: Doubleday, 1961), p. xiii.

13 Frank Parkin, *Class Inequality and Political Order* (New York: Praeger, 1971).

14 See Robert Boguslaw, *The New Utopians: A Study of System Design and Social Change* (Englewood Cliffs, N.J.: Prentice-Hall, 1965).

15 See Gerald R. Leslie, Richard F. Larson, and Benjamin L. Gorman, *Order and Change* (New York: Oxford University Press, 1973).

16 Ibid., p. 128.

17 See Talcott Parsons, *The Social System.*

18 Leslie et al., *Order and Change*, p. 130.

Culture

Social structure represents the *is* of society, the actual patterns and types of relationships people create and enter into. Social structure involves a systematic ordering of positions, groups, roles, and institutions within a society, and the process of social interaction that creates this ordering leads to differences of power among social groups. As new members enter through birth and immigration they must develop an understanding of the basic organization of social structure, if they are to become productive. (See chapter 11.)

Sociologists use the concept of culture to describe "oughts" of a society. Upon arriving in a city, the proverbial visitor from outer space would need to know a great deal about the culture of the natives as a preliminary to knowing how to behave. It would be important to know how people communicate with each other, both verbally and in written form. It would be necessary to become familiar with the newspapers of the city as well as letters, television reports, and street-corner orators. Culture includes information about sports and food, humor and taboos, pets and literature, love-making, dress, architecture, hobbies, speed limits, and much more.

Culture could be called a mental map, one that guides us in our relations to our surroundings and to other people. This map, necessarily must be shared by a large number of people, since it gives the boundaries of social interaction. Individuals and groups may have slightly different maps, reflecting their own biographies, but the general outline and broad details must be similar in order for social interaction to reinforce the structure. When we encounter people using different maps we know we have crossed from one culture or subculture into another.[1]

Some contemporary sociology textbooks find it convenient to use the definition of culture offered by Edward Tylor in 1871: "Culture is that complex whole which includes knowledge, belief, art, morals, law, custom, and any other capabilities acquired by man as a member of society."[2] The point is that the term culture, as used by sociologists, is by no means equivalent to what is meant by the phrase "the finer things in life." Sociologists equate television shows and movies with symphony orchestras and ballet companies as valid components of a country's culture.

The importance of culture in shaping beliefs and behavior is most vividly demonstrated when different cultures come into contact with one another. One's own culture is often taken for granted, operating at a subconscious level of the personality to create certain expectations. When these expectations are shaken by contact with a culture embodying fundamentally different expectations the result can be a profound disorientation and anxiety, which we call *culture shock*. When Americans come into contact with cultures that place a lower value on children, they are often horrified by an apparent disregard for human life. This is a kind of culture shock, for it is not really true that human life is callously disregarded in such a society but merely that human life in general is valued much differently.

Many Peace Corps volunteers, for example, have experienced culture shock when confronted with the treatment of children in other societies. In the United States, where great value is placed on the care and protection of the young, we expect children to be fed before adults if food is in short supply and assume that they are to be protected at the expense of our own lives if necessary. But in some developing countries with few resources and large populations, cultural priorities can be quite different. Healthy adults are often valued above children, since adult labor is essential to provide the meager existence of the community. Children, though they represent a potential source of production, can at times be considered a drain on limited resources.

Most groups, and certainly most cultures, tend to consider their own way of life as the best and most natural way of living. People in other societies, with their seemingly strange ideas, beliefs, and practices, are sometimes viewed with suspicion and hostility. This tendency to value highly one's own way of life while devaluing that of others is known as *ethnocentrism*.

During the Nazi period in Germany the virtues of German culture were seen to embody the supposed superiority of the "Aryan race" while other cultures were deemed inferior and polluting. These attitudes and policies were used to justify murder and military conquest. In less virulent form, ethnocentrism can lead to the image of the "ugly American" who travels around the world refusing to learn the languages of other countries, constantly using his own culture as the standard for judgment, and ignoring or demeaning other cultures.

The opposite of ethnocentrism is *cultural relativism*, which holds that there is no universal standard that an outside observer can use to evaluate a culture: each must be judged and evaluated according to the values and goals it defines for itself and in terms of whether it facilitates or inhibits the attainment of those values and goals.

Cultural relativism is a useful framework for sociologists studying different societies, since it can help them to understand the ways in which culture orients individuals to their particular social structure. This does not mean that people sharing one culture must never employ their own standards to decide on a course of behavior toward those who share a different culture; it simply means that they should try to understand why others have different standards.

Since culture is a guide for how we think and act within a particular social structure, changes in that structure tend to bring about changes in culture. One of the classic examples of the dependence of culture on social structure is a study by Ralph Linton of the Tanala tribe of Madagascar.[3] Initially, the Tanala produced their food by employing a technology of dry-rice cultivation. The natural resources employed in food production consisted of jungle land that had to be cut down and burned before the rice could be planted. This land remained fertile only long enough to grow a couple of crops, after which new land had to be cleared, while the jungle was allowed to reclaim and refertilize the old land. When the land around a village became exhausted, the Tanala moved their village to a new location surrounded by fertile jungle. Within the tribe, ownership of land belonged to the village as a whole, and the division of labor was based on "joint families" (several households connected by a common head of the family) who worked the land and owned the crops they grew. According to the culture of the Tanala, then, the most highly valued part of society was the joint family, while land had little value.

After associating with a neighboring tribe, the Tanala adopted a new technology of wet-rice cultivation. This technology required only small plots of land for planting, and the same land could be used time and again. As the new technology was adopted, it became possible for single household units to produce enough food for themselves on a small plot of land, and the joint family structure began to break down. Within the tribe as a whole, a distinction emerged between those involved in wet-rice cultivation and those who continued to engage in dry-rice cultivation. The landholders engaged in the former opposed moving the village as dry-rice land was exhausted, and those engaged in the latter had to travel farther and farther into the jungle to clear new land, returning to the village at night. Eventually, the dry-rice farmers took their families with them and established new villages; and the single household organization became the primary unit of the wet-rice farmers. This in turn led to changes in kinship, government, and other social institutions.

Changes in production and social relations among the Tanala were accompanied by changes in culture. The single family replaced the joint family as the valued social unit, and ownership of land became highly valued. These changes in the culture of the Tanala were produced by changes in the relations of production, authority, and control within the social structure, and in turn reinforced the changes in social structure.

As the example indicates, culture is a social product emerging from experiences of a people. It grows out of the same processes of interaction that shape social structure, and its function within a society is to give an orientation to individuals and groups as to how to respond to concrete situations.[4]

| Elements of Culture | To say that culture is like a mental map is to say that culture represents a subjective dimension of society. Sometimes culture is referred to as social consciousness, mediating between individuals and their social environment. This mediation distinguishes human beings from other animals. There are three ways this is done: (1) *cognitively*, through a system of symbols conveying meaning; (2) *evaluatively*, by providing cultural values that |

individuals can strive for; and (3) through *action orientations*, norms that prescribe particular behavior in specific situations.[5]

Symbols and Language

Animals communicate through the use of natural signs that produce instinctive responses. Human beings are capable of symbolic communication. In the most general sense, a symbol is anything that stands for or represents something else.

Sociologists distinguish between referential symbols and expressive ones. A referential symbol refers to a specific object—for example, the word "boat." Expressive symbols, on the other hand, are open-ended and connotative. Expressive symbols such as the words "God" or "pride" connote a wide variety of associations among different people. For some an expressive symbol will have a very specific and personal meaning; for others it will have more diffuse positive associations; and for still others it may have negative associations. "Uncle Sam" is another symbol that may evoke different associations. For some it means America, democracy, freedom, and other positive associations, some of which are symbols themselves. For others Uncle Sam means exploitation, imperialism, and other negative associations. The burning of American flags, and the reactions to such acts, illustrate the importance that can be attached to expressive symbols.

The open-endedness of expressive symbols is an indication of the fact that culture intervenes, or mediates, between a symbolic stimulus and the behavioral response to that stimulus. For people to have a similar response to any symbol, they must first understand its meaning and value. In this sense, symbols contribute to social solidarity, affirming the ideals and values shared by members of a society. At the same time, as the flag-burning example illustrates, different groups may attach conflicting meanings and values to the same symbol. Symbols are rooted in a cultural context, and their meaning depends on that context; they shape and strengthen culture, but they also derive from culture.[6]

Because they can contribute to social solidarity, the ability to manipulate symbols is power in a society. Those who control the means of communication play an important role in defining the meaning of symbols within a culture.[7] To the extent that the symbols are accepted by a variety of social groups, they represent legitimate aspects of culture, but for groups that reject the symbols, they become illegitimate. When we examine the concept of subculture we will see how different groups may use conflicting symbols within the same society.

For symbols to be useful, they must be communicated, and the most important element of human communication is language. We normally take language for granted as a way of expressing ideas and feelings and of communicating messages. Even though there are many different languages in the world, common sense tells us that these different languages describe the same underlying reality, that the different words and sounds in different languages actually apply to the same things. With this assumption, we are able to translate one language into another.

Although most American sociologists probably agree with this common-sense view, many in this country and elsewhere do not. These, in general, accept the Sapir-Whorf hypothesis that language is not only a vehicle for communicating thoughts, but is also a shaper of the content and style of thought.[8] They maintain that language constructs reality by determining the kinds of objects we carve out of experience, that language itself shapes the kinds of messages that can be conceived or conveyed.

The Sapir-Whorf hypothesis suggests that culture may play an independent role in shaping thoughts and behavior to the extent that language accentuates some features of experience and helps form our conceptions of reality. It is important to remember, however, that differences in the structure of a language usually reflect the different experiences of a people. In the English language, for example, the single word "snow" applies to many different kinds of white frozen flakes. Eskimos, however, use different words to describe different types of snow, because their lives and livelihood are affected by each kind in different ways. Heavy, wet snow has one implication; dry, powdery snow quite another.[9] In short, while the language of a people shapes and constrains the realities they can conceive and communicate, that language is itself shaped by the realities they have encountered.

Symbols and language, then, are part of the cognitive dimension of culture that mediates between individuals and their social environment. To the extent that individuals share the same symbols and language, they are part of a common culture and are likely to respond similarly to their social environment. Indeed, symbols and language reinforce a common understanding of that environment. Individuals who share a common linguistic and symbolic representation of their environment may, however, evaluate that environment in different ways.

Cultural Values

This evaluative aspect of culture takes the form of *cultural values*—widely held beliefs that some activities, relationships, or goals are important to the maintenance of the social structure. In most societies there is general agreement about the cultural values that dominate the culture. At times of crisis, however, existing values are often called into question and new values proposed and slowly adopted.

Conventional attitude studies have, over the years, found a number of traditional cultural values shared by Americans—for example, beliefs that children should respect their parents; that society needs some legally based authority to prevent chaos; that business is entitled to make a profit; that the right to private property is sacred; that hard work will always pay off; that organized religion is important.[10] In studies of American college students conducted between 1968 and 1971, Daniel Yankelovich found some of these values called into question.[11]

Thus, from 1968 to 1971, the proportion of students believing that hard work always pays off declined from 69 percent to 39 percent. A belief that organized religion is important declined from 42 percent in 1969 to 35 percent in 1971. Even where a majority of students shared the traditional cultural values, a growing number did not. The proportion of students who did not believe that society needs some legally based authority to prevent chaos rose from 8 percent in 1969 to 14 percent in 1971, and the proportion who did not believe that private property is sacred rose from 25 percent to 31 percent in the same period.

The Yankelovich study also found a growing majority of students favoring more emphasis on self-expression, more sexual freedom, and less emphasis on money, as well as a questioning of traditional forms of marriage and child-rearing. Other studies have found similar shifts in values concerned with sex, the family, work, and politics during the last decade.

Some sociologists have concluded that such shifts in values represent a generational conflict between the young and the old, but this conclusion seems unwarranted. It turns out that value conflicts between children and parents are not very pronounced compared with value conflicts between different class and ethnic groups. Middle-class children tend to share with their parents cultural values emphasizing self-direction and independence, although they disagree about strategies for realizing these values. Working-class children tend to share with their parents cultural values emphasizing conformity and obedience. Melvin Kohn has argued that these differences reflect the different positions and power of social classes in the American social structure.[12]

Cultural Norms

Where cultural values involve very broad beliefs, *cultural norms* are specific behavior patterns with intense positive valuations. Norms may be based directly on cultural values, but they may also be purely technical arrangements for organizing work. William Graham Sumner, as we have previously noted, distinguished between norms not treated as crucial to the maintenance of social structure, which he called folkways, and norms that demand conformity, which he called mores.[13] A norm specifying appropriate ways of dressing might be an example of a folkway, while a norm prohibiting incest is likely to be a mos, the singular of the word mores. The difference is that any violation of the mores is severely punished either by law or by custom. Violations of folkways are punished very mildly by expressions of public opinion, if at all.

Culture and Social Control

Culture is not part of nature; it must be made. Before symbols, values, and norms can be integrated into the fabric of a society, they must be created and propagated. The creation and propagation of culture takes place within social institutions. Inevitably, then, questions of social power within these institutions are involved. Maintenance of the social structure of a society depends upon the authority and control that give some positions and groups more power than others. Many of these controls tend to become formalized in government. We refer to such a formalized social structure as the dominant one. Similarly, we can speak of a dominant culture as the system of symbols, values, and norms that sanctions and reinforces the dominant social structure.

The strength of a dominant culture lies in the fact that it is not abstract, but is reinforced by experience. It constitutes a sense of reality for most people in society beyond which it is difficult for them to move in their daily lives. Since the dominant culture gives us a sense of what is natural in society, it has been an important focus for sociological study.[14]

Historically, in western industrialized societies, there has been a division between a high culture available only to an educated elite, and a popular culture, available to all. In our contemporary world, there has been an ever-growing gap between high culture and popular culture. Without the overarching and comprehensive cultural system associated with religious institutions in earlier times, popular culture exists as isolated sets of symbols, values, and norms corresponding to special social relationships. People do not always connect the rationality of one area of life with that of another, and often seem to believe and behave in contradictory ways. In modern industrial societies, the dominant culture no longer provides an underlying comprehensive understanding of social structure, but instead tells us that life can go on without our full understanding.

Herbert Marcuse has argued that these changes in the nature of the dominant culture have increasingly given it the capability of absorbing and deflecting all opposition.[15] In earlier times, he explains, culture always contained certain critical contradictions. Art, for example, by portraying cultural symbols and values in an ideal form, to some extent constituted a denial of the real world of daily experience—it abstracted portions of that experience and gave them meaning. Going to concerts or viewing paintings was an escape from the real world. Precisely because they were escapes they also represented a critical comment on the real world.

In modern society, however, art has become commercialized. One hears Beethoven in elevators, views Rembrandts in restaurants, and hears great literature quoted in television commercials. High culture, Marcuse tells us, has become absorbed into popular culture.

Where the dominant culture of early industrial society, primarily Protestantism, required a denial of inner needs in the interest of hard work, the dominant culture of advanced industrial society encourages the immediate gratification of contrived needs—in the same interest. Sexuality is intensified and emphasized. Fewer restrictions are placed on sexual gratification, but genuine passion is reduced. According to Marcuse, the expanding cultural freedom of contemporary American society really reflects a contraction of freedom, because immediate gratification of needs is used to hide the continued disparities of power and the growing irrationality of the social structure as a whole.

Marcuse is very pessimistic about the possibilities of challenging this dominant culture, because he sees it as capable of absorbing and commercializing all challenges. Revolutionary symbols and values are converted into revolutionary hair sprays and toothpaste; symbols and values calling for a more natural and less material focus in life are used to sell margarine and makeup. When the news media discovered the accumulation of hippies in Haight-Ashbury in 1966, tourist agencies sponsored bus tours through the area so that others could see the counterculture.

Social control exercised through the instrumentality of a culture can be even more complete and restrictive than the most tyrannical of conventional despotisms. People living within the framework of twentieth-century technologically oriented cultures are persuaded that "discontent about anything other than superficial inconvenience is inadmissible, a sign of unfortunate maladjustment or a failure of reason."[16] Thus, Theodore Roszak maintains that although some minorities may be kept in line by brute intimidation, that is not what keeps middle America loyal. He reports conversations with people whose entire loyalty to the existing order seems to rest on stereophonic radiophonographs or the convenience of frozen food. "They seem not to be able to contemplate their existence without such baubles—so trivial and cockeyed have their priorities become. In the absence of a vacuum cleaner, life could not go on. Clearly what is seriously wrong with them is the very seriousness with which they take trivialities . . . having sold their souls for an electric dishwasher, what can they do but pretend the foolish thing is worth the price?"[17]

The argument of Marcuse, Roszak, and others implies that culture, although a product of social interaction and a reflection of social structure, increasingly has developed an autonomy from social structure and an independent ability to shape human behavior. The fragmentation of culture has made the dominant culture more flexible and more capable of absorbing opposition than in earlier times. To the extent that this argument has merit, social change increasingly can be controlled and channeled in directions that do not threaten the existing relations of authority and control in society.

Culture and Social Change

Despite questions about the ability of the dominant culture to absorb all opposition, it is clear that there are always sources of cultural differences and potential conflict within a society, precisely because the function of culture is to orient individuals and groups to concrete situations they may face. The different power positions of different social groups insures that they are confronted by quite different situations much of the time, and this results in adaptations of the dominant culture to the conditions of different groups.

Subcultures and Countercultures

A *subculture* contains some of the dominant cultural symbols, values, and norms, but it also contains values and norms particular to itself. Two major sources of subcultural differences are class and ethnicity. During the nineteenth and early twentieth centuries, for example, there was a vast migration of European immigrants to the United States. These immigrants brought with them their own native cultures, which gradually were assimilated into the dominant American culture. In the process of this assimilation, many of these groups retained features of their native culture, and these came to constitute a distinct subculture. What made this possible was that these immigrants were not simply dispersed throughout the society, but tended to live together and to hold similar jobs. They were assimilated as groups rather than as individuals, and the assimilation of culture took the form of the modification of their native culture, rather than its total destruction.

Because the function of culture is to provide an orientation of different ways of responding to concrete situations, the nature of situations confronted by groups has an impact on the formation of subcultures. When distinct groups experience very different situations they are likely to develop cultural differences, even within the same society. These different experiences are often class differences, which shape not only occupational experiences but also the life chances and conditions of families. When people in similar class circumstances adopt the dominant culture, they modify it in ways to make it applicable to their experiences. When class differences correspond to ethnic and racial differences, the subcultures that develop tend to be even more distinct from the dominant culture.

Subcultures tend to be both distinct from, and compatible with, the dominant culture of a society. They have their own unique features, but at the same time they accept the major symbols, values, and norms of the dominant culture. Sometimes, however, subcultures develop values and norms that are in conflict with those of the dominant culture, and sociologists use the term counterculture to describe such a subculture.[18] During the 1960s, this term was used to describe the adoption by college students of new values and norms regarding sexual relations, work, and politics that were consciously challenging the dominant values and norms in these areas. As we noted earlier, however, many sociologists believe that the dominant culture has been able to absorb these "alternate life styles" within its framework in a way that does not threaten the dominant social structure.

Residual and Emergent Cultures

Social structure is a historically developing and changing process of social interaction. Cultural differences arise from existing differences in group situations and from changes in social structure.[19] Residual culture is a culture based on some earlier social structure that persists in the present. Certain religious values, for example, continue to be held by significant groups even though those values are no longer part of the dominant culture. Similarly, in certain regions of the United States, rural values and norms continue to influence the lives of many people, even though they run contrary to the dominant values and norms oriented to industrial society.

Residual cultures, unlike some ethnic subcultures, survive because of group assimilation and because remnants of the earlier social structure remain. Despite the fact that the United States represents the most highly developed form of industrial capitalism, small segments of society remain tied to semifeudal social relations—tenant farmers and sharecroppers in the South; migrant laborers in the West and Southwest. In addition, there are growing numbers of chronically unemployed who are not integrated into the dominant social structure. These and other unintegrated sectors of the population continue to develop residual cultures that serve as alternatives to the dominant one. The long-term trend, however, is for such cultures to die out or to become absorbed into the dominant culture.

Another source of different cultures is the emergence of new social relations within the framework of the dominant relations of authority and control. At the end of the 1940s, for example, C. Wright Mills observed that the old middle class of self-employed businessmen was being replaced by a new white-collar stratum of salaried clerks and office workers.[20] The conditions of this group led them to develop new symbols, values, and norms that were at variance with those of the existing, dominant culture. In the decades since, there has been a sharp growth of "professional, technical" workers whose conditions are quite different from those of the independent professionals (doctors, lawyers, and so on) of earlier times. These new professionals do not have the degree of autonomy of control over their conditions of work that typified earlier professionals, and they, too, have developed cultures divergent from the dominant one.

Positivism and Culture

One of the disagreements between positivist sociologists and the critical sociologists (whose views we have summarized), concerns the degree of autonomy of culture. Functionalist interpretations, in particular, have tended to emphasize the impact of culture in shaping behavior, while at the same time playing down the extent to which culture is dependent on social structure. This also leads, on occasion, to an overemphasis on those aspects of culture shared by all members of society, at the expense of focusing on those aspects that cause conflict among groups.

One leading text claims that "a society is a group of people who share a common culture." [21] Instead of examining relationships between a dominant culture and a dominant social system, or relationships between dominant and subordinate cultures, positivists often focus on what they call the "cultural universals" shared by all "normal" members of a society.

Culture, in these terms, is the glue that holds society together. Culture makes possible social interaction by providing a shared system of beliefs, customs, values and activities. Such a "positive" view of culture encourages two types of sociological inquiry: first, since the existence of a shared culture seems normal from such a perspective, it encourages research to explain any deviations from this normal state; and, second, it encourages the view that anything threatening the stability of a culture is negative, since the breakdown of culture implies the breakdown of society.

Accordingly, a major focus of research by functionalists has been directed toward explaining deviance. In Talcott Parsons' formulation, the starting point for analysis is the existence of an integrated, self-maintaining, social system, defined so as to coincide with the society studied; anything that does not contribute to this integration is negative or deviant, to be studied only in relation to its positive counterpart, the integrated society.[22] In this approach, social conflict and social problems seem to be individualized, and they are ultimately explained in terms of psychological aberrations of individual persons.

By denying the social structural basis of culture, positivists ignore the fact that what they call deviance is, to a large extent, generated by social interaction. The ongoing process of creating and changing social structures leads to different conditions, experiences, and power for various social groups. The dominant culture of a society embodies symbols, values, and norms that support existing inequalities of power and position. To assert that all opposition to that culture is deviance is to claim that opposition to inequality is somehow abnormal and wrong. Such a claim is reasonable only to those satisfied with existing inequalities.

Applied Sociology and Culture

Working in the positivist and often in the phenomenological tradition, applied sociologists have employed the notion of deviance to study many social problems. One of the largest efforts to apply positivist formulations of cultural deviance to social problems occurred during the 1960s. As the visibility of poverty amidst plenty was increasingly highlighted by journalists and social scientists, the federal government generated a War on Poverty, aimed at eliminating pockets of poverty throughout the United States. Sociologists were asked to prescribe effective strategies for attacking the problem, and this required them to explain the causes of poverty.

As we noted in chapter 3, many applied sociologists argued that a major source of the difficulty was a "culture of poverty." This theory held that many slum dwellers had developed a special set of values, norms, and behavior that made them incapable of "making it" in the larger society. The poor assumed attitudes toward work and success that made it impossible for them to hold normal jobs and led them to spend money as fast as they received it. Their children shunned education and dropped out of school. This began the process of passing the family's poverty on to the next generation.

During the 1960s a number of government programs were developed for the purpose of altering the culture of poverty and adapting poor families to the dominant culture. But the culture of poverty proved remarkably resistant to change. Families saw no reason to change their values and norms in the absence of any concrete evidence that doing so would change their conditions. On one level it appeared that a vicious circle had developed. While some sociologists argued that poverty could not be eliminated until the culture of poverty was altered, others insisted that the culture of poverty could not be altered until poverty was eliminated.

According to this latter view, the poor are victims of the unequal distribution of power and wealth in American society. If they seem to have a culture that condones illegitimate children, broken families, and living together out of wedlock, it is because marriage and divorce are expensive luxuries they cannot afford. They do not wish their children to become drug addicts or criminals, but they cannot afford to live in the "better" neighborhoods and their children cannot support themselves on legal jobs. If they spend money as fast as they receive it, why shouldn't they? They are always in debt, and if they try to save money it will simply be claimed by creditors.

The attempt to cure social problems by altering culture is rooted in the belief that culture is an independent variable affecting social organization and structure. As the example of the culture of poverty illustrates, however, it is extremely difficult, if not impossible, to change culture patterns when the new patterns are not relevant to the daily experience of the people involved. It would seem that human beings will tolerate culture patterns to the extent that these help orient them to the situations they confront and help them deal with situations effectively.

As we have previously noted, one analysis, offered by sociologist Daniel Patrick Moynihan, sought to explain the relatively high poverty rate among black Americans. Moynihan concluded that the main factor preventing improvement in the position of blacks was the weakness of black family structure:

> At the heart of the deterioration of the fabric of Negro society is the deterioration of the Negro family. It is the fundamental source of weakness of the Negro community at the present time. ...The white family has achieved a high

degree of stability and is maintaining that stability. By contrast, the family structure of lower class Negroes is highly unstable, and in many urban centers is approaching complete breakdown.[23]

The basic position taken by Moynihan was that while unemployment and family income historically were simply factors contributing to the weakness of the Negro family, after 1960 these weaknesses took on a life of their own and caused continued poverty. His evidence for this claim was based primarily on the finding that, until 1960, rising unemployment and declining family income were related to increasing divorce, higher welfare rates, and other indicators of family instability among blacks. Between 1960 and 1964, however, unemployment declined slightly while welfare Aid to Dependent Children cases continued to rise.

Moynihan concludes from these figures that the weakness of black family structure was primarily responsible for continued poverty:

Obviously not every instance of social pathology afflicting the Negro community can be traced to the weakness of family structure. . . .Nonetheless, at the center of the tangle of pathology is the weakness of the family structure. Once or twice removed, it will be found to be the principal source of most of the aberrant, inadequate or anti-social behavior that did not establish but now served to perpetuate the cycle of poverty and deprivation.[24]

Moynihan's commitment to the functionalist view of deviance is evident. The difficulty is not seen as arising from structured inequalities in our society, but from those who are poor: "The present tangle of pathology is capable of perpetuating itself without assistance from the white world." [25] Poverty, at least among blacks, is not produced by our social structure but by deficiencies in the black way of life.

Charles Valentine and many others have noted that the statistics on which Moynihan bases his arguments are misleading and inaccurate.[26] For example, although ADC cases rose between 1960 and 1964, other family statistics such as divorce rates continued to parallel the unemployment trends, as they had before that time. Moreover, even during the period in question, black family income declined relative to white income. Valentine argues that Moynihan's own study provides support for the claim that statistics on family structure respond to basic economic trends rather than the reverse.

Although Moynihan's study is a relatively simplistic example of the culture of poverty approach, even the more sophisticated versions have been unable to demonstrate convincingly the existence of a culture of poverty independent of the conditions of social structure creating such a culture or the existence of a culture of poverty even where poverty exists. Elliot Liebow, for example, argues that blacks in a study he conducted share the dominant culture of the society, and feel themselves to be failures precisely because they cannot achieve the symbols, values, and norms of that culture.[27]

Critical Perspectives on Culture

Throughout this chapter, we have repeatedly touched on one of the main disagreements between pure scientists, applied scientists, and critical scientists about the social relations of culture—whether or not culture can be viewed as an independent variable that affects social organization. For the critical scientist, culture is a social product that cannot be entirely divorced from the social environment. It mediates between individuals and their environment, but it cannot be composed of symbols, values, and norms that run directly counter to an individual's daily experiences.

Culture does, however, help to foster solidarity among the members of a group or in society as a whole. Cultural symbols, language, values, and norms all create a shared set of mental representations that orient the behavior of groups and individuals. Because of this function of culture, pure and applied scientists have tended to view somewhat negatively any influences that may weaken or destroy culture. Critical scientists, on the other hand, have tended to argue that weakening the dominant culture can be one way of calling into question the existing relations of domination and subordination within a society.

Contemporary critical sociologists are becoming increasingly aware of the relevance of cultural change as a necessary prerequisite for significant political or economic change. Stanley Aronowitz suggests that if American workers are to make a break with the past, then militancy or even widespread acceptance of leftist ideas will not be sufficient. "It will arise," he tells us, "out of new conditions, rooted in new social relations and in the development of a conscious opposition culture generated by the workers themselves. This culture is ... the matrix of language, arts, and political sensibility that constitutes the world outlook for an entire class. The fundamental condition for its emergence must be located among the sinews of society—not outside it." [28]

One central difficulty involved in all this, Aronowitz says, begins with the existence of "distorted" communications transmitted and received in this society. The symbols used reflect existing social divisions within the social system. These symbols are abstractions that appear to be the only basis for intellectual analysis. They are used to construct a cultural reality that seems to be fixed irrevocably and eternally. Workers, then, are tied to the existing system by the material necessities of life and by the workers' own perception of themselves in relation to the system.

> The appropriation of all culture in the service of commodity production is the distinguishing feature of late capitalism. Nearly all human activity seems to be directed toward the single end of perpetuating the production-

> *consumption cycle. . . . Culture becomes debased by advertising and finds space*
> *for even its most traditional forms only to the extent that it is "sponsored"*
> *by a commercial interest.*[29]

When culture becomes centralized and standardized, there occurs, Aronowitz notes, a curious effect on traditional regional, ethnic and other kinds of language variations that historically have distinguished various parts of the working population. Mass communications have tended to incorporate these dialect patterns into homogenized uniformity, in which old phrases lose their distinctive meaning and become incorporated into common speech patterns without the support of traditions that can add to their meaning. Private life becomes increasingly more controlled in subtle ways through standardizations in entertainment and other leisure-time activity. Developing alternate cultural values involves conscious efforts to resist the subtle "brainwashing" of unrelieved uniformity in the dominant culture.[30]

Summary

Culture is the "ought" of society. It is like a mental map that guides us in our relations to others and to our surroundings in a particular society. When people from different cultures come into contact, the result can be culture shock—profound disorientation and anxiety. The belief that one's own culture is better than others is known as ethnocentrism, while the view that each culture must be judged according to its own standards is known as cultural relativism.

Culture reflects social structure, and the function of culture is to give an orientation to individuals and groups as to how to respond to concrete situations. Culture mediates between individuals and their social environment by providing symbols, values, and norms to orient behavior.

Symbols are anything that stand for something else, and symbolic communication is what distinguishes human beings from other animals. To the extent that individuals share the same symbols and language, they are part of a common culture and are likely to respond similarly to their environment. Cultural values are widely held beliefs that some activities, relationships, or practices are important to the maintenance of the social structure. Cultural norms are specific behavior patterns people are expected to follow.

Because culture is produced and propagated within social institutions, culture is involved in the power relations of society. The dominant culture is a culture that sanctions and reinforces the dominant social structure. Many critical sociologists believe that the dominant culture in contemporary America has become so flexible that it is capable of absorbing and blunting all potential sources of opposition. Others, however, maintain that the continuing process of change in social structure will produce new sources of cultural conflict and opposition.

Subcultures contain some of the dominant symbols, values, and norms, but also contain some values and norms unique to themselves. Countercultures are subcultures that directly conflict with the major culture.

Positivist sociologists tend to reject the notion that culture simply reflects social structure, and argue that culture is independent of social structure. They identify one basic culture with any one society. Major conflicts with that culture are treated as deviance. Functionalists, in particular, conceive of deviance as an individual aberration from the normal or dominant culture, while critical sociologists argue that deviance is generated by inequalities in the social structure.

Applied sociologists have been largely unsuccessful in their efforts to change culture patterns when these changes have been unaccompanied by changes in the relevant social structure.

Critical sociologists have become increasingly more sensitive to the importance of changes in culture, perhaps as a necessary preliminary to significant changes in the social structure.

For Further Study

A good introduction to current anthropological thinking about the nature of culture is James F. Downs, *Cultures in Crisis* (Beverly Hills, Calif.: Glencoe Press, 1975). An interdisciplinary summary of positivist thinking can be found in Louis Schneider and Charles Bonjean, eds., *The Idea of Culture in the Social Sciences* (Cambridge, England: Cambridge University Press, 1973). A sociological text emphasizing the positivist view, by Leonard Broom and Philip Selznick, is *Sociology* (New York: Harper, 1973).

Probably the best-known work by a critical sociologist treating the concept of culture is by Herbert Marcuse, *One-Dimensional Man* (Boston: Beacon Press, 1964). A more recent work attempting to extend Marcuse's analysis is by Bruce Brown, *Marx, Freud, and the Critique of Everyday Life* (New York: Monthly Review Press, 1973). Norman Birnbaum has also attempted to adapt Marcuse in *Toward a Critical Sociology* (New York: Oxford University Press, 1971). In Europe, some anthropologists and sociologists have tried to merge Marcuse's emphasis on the semiautonmous role of culture in society with more orthodox Marxist perspectives. The most developed effort is that of Tullio Seppilli and Grazietta Guaitini Abbozzo, *Conceptual Scheme of a*

Theory of Culture (Perugia, Italy: Institute of Ethnology and Cultural Anthropology, 1974).

The role of symbols and language as elements of culture has been the focus of the new science of semiology, as well as of more traditional social sciences. A good example of the latter is Benjamin L. Whorf, *Language, Thought and Reality* (New York: Wiley, 1956). For the perspective of semiology, *see* Roland Barthes, *Mythologies* (New York: Hill & Wang, 1972).

There are many excellent case studies of the impact of culture on social structure. A classic study is by Ralph Linton, *The Study of Man* (New York: D. Appleton & Co., 1936). A more recent, tongue-in-cheek example is by Daniel J. Boorstin, *The Image: A Guide to Pseudo-Events in America* (New York: Harper, 1961). One of the best-known studies by a subjective sociologist is Howard Becker, *Outsiders* (New York: Free Press, 1963). A good case study by a critical sociologist is by Stanley Aronowitz, *False Promises: The Shaping of American Working-Class Consciousness* (New York: McGraw-Hill, 1973).

The debate over the "culture of poverty" is best summarized by Charles A. Valentine, *Culture and Poverty* (Chicago: University of Chicago Press, 1968). A study supporting the notion is by Daniel Patrick Moynihan, *The Negro Family: The Case for National Action* (Washington, D.C.: U.S. Department of Labor, 1965). A case study rejecting the notion is by Elliot Liebow, *Tally's Corner* (Boston: Little, Brown, 1967). For an examination of an important social problem by an applied sociologist, *see* David J. Pittman, "Drinking Patterns and Alcoholism: A Cross-Cultural Perspective," in *Alcoholism,* ed. David J. Pittman (New York: Harper, 1967).

Notes

1 See James F. Downs, *Cultures in Crisis,* (Beverly Hills, Calif.: Glencoe Press, 1975); also see Tullio Seppilli and Grazietta Guaitini Abbozzo, *Conceptual Scheme of a Theory of Culture*, (Perugia, Italy: Institute of Ethnology and Cultural Anthropology, 1974).

2 Edward Tylor, *Primitive Culture* (New York: Harper, 1871).

3 See Ralph Linton, *The Study of Man* (New York: D. Appleton & Co., 1936).

4 See Seppilli and Abbozzo, *Theory of Culture.*

5 Ibid.

6 See Edward Sapir, "Symbolism," in *Encyclopedia of Social Sciences* Vol. 14 (New York: Macmillan, 1935), pp. 492–495.

7 See Hugh Dalziel Duncan, *Communication and Social Order* (New York: Oxford University Press, 1962).

8 See Edward Sapir, "The Status of Linguistics as a Science," in *Selected Writings of Edward Sapir,* ed. Daniel D. Mandelbaum (Los Angeles: University of California Press, 1958); also see Benjamin L. Whorf, *Language, Thought, and Reality* (New York: Wiley, 1956).

9 Whorf, *Language, Thought, and Reality.*

10 See Angus Campbell, et al., *The American Voter* (New York: Wiley, 1960).

11 Daniel Yankelovich, *The Changing Values on Campus* (New York: Washington Square Press, 1972).

12 Melvin L. Kohn, *Class and Conformity* (Homewood, Ill.: Dorsey Press, 1969).

13 William Graham Sumner, *Folkways* (New York: New American Library, 1960).

14 See Norman Birnbaum, *The Crisis of Industrial Society* (New York: Oxford University Press, 1970).

15 Herbert Marcuse, *One-Dimensional Man* (Boston: Beacon Press, 1964).

16 Theodore Roszak, *Where the Wasteland Ends* (Garden City, N.Y.: Doubleday, 1972), p. 433.

17 Ibid.

18 See Milton J. Yinger, "Contraculture and Subculture," *American Sociological Review* (October,1960): 625–635.

19 For a discussion, see Raymond Williams, "Base and Superstructure in Marxist Cultural Theory," *New Left Review*, 82 (November–December, 1973): 3–16.

20 C. Wright Mills, *White Collar* (New York: Oxford University Press, 1956).

21 See Paul B. Horton and Chester L. Hunt, *Sociology,* 2d ed. (New York: McGraw-Hill, 1968), p. 63.

22 See Talcott Parsons, "Culture and Social System Revisited," in *The Idea of Culture in the Social Sciences,* eds. Louis Schneider and Charles Bonjean (Cambridge, England: Cambridge University Press, 1973).

23 Daniel Patrick Moynihan, *The Negro Family: The Case for National Action* (Washington, D.C.: U.S. Department of Labor, 1965), p. 5.

24 Ibid., p. 30.

25 Ibid., p. 47.

26 Charles A. Valentine, *Culture and Poverty* (Chicago: University of Chicago Press, 1968).

27 Elliot Liebow, *Tally's Corner* (Boston: Little, Brown, 1967).

28 Stanley Aronowitz, *False Promises: The Shaping of American Working-Class Consciousness* (New York: McGraw-Hill, paperback ed., 1974), pp. 14–15.

29 Ibid., p. 15.

30 Ibid., pp. 15–16.

Socialization

Although the dominant culture is an already-existing reality to the newborn infant, it still must be transmitted to the infant. The set of processes by which this transmission of culture occurs is called "socialization." Socialization is one of the major categories that sociologists employ to organize their concepts about society. Human beings are social creatures, and many different social institutions are involved in socialization. Unlike many other animals, human beings have few behavior patterns that are shaped exclusively by biological characteristics. They need help and direction to adapt effectively to life in society.

In saying that human beings are social animals, we do not mean to suggest that they are simply empty vessels waiting to be filled with whatever behavior patterns are demanded by society. Human beings do have biological characteristics that, in some measure, determine what they can become. Human personality and behavior are shaped by the interaction of biological characteristics and the socialization process.

Biologically Determined Behavior

It is often noted that human beings show a relative lack of instinctive behavior, as compared with other animals. Instinct refers to a complex pattern of behavior, such as nest-building by birds, for which some species are programmed biologically. Although human beings have physiological reflexes, such as eye-blinking and perspiration, it is fashionable to deny that they have biologically fixed behavior patterns comparable to nest-building. Conversely, it is often assumed that other animals behave instinctively rather than by learning.

More recent studies have opened these assumptions to question.

Scholars have confused themselves by attempts to set the brain of man on a pedestal dedicated to rationality and to dismiss the brains of other animals, including other primates, as occupants of a corral fenced by instinct. Only within the past few decades have scholars begun to recognize that all brains fit somewhere on a continuum: with instinctive patterns dominant at one end, and on the other progressively greater reliance on conditioned instincts, accumulated experience, deliberately sought knowledge, and logical or creative thought.[1]

One of the simplest forms of life is the flatworm. It has a nervous system and a brain and can learn through simple conditioning. If it is given a mild electric shock preceded by a flash of light, it learns to react to the light in anticipation of the electric shock. Beyond this, if the worm is cut in half, each half grows a new half necessary for a whole—either a head or a tail. Experiments have shown that when a conditioned worm was cut in half, the newly constructed halves responded to light in anticipation of a shock, even though they had not existed when the conditioning took place. Similarly, experimental evidence suggests that it is possible to transfer the conditioned response of one rat to another by extracting ribonucleic acid molecules from the one rat and injecting them into the other. Such findings raise the question of when a conditioned response must be treated as part of a "genetically established instinct pattern." [2]

In attempting to define a typical pattern of behavior that is characteristically and exclusively human, many theorists have referred to human beings as tool-using animals. Since nonhuman animals rely exclusively on instinct rather than on learned behavior, the argument goes, they do not use tools. The use of tools requires learning. However, numerous examples contradict this argument. For example, chimpanzees and baboons are known to use sticks for recovering honey from otherwise inaccessible hives in hollow trees. Chimpanzees also collect and trim straws or twigs with which they fish for termites by poking them into termite nests. They use crushed leaves as a sponge to soak up water or wipe dirt from their bodies. The Galapagos Islands finches manufacture probes with which to get grubs out of crevices into which their bills will not fit. They do this by holding a twig down with one foot and trimming it with their bills. The spotted woodpecker of Great Britain hacks a V-shaped crevice in the bark of trees to keep pine cones from bouncing as it pecks seeds out of them. The Javanese crab monkey uses stones as hammers. The South Pacific Coast sea otter uses stones as anvils on which to crack bivalves. Beaver dams are manufactured devices, as are beehives and the nests of wasps, birds, chimpanzees, and gorillas.[3] There are many more examples like these. The sharp distinction once made between instinctive and learned behavior has been largely abandoned by contemporary scientists.

Imprinting is a form of behavior that seems to occupy an intermediate role between learned and instinctive behavior. It has been defined as a form of learning on the part of young animals who are in the process of becoming aware of the characteristics of their parents. Recent experiments have demonstrated that young animals can learn to respond to a variety of objects, including black boxes, as if they were parents. At least one writer has, accordingly, redefined imprinting as "learning by young to respond in a filial manner to an object." [4]

The usual procedure for studying imprinting under controlled conditions is to arrange that a newly born infant not see a member of its own species, but have the opportunity to see some other object. The object may be anything from a squawking model bird to a silent black box. Ducklings can be influenced to follow a matchbox or a man. Some species follow only patterns resembling their own adults; others follow virtually any visual pattern. Imprinting can also occur with respect to sounds. For example, birds follow artificially created clucks or quacks. Experimenters have concluded that imprinting occurs quite early in life and only for a brief period. There are only a few hours of the day during which imprinting seems to occur.[5]

In some species, sexual behavior can be affected in a lasting manner during the sensitive period for imprinting. It has been reported that male ducklings forced to associate exclusively with male ducks during the imprinting period will behave homosexually in their adult life. A jackdaw reared by human beings and prevented from seeing other jackdaws becomes sexually imprinted in favor of human beings. Even if it is induced to have relations with other jackdaws, in the mating season the following year, it will court only human beings, although other jackdaws are available. Budgerigars (small Australian parrots) imprinted in favor of human beings can be induced to mate and breed in a covered cage, but at the sight of a human being both birds will start courting the human.[6]

Imprinting has been defined by four characteristics: (1) It occurs during a very brief and definite period early in the individual's life; (2) Once established, it tends to persist and, in some rare cases, seems to be irreversible; (3) Although it occurs early in life, it can affect behavior that is as yet undeveloped, such as sexual behavior and other forms of adult social behavior; and (4) It resembles a form of generalized learning, in that it is a way of responding to the broad features of a situation and only later allows finer discriminations to be made.

Some investigators think that human children become attached to other human beings in a way that is like the imprinting process in other mammals and in birds.[7] The attachment behavior in human infants seems to occur as follows:

> **1** Social responses are first called forth by a variety of stimuli. Later, they are elicited by a much narrower set of stimuli. After some months have passed, they can be evoked only by one or two particular individuals.

2 Evidence indicates a marked bias to respond socially to some kind of stimuli more than to others.

3 The more an infant interacts with a person, the stronger his or her attachment to that person becomes.

4 Learning to discriminate among different faces usually occurs after a period of intensive listening and staring. This suggests that perceptual learning plays a part in the process.

5 Most infants become attached to a preferred figure during the first year of life. There seems to be a sensitive period during the first year during which attachment behavior develops most readily.

6 The sensitive period begins at least six weeks after birth, and perhaps weeks later.

7 Starting at about six months of age, and especially after eight or nine months, babies often respond to strange persons with fear. The fear reaction is stronger than it was when they were younger. The development of attachment to a new figure becomes more and more difficult toward the end of the first year and thereafter.

8 Once a child has become strongly attached to a particular person, that person is characteristically preferred over all others. The preference tends to persist even when the child and the person have been separated.[8]

Social Interaction and Behavior

Instinctive behavior and imprinting are processes that are found, to some extent, in all animals. These processes exist at birth and result in certain general types of behavior by all infants. During the early years of life, however, these general behavioral responses are modified and take on specific forms that result from the interaction between infants and their physical and social environments. The nature and extent of interaction between infants and adults—the kind of care infants receive—is especially important in shaping their behavior in later life.

A study frequently cited to demonstrate the consequences of lack of parental care and affection was reported by Rene A. Spitz in the 1940s.[9] Spitz observed 164 infants, most of whom were being raised at one of two institutions—"nursery" and "foundling home." The other infants were raised at the homes of their own parents. Spitz reported that the children raised at "nursery" and at the homes of their parents developed in a normal fashion and made generally satisfactory adjustments to life. The children in "foundling home," however, encountered great difficulties. Despite the fact that they were being raised in an impeccably clean environment where many precautions were taken to prevent the spread of contagious disease, the children demonstrated an extreme susceptibility to infection and illness from the third month on. After a year, very few were able to walk, talk, or eat alone. None were toilet-trained. This was a sharp contrast to the children raised at home and at "nursery." These marked differences persisted in a follow-up investigation conducted for two additional years at four-month intervals.

"Nursery" was a penal institution for delinquent girls. Often these girls were pregnant at the time they were admitted. Their children were delivered in a nearby maternity hospital and were subsequently cared for in "nursery" from birth to the end of their first year. "Foundling home" was simply a foundling home. Some of the children had a background similar to those at "nursery", but many others came from socially well-adjusted mothers whose only handicap was an inability to support themselves and their children. (Spitz points out that this cannot be viewed as a sign of maladjustment.) In short, the parental background of the children in the two institutions did not favor "nursery." On the contrary, it showed a marked advantage in favor of "foundling home."

What about the conditions in the two institutions? "Nursery" provided virtually every child with one or more toys. From their glass-enclosed cubicles, the children could see trees, landscape, and sky, in addition to observing everything else going on about them. They could see other children, mothers carrying children and feeding or playing with them. At the age of six months, the children were transferred to the wards of older babies, where a number of children were together in the same room and were allowed to play with each other. "Nursery" was run by a head nurse and three assistants, whose primary job was to teach the children's mothers to take care of their children and to supervise them as they did so. If a mother was separated from her child for any reason, another mother or a pregnant girl cared for the child. Thus, each child had full-time care by its own mother or by a substitute who the head nurse felt really liked the child.

In "foundling home," bedsheets were hung over the foot and the side railing of each cot. The child lying in the cot was thus effectively screened from the world. In effect, babies lay in solitary confinement until they could stand up in bed. The only object a child could see was the ceiling. A head nurse and assistant nurses had the entire care of about forty-five babies. Although the babies might be breast-fed by their own mothers or wet nurses for the first few months, they were then moved to the single cubicles of the general ward, where they shared a nurse with at least seven other children. The babies lacked any human contact for most of the day.

Spitz thought that the two institutions were radically different with respect to mother-child relations. Since the mothers of the children at "nursery" had few other emotional outlets, they provided each child an abundant amount of motherly attention and care. "Foundling home" did not provide a mother or even a substitute mother,but simply one-eighth of a nurse. Spitz concluded that the physical and emotional experiences of infants were crucial factors in determining how they adapted to life in human society. Other studies have indicated that the importance of early parent-child interaction is not confined to humans.

Harry F. Harlow and his associates were really more interested in baby rhesus monkeys than in love of any kind.[10] They had been conducting research with these animals and, at one stage of the research, separated the infant monkeys from their mothers a few hours after birth. Bottle- fed monkeys seemed to have a lower mortality rate than breast-fed monkeys, and the experimenters were curious about this. The newborn monkeys were placed in individual cages, and a folded gauze diaper was placed on the floor of each cage. The infants became very attached to these diaper pads, and were very upset when the pads were removed for laundering. The infant monkeys seemed to behave very much like human infants who become at-tached to blankets, pillows, rag dolls, or teddy bears. This led Harlow to design a whole new series of experiments. He began by making two kinds of artificial mother dolls. One was a bare wire cylinder with a wooden head and face. The other was made in much the same way but was cushioned with terry cloth. Eight newborn monkeys were placed in individual cages, and each had equal access to a cloth or a wire mother doll. Four infants received milk from a wire mother; the other four from a cloth mother. In each case, the milk was made available through a nursing bottle whose nipple protruded from the mother's "breast."

Harlow reported that both mother dolls proved to be equivalent in physiological terms. Monkeys in both groups drank the same amount of milk and gained weight at a similar rate. But monkeys in both groups spent much more time clinging to and climbing on the cloth mothers rather than the wire mothers. Those required to get milk from the wire mothers spent no more time with them than it took to be fed; they then clung to the cloth mothers. As a matter of fact, Harlow concluded that the cloth dolls proved to be highly satisfactory mothers. They were always available for cuddling; they never scolded; they never bit in anger.

But the monkeys did not look to the cloth mothers only for love. When exposed to stressful situations, they ran to these mothers for comfort and security. The experimenters presented strange objects to the monkeys periodi-cally. One such object was a toy teddy bear, which moved forward while beating a drum. All the monkeys became terrified, and all sought reassurance from the cloth mothers. At an early stage of the experiment, an infant might run to the wire mother, but even if it did so, it would soon leave it for the one covered with cloth. After its fears had been relieved by contact with the cloth mother, a monkey would then turn and look at the teddy bear with no signs of alarm. It might, on occasion, leave the protection of the mother and approach a strange object. From time to time, other objects were placed in the cage. These included crumpled pieces of paper, wooden blocks, and doorknobs. If the cloth mother was in the room, the monkeys would almost invariably run and cling to her. Later, they would begin to examine the object. If the cloth mother was not in the cage, the monkeys would rush across the room, throw themselves face down on the floor, and scream while clutching their heads and bodies.

Other experiments conducted by Harlow indicate that infant monkeys prefer rocking mothers to those that do not move, and that those deprived of all physical contact with a mother surrogate at an early age may have difficulty in forming affectional responses in later life. Later studies by Harlow and others suggest that monkeys deprived of close contact with mothers during the first year of life grow up to be ineffective and even brutal toward their own first-born children.[11]Some evidence is also presented suggesting that heterosexual behavior in adult monkeys is heavily influenced by experiences in infancy. Thus, if infants are raised in isolation or with no interaction with other infants, they tend to encounter great difficulty in establishing satisfactory adult heterosexual relationships.

Nature Versus Nurture

As these examples suggest, the behavioral patterns found in all animals at birth take on form and substance in a process of social interaction—particularly in parent-child interaction. The question that has concerned sociologists, psychologists, and anthropologists is the extent to which distinctively human behavior is a result of biologically determined patterns, and the extent to which it is determined by social interaction. It is very difficult to answer this question, since all human beings live in society. A "scientific" answer would require us to be able to compare human infants raised in society with human infants raised in isolation from society. What would it mean to be "in isolation from society"?

Ethical principles do not allow the deliberate isolation of human infants for scientific purposes. When this occurs for other reasons, as in the case of the children studied by Spitz, it may be possible to make important observations. If a human infant were isolated from all contact with other human beings, one might be able to determine the extent to which human nature is instinctive or is due to the socialization process. But, since experiments have not been available in this area, differences of opinion continue to exist about the precise relationship between biological or inherited factors and environmental conditions. One reviewer of the available literature in this area concludes that human beings have no human nature but simply a history.

> *The fact is that human behavior does not depend on heredity to the same extent as animal behavior. The system of biological needs and functions carried by the genotype and passed on to man at birth relates him to all other living creatures rather than defines him as specifically human, and it is this very absence of predetermined characteristics which mean that man's possibilities are unlimited.*[12]

There are some well-documented cases of children who were apparently abandoned and either raised in complete isolation or in the company of animals. These children are known as feral or wolf children. Lucien Malson, a contemporary French sociologist, has reviewed in some detail the cases of three feral children about whom "one can have no serious doubts. ... They are as dependable as any reliable historical record."[13] Kingsley Davis, a distinguished contemporary American sociologist, reported two cases he has personally witnessed. What can we learn from these cases?

Kaspar of Nuremberg. Kaspar Hauser was found on May 26, 1828.[14] He had apparently been raised in complete isolation in a dark cell and was at that time apparently just short of seventeen years of age. Although he had the body of a man, his mind seemed to be at the level of a three-year-old. He could do only one thing with his hands—pick up objects with his thumb and index finger. He spent most of the day sitting on the ground with his legs stretched out in front of him. He was taken to the home of a Dr. Daumer, who began to reeducate him. After a few months, it is reported, his face lost its noticeable prognathism and acquired some symmetry. He learned to draw, climb stairs, and speak. He tended to speak of himself in the third person, and acquired the use of "I" only very slowly. During the next three years, he learned arithmetic and Latin and recalled a few details about his early life. He had lived in a "hole" or "cage" on a diet of bread and water. His daily food had been brought to him by someone he never saw—the first person he remembered—the Man. He was stabbed with a knife one day in 1833 while walking in the park and died the following day.

Amala and Kamala of Midnapore. Amala, aged one and a half, and Kamala, aged eight and a half, were found on October 9, 1920, by a Reverend Singh near the village of Codamur.[15] They were found in the company of two wolf cubs and a she-wolf in a cave. Singh took them to an orphanage he ran in Midnapore, arriving there on November 14, 1920. The skin on the hands, knees, and elbows of both children was heavily calloused. Their tongues hung out; they frequently panted and bared their teeth. For short distances they moved on their knees and elbows; for longer distances or for running they used their hands and feet. They lapped up liquids and ate in a crouching position. They snarled at human beings and, when anyone approached, arched their backs in a menacing fashion and shook their heads rapidly back and forward.

Amala, the younger one, died on September 21, 1921. Kamala died eight years later, on November 14, 1929. Reverend Singh and a Dr. Sarbadhicari kept a careful record of Kamala's development throughout her stay at the orphanage. Singh's journal indicates that she became progressively more human and, after ten months, was able to reach out her hand and take food. By February, 1922, she could kneel, and by March, she was walking on her knees. By January, 1926, she had learned to walk, and she eventually learned to drink from a glass and carry out many simple errands. Toward the end of her life, she had acquired a vocabulary of about fifty words and was able to speak with the doctors who looked after her. Malson and others have concluded that the increase in her mental faculties between the time she was found and the time of her death indicates that her original condition was due to lack of an appropriate family early in life.

Victor of Aveyron. Victor was captured by some hunters in July, 1778. He was about eleven or twelve years of age when he was noticed, playing entirely alone and naked in the woods near a small town in France. He escaped and was subsequently recaptured on January 9, 1800. He was initially diagnosed as a congenital idiot and was subsequently given to the care of Jean Itard, a senior doctor at the National Institute for the Deaf and Dumb in Paris. Itard has left two reports describing Victor's progress.

Upon initial examination, Victor seemed to be totally deaf. He could utter only a guttural and uniform sound. He seemed to be totally indifferent to smells of various kinds and seemed unable to direct his attention to anything. He imitated nothing and could not open a door or get on a chair to take food placed out of reach of his hand. All his habits seemed to bear the stamp of a wandering and solitary life and an aversion to human society. It was concluded that he had probably been abandoned at about the age of four or five but had forgotten whatever words and ideas he had acquired at that time.

In time, Victor learned to communicate his needs and exchange thoughts by pointing to words and objects. He remained unable to speak and could distinguish only some kinds of sound. But it became clear that he was no idiot, congenital or otherwise. He did have considerable difficulty in establishing satisfactory emotional relationships with members of the opposite sex. He had not learned to distinguish between the sexes, and Itard was reluctant to give him much education for fear he would try to satisfy his sexual needs as publicly as he did his other needs. Itard reports that Victor remained fundamentally selfish, although he did become responsive to gratitude and friendship and seemed to enjoy being useful. But he showed eagerness to help only when the services demanded of him were consistent with his own immediate needs. Apparently he did not develop feelings of pity or any inclination to be helpful in any selfless way.

Victor died at the age of forty. An autopsy showed no physiological reasons for his backwardness. Itard and Malson both concluded, on the basis of this case, that human beings are essentially what they have been made by the circumstances and conditions in which they find themselves—that the lessons and examples a human being requires are provided "only by his human surroundings and by the magic of his relationships with others."[16]

Anna and Isabelle. Anna and Isabelle are the two children reported by Kingsley Davis.[17] Anna was an illegitimate child whose birth displeased her grandfather. He had her locked in an upstairs room, where she received only enough care to keep her alive. She was seldom moved from one position to another; her clothing and bedding were filthy; she apparently received no training, education, or friendly attention. She was found when she was almost six years old. She could not walk, talk, or do anything to demonstrate intelligent behavior. She was believed to be deaf and possibly blind. She died about four and one-half years later, and it is not known to what level of development the socialization process could have taken her. Davis concludes that, although the socialization process did not start until Anna was six, it did a great deal toward making her a person. At the time of her death, she could behave somewhat like a normal child of two or three years of age. She could follow directions, string beads, identify several colors, build with blocks, and distinguish pictures she liked from those she did not like. She had a good sense of rhythm, played with a doll, talked mostly in phrases but could repeat words and try to carry on a conversation. She washed regularly, brushed her teeth, walked, and could run somewhat.

Isabelle was found at about the same time as Anna under very similar circumstances. She was an illegitimate child about six and a half years old, and she had been kept in isolation for the same reason. Her mother was a deaf mute, and they lived together in a dark room. Isabelle, accordingly, had no opportunity to learn speech. She could, however, communicate with her mother with the use of gestures. In lieu of speech, she made only strange croaking sounds. She appeared to be deaf, but after it had been established that she was not, the specialists who examined her pronounced her to be feeble-minded. Nevertheless, she was given a systematic training program. After a few initial difficulties, she went through the stages of learning characteristic of normal children from the ages of one through six, but much more rapidly. In a little over two months, she was using sentences; in nine months, she could identify written words and sentences. She could count to ten and retell a story after hearing it. In sixteen months, she had a vocabulary of 1,500 to 2,000 words. By the age of eight and one half, she had reached a level of educational development considered normal for her age. Her I.Q. tripled in a year and a half.

In comparing these two girls, Davis observes that, in both cases, there existed an initial very low, virtually blank intellectual level. Both girls appeared to be feeble-minded, yet both subsequently reached a much higher level. Nevertheless, Isabelle reached a normal level in two years, while Anna was still quite deficient after four and a half years. Davis suggests that the difference might be attributed to the fact that Isabelle had a more friendly relationship with her mother in infancy and also that she was apparently given much better training after she was found. It may also have been the case that Anna had less innate capacity. In any event, Davis concludes, Isabelle's case shows, as Anna's does not, that being isolated until the age of six and failing to acquire any form of speech or shared meaning with other human beings until that age does not preclude the possibility of subsequently learning to speak and becoming a normal member of society.

All of these examples show how essential contact with other humans is for the formation of characteristics we call human. In particular, these examples suggest that language and the formation of a self-concept are almost totally dependent on interaction with other people.

Theories of the Socialization Process

The research we have discussed suggests that socialization processes play a crucial role in shaping the behavior patterns of human beings. What are these processes? What are the mechanisms by which culture is transmitted to individual members of a society and internalized as part of their own personalities? Once again, sociologists of different theoretical orientations disagree about these mechanisms. Before discussing these disagreements, it is important to understand some of the major theories about socialization that lead to differences of emphasis and interpretation.

Charles Horton Cooley

Charles Horton Cooley (1864–1929), is a landmark figure in the history of American sociology. In his book, *Human Nature and Social Order,* Cooley considered the problem of what it means to be an individual.[18] A separate individual, he observes, is an abstraction rather than a directly observable object. The same is true for society. To establish a dichotomy between society and the individual is meaningless, since to do so is to convey the notion of two separate entities or forces, and this is nonsense. Related to this is the belief that individuals exist before society does. Cooley argues that this, too, is nonsense. There is no good reason for asserting that either one exists before the other.

For many people, the object called "I" is the material body of a person. But this is not the case at all. Even in common speech, "I" refers to the physical body only infrequently. More often it refers to opinions, purposes, desires, claims, and related ideas that have no direct reference to the body. Self-feeling always has its major focus within social existence rather than outside it. There is no sense of "I" without the concomitant sense of "you," "he," "she," or "they." On this subject, Cooley quoted Goethe approvingly:

> A person knows himself only in other people,
> Life alone teaches one what he is.[19]

Exactly how does this occur? Cooley invokes the concept of the *looking-glass self*. I see myself in a looking-glass; I am interested in what I see; I am pleased or displeased, depending on whether what I see corresponds to what I would like the image to be. In the looking-glass process, the child imagines another person looking at her. The child sees her own reflection by imagining what it is that the other person sees. Three things happen: (1) the child forms an image in her own mind of her appearance to the other person; (2) the child imagines how the other person judges that image; and (3) the child develops some sort of self-feeling, such as pride or mortification.[20]

It is the importance of the other person, and some notion about the values of the other person that makes the essential difference to the child's feelings. Cooley illustrates this point by suggesting that we are ashamed to seem evasive in the presence of a straightforward person, cowardly in the presence of a brave one, gross in the eyes of a refined one, and so on. The decisive consideration is not what the other person really thinks, but rather what we imagine the other person thinks.

Children study the connections between the things they do and the actions of other persons. That is, they learn to perceive the power they have over others. They take over the visible acts of parents, nurses, or others over whom they find that they have some control, much as they take control over their own limbs or toys. They then experiment with the different things they do with others. Tugging at a mother's skirt, wriggling, gurgling, stretching out one's arms—all these become ways one can get others to react. Like a more experienced scientist, the child learns that different persons are affected by different things. Some are affected by tears, others by smiles or even punches. This entire process moves from the naive to the subtle. Initially, the children do things simply for effect; later they try to hide their actions by simulating such attitudes as affection, indifference, or contempt. Overly obvious efforts to obtain favorable reactions ultimately are perceived by the child as being inappropriate and leading to unfavorable consequences.[21]

George Herbert Mead

George Herbert Mead (1863–1931) agreed that the self is something different from the physiological organism.[22] He emphasized that the self is something that develops, and that it is not initially present at birth. It develops as a result of a person's relation to other persons and to social experience as a whole. Many things that happen to people do not involve the self. Experiences that are completely sensual or habitual do not necessarily involve the self. The body can be present and even operate in an intelligent fashion without the self. This is the kind of behavior engaged in by animals other than human beings. Each part of the body is completely distinguishable from the self, and individual parts of the body can be lost without losing any significant part of the self.

The distinguishing feature, Mead emphasized, is that the self is an object to itself. "Self" is a reflexive, which means that it can be both an object and a subject. This makes it different from other objects. Historically, this difference has been noted by referring to consciousness—an experience with or of one's self. But the basic problem of understanding the self or self-consciousness is the problem of understanding how people can get outside of themselves and experience things in a way that allows them to become an object to themselves. This is a social process, according to Mead. To accept Mead's thought on this subject, or Cooley's, is to reject a long line of fashionable metaphysical speculation. Traditionally, human society and social organization have been seen as something imposed on the ready-made individual.

The Generalized Other. Although Mead admired much of Cooley's work, he was critical of the concept of a "looking-glass self."[23] Mead thought that this concept was too physical. He saw Cooley's analysis as an "affair of consciousness." Other people exist only in a person's imagination, and it is only in the imaginations of others that the person is affected. Mead called his own approach "social behaviorism." This term is used to refer to descriptions of behavior at the distinctively human level. Its basic datum is the social act. "For Mead, both the content and the very existence of distinctively human behavior are accountable only on a social basis."[24]

According to Mead, the development of the self proceeds through three stages:

> **1** *A preparatory stage* (age about 2–4). **During this period, infants engage in meaningless imitation of the acts of persons in their immediate environment, without understanding what the behavior means. For exam-**

ple, they may read a newspaper, smoke a pipe, or powder their noses. The child is on the verge of placing himself or herself in the position of other persons and doing what they do.

2 *A play stage* (age about 5–6). Here, the child starts to play the role of mother, father, teacher, clerk, physician, and so on. It is thus possible for children to examine themselves reflexively in each of these roles and refer to themselves in the third person. This represents the early formation of a self, but it is still fragmented. Children make many separate objects of themselves and have no unified conception of what they are as complete persons.

3 *A game stage* (age about 8–9). Children find themselves in situations where they must respond to the expectations of several different people simultaneously. For example, in the game of baseball, each player must understand the expectations of several other players. Previously, it was necessary for a child to internalize only the expectations of important individual others; they now must construct a "generalized other"—"a generalized role or standpoint from which they view themselves and their behavior."[25]

Having constructed the generalized other, children behave in an integrated fashion. They can see themselves consistently, even if they find persons who see them differently than they see themselves.

The "I" and the "Me." The self is in a sense contradictory. On the one hand, it is spontaneous, creative, and unprogrammed. It is free to do anything it wishes. That is its truly human aspect. On the other hand, however, there is a part of the self that has developed from the reaction of other persons; it has become essentially programmed, predictable, and preestablished. It is the first part that Mead calls the "I," the second part is the "me."

> It is because of the "I" that we say that we are never fully aware of what we are, that we surprise ourselves by our own action. It is as we act that we are aware of ourselves... The "I" is the response of the organism to the attitudes of others: the "me" is the organized set of attitudes of others which one himself assumes. The attitudes of the others constitute the organized "me." [26]

Before the development of the generalized other, there is really no distinction between the "I" and the "me." The generalized other gives the individual, "me," an awareness of self. It is based on the attitudes and expectations of the others to whom the "I" responds. It is the "I" that does the responding. The response that "I" makes is not previously determined or specified. "I" may not even know exactly what "I" will do under any given set of circumstances.

The "I" is something that is never entirely calculable . . . the "I" is always some-thing different from what the situation itself calls for . . . The "I" both calls out the "me" and responds to it. Taken together they constitute a personality as it appears in social experience.[27]

The Oversocialized Conception of Man

Mead's distinction between the "I" and the "me" provides us with a shorthand way of examining the extent to which human beings have been socialized. A classic article by sociologist Dennis H. Wrong points out that socialization may mean two quite distinct things: (1) transmitting to an individual the culture they entered when they were born, and (2) acquiring distinctively human attributes by interacting with others.[28] When these two are confused, "an oversocialized view of man is the result." Despite socialization, human beings are not completely molded by the values and customs of the society in which they grow up. Even when they know what society expects, human beings do not necessarily conform. People frequently do not try to please others by conforming to their expectations. Wrong insists that we remember the "I" while trying to understand the process by which the "me" comes into existence.

Sigmund Freud

Sigmund Freud (1856–1939) was a physician who was primarily concerned with helping his patients become well. His socialization theories were devel-oped on the basis of observations he made in the course of his efforts to treat patients. He was thus quite different from the other theorists we have mentioned. He developed a theory of socialization to explain his therapeutic procedures. Perhaps the most fundamental premise of psychoanalysis is the assumption that it is possible to make a distinction between conscious and unconscious mental processes. Conscious states are characteristically very transitory. An idea that is conscious at one moment may not be so a moment later, and it may then reappear. What happens to it during the interval when it is not conscious? Freud suggests that it is latent—that is, capable of becoming conscious at any time—or we may simply say that it is unconscious.[29]

Freud observed that some ideas or mental processes seem to exist and have all the effects of ordinary ideas, while remaining unconscious. Some force seems to oppose them and keep them from becoming conscious. Freud saw psychoanalysis as a means for making these ideas conscious. The state in which these ideas exist before becoming conscious he called "repression"; the force that starts and maintains the repression is "resistance." Freud felt that, for each person, there exists an integrated organization of mental processes called the "ego." Consciousness is attached to the ego, which supervises its own processes. It is the ego that goes to sleep at night, although it is also the agency that censors dreams, and it is the source of repressions. In working out the implications of these ideas, Freud introduced some new terms to describe the processes involved.

The term "id" in some ways replaces the former notion of the unconscious. It is

> the dark, inaccessible part of our personality . . . a chaos, a cauldron full of seething excitations. . . . It is filled with energy reaching it from the instincts, but it has no organization, produces no collective will, but only a striving to bring about the satisfaction of the instinctual needs subject to the observance of the pleasure principle.[30]

The id is no respector of conventional laws of logic or physics. It does not recognize the passage of time and is completely indifferent to moral considerations. It makes no value judgments and does not distinguish between good and evil.

The ego is the part of the id that has been modified by the influence of the external world. It tries to substitute the reality principle for the pleasure principle, which operates freely in the id.

> The ego represents what may be called reason and common sense, in contrast to the id, which contains the passions . . . its relation to the id is like a man on horseback who has to hold in check the superior strength of the horse.[31]

It is the task of the ego to represent the external world to the id. Freud compared its relation to the id with that of a rider to a horse. The horse supplies the energy, but it is the rider who must decide upon the goal and who must assume responsibility for guiding the horse's movements. Frequently, however, the ego must guide the id along the path it wants to take.[32]

The "superego" is the moral component of the self. It develops as a result of the socialization process during which children adopt their parents' notions of good, evil, and conscience. By adopting the moral standards of their parents, children replace parental authority with their own. The basis of the process of developing a superego is called "identification." The child's ego assimilates that of the parent, behaves like the parent in some ways, imitates the parent, and, in effect, absorbs the parent.[33] The superego observes the self and acts as its conscience. It is continually opposed by the id, which would have the self indulge in uninhibited pleasure-seeking. The ego mediates the id-superego conflict and tries to find a path for the self that is possible and satisfactory, given the reality in which it finds itself.

Although Freud's "superego" seems to resemble Mead's "me," in the sense that both represent the wishes of society, there are important differences in the concepts of these two authors. The superego is seen as battling a repressive, pleasure-seeking, and almost blindly biological id. Mead's "me," on the other hand, is a force providing necessary direction, often of a gratifying nature, to the "I." As one writer has put it, "Freud views the Id and the Superego as locked in combat upon the battleground of the Ego; Mead sees the 'I' and 'me' engaged in close collaboration."[34] This difference in perspective may be a result of the different concerns of these two thinkers. Freud's interest in the socialization process and the self stemmed from his concern with tension, anxiety, and abnormal behavior. Mead was primarily concerned with understanding the nature of behavior; his interest did not arise out of clinical concerns.

Operant Conditioning and Social Exchange Theory

Imagine, a young, untutored pigeon in a laboratory cage. The pigeon is born with a tendency to peck, and it pecks its way about the cage to explore its environment. At some point, it pecks a round red object and finds that it immediately receives some grain that can be eaten. For B. F. Skinner, George Caspar Homans, and others, "the pigeon's behavior in pecking the target is an operant; and the pigeon has undergone operant conditioning."[35]

Actually, to get closer to everyday language, Homans calls any particular sort of learned behavior, like pecking at the red object, an activity. Among other things he is interested in the "variables that determine the rate of emission of an activity."[36] There are two main kinds of such variables: (1) the state of the animal (how hungry the pigeon is): and (2) the rate of reinforcement (how frequently the pigeon is given food after pecking the object).[37]

Homans sees social behavior as an exchange of activity between two or more persons. This exchange may be more or less rewarding or costly, and the activity may be either tangible or intangible. This concept is derived from behavioral psychology and elementary economics. Both of these disciplines see human behavior as a function of its payoff. The amount and kind of behavior that occurs depends upon the amount and kind of reward and punishment it summons. When behavior summons the behavior of another person (which is determined in the same way), the behavior becomes social.[38]

Since behavioral psychology uses a set of propositions derived mostly from studies of animals in nonsocial situations, it must be extended and adapted to apply to the behavior of human beings in social situations. In these situations, the behavior of one person affects and is affected by the behavior of another person. Elementary economics is a set of propositions purporting to describe the behavior of human beings in a perfect market, where what one buyer or seller does has virtually no effect on market price.

Operant conditioning and social exchange theory both view the socialization process as a series of exchanges between parents or other persons and children. The nature of the reinforcements used in relation to the operant or activity are subject to study. Within this framework, the self is a "repertoire of behavior appropriate to a given set of contingencies." [39] Thus, what is known as the "self" arises from the contingencies responsible for the behavior (contingencies refer to the environment and how it rewards behavior).

> *Two or more repertoires generated by different sets of contingencies compose two or more selves. A person possesses one repertoire appropriate to his life with his family, and a friend may find him a very different person. . . . The problem of identity arises when situations are intermingled as when a person finds himself with both his family and his friends at the same time.*[40]

Phenomenology and Socialization

As mentioned in chapter 9, subjective theories tend to emphasize the socialization process. Because these theories view interaction as the crucial process shaping social structure and culture, socialization processes are seen as the critical factor. The theories of Cooley and Mead, in particular, have provided a starting point for applying phenomenological perspectives to the study of socialization.

The phenomenological perspective on socialization emphasizes the lifelong nature of the process. The self is viewed as dynamic and changing. Although childhood experiences are undoubtedly the most crucial ones in determining the direction taken by individuals, socialization continues in later life through peer group experiences and other types of interaction. Many contemporary encounter groups and other forms of therapy represent attempts at adult socialization. Such efforts seek to convince individuals to reject their old selves and to replace them with new, and presumably healthier ones.[41]

One example of the importance of socialization to the full development of human capacities is provided by the Frank Porter Graham Child Development Center at the University of North Carolina in Chapel Hill. The center opened a day care service in 1966 to provide comprehensive services to selected groups of infants and very young children.[42] It was planned as a pilot facility that would ultimately provide "optimal" socialization experiences and care for many children. Eleven children admitted in 1966 and twenty enrolled during 1967 and 1968 were studied under controlled conditions.

Two separate control groups of infants with similar backgrounds and other characteristics were studied and tested.

Results of the study suggest that the infants who received the enriched group care at the center performed much better on intelligence test scores than did the infants in the control groups. Black children in the control groups who came from primarily poor families had an average I.Q. score of 77.6 on the Peabody Picture Vocabulary Test. Black children from similar backgrounds who participated in the center program had an average score of 107.4 on the same test. When the Stanford-Binet I.Q. test was used, the same control group of children had an average score of 86.1, while the same children in the center program had an average of 119.7.

It was not possible to tell from this study whether the crucial difference was the day care program, the educational program, or the health program. What it did show was that a comprehensive program including all three elements seemed to have dramatic consequences for the socialization and development of the children.

Positivism and Socialization

Since socialization processes involve the mechanisms that directly link individual behavior to social structure and culture, they lend themselves to applied sociology in a more immediate way than do the other basic categories of social relationships. Positivist sociologists have attempted to apply socialization theories to child-rearing practices and to various forms of behavior modification. Two examples illustrate their approach.

Autistic Children

Operant conditioning and social exchange theory have been applied to the treatment of autism. Infantile autism has been described as a form of schizophrenia affecting children by making them appear to be completely absorbed with themselves, uninterested in other human beings and "unreachable in a shell of their own."[43] Sociologist Robert Hamblin and his associates, influenced by operant conditioning and exchange theories, attempted to change the behavior of children affected by this disorder. Their work was based on the assumption that autism was a result of faulty socialization practices and could be affected through the use of appropriate reinforcement.

Autistic children treated in their laboratories had a variety of symptoms. They engaged in:

ritualized hand motions, stereotyped positions, repetitive noise making, rocking, stereotyped dancing, indiscriminate mouthing of objects, unusual eye movements, bizarre food preferences, drooling, sniffing, dry-eyed crying, creepy touching, lining up subjects, spinning objects, irrelevant laughing or smiling and such self-injurious practices as hand biting and head banging.[44]

These behavior patterns were viewed by the sociologists as attention-getting devices and as a means of trying to obtain "illicit" attention. Efforts were made to have the children give up these behaviors and instead use normal attention-getting patterns. A child was rewarded with a bite of food when instructions were followed. These instructions might include orders to fit a piece into a puzzle, look directly at the teacher's eye, or say something. In addition to food, other means of rewarding behavior were used, including the use of tokens that the children could exchange for desired food. Hamblin and his associates developed a program of eight stages of planned development, after which autistic children should reach a normal level of development for their age levels.[45]

Operation Head Start

In 1965 the United States federal government began a program designed to modify the socialization of economically disadvantaged children. A national planning committee had reported to the Office of Economic Opportunity that there is considerable evidence that the early years of childhood are the most critical in the poverty cycle. During these years, development occurs at a very rapid rate. For the children of poverty, there are obvious deficiencies which lay the foundation for a pattern of failure—and thus a pattern of poverty—throughout their lives.[46]

The federal antipoverty program then launched Operation Head Start, which provided most of the financing for a large number of child development centers around the country. These centers were intended to improve the health and physical condition of children of poor families, increase their self-confidence and ability to relate to others, increase their verbal and conceptual skills, encourage parents to engage in activities with their children, and provide various social services to the families of these children.

Years later, Head Start remained a controversial program. Some specialists pointed to the unfavorable experiences with institutional care of children reported by Spitz and others, and insisted that day care centers would be detrimental for young children. It was argued that, if the mothers of these children had to work because of economic distress, then the solution would be to make it unnecessary for mothers to work, presumably by giving them direct economic support.[47]

One major evaluation of the Head Start program was made by the Westinghouse Learning Corporation and Ohio University.[48] Former Head Start children, then in the first, second, and third grades of school, were tested on a series of cognitive and affective measures. Their scores were compared with those of a control group. This *ex post facto* design was opposed by many Head Start administrators, who felt that a longitudinal study would be more desirable from a methodological point of view. But the *ex post facto* design would give answers within a year, while a longitudinal study would take many years to complete. The study was also criticized because of the alleged weakness of available test instruments and the failure to include such other Head Start goals as health, nutrition, and community involvement. Nevertheless, the study was carried out quietly, beginning in June, 1968, the third year of the Head Start program. President Nixon was preparing a major address on the poverty program—an address that would include a discussion of the Head Start program. White House aids inquired about the study and were alerted to the fact that the results seemed to indicate that no significant differences existed between the Head Start children and the control group children. In his Economic Opportunity Message to Congress on February 19, 1969, President Nixon referred to the study and stated that the long-term effect of the Head Start program appeared to be extremely weak.

This announcement led to a nation-wide controversy. The researchers were greatly embarrassed because their very tentative findings had been used as the basis for a presidential pronouncement. However, the final report, issued the following June, seemed to confirm the preliminary findings.

Critical Perspectives on Socialization

Although phenomenological theorists draw heavily on the work of George Herbert Mead, and positivist sociologists point to Mead's description of himself as a "social behaviorist" as evidence that he shared their perspective, critical sociologists dispute these claims. In their view, Mead was a dialectical theorist. The traditional separation of phenomena into mind and physical nature was not a distinction Mead could accept. He saw the individual as a sensitive, social being who constructed the environment, just as the natural and social environment constructed the individual.

Critical sociologists maintain that Mead saw a dialectical relation between persons and the world in which they live. Thus, he did not see the past as inevitably and rigidly determining the future. The past determines human action only to the extent that human beings select from the past as they prepare for the future. Individuals do not simply acquire a consciousness of what objectively exists in the environment, but rather they select and construct their environment.

While positivists focus on childhood socialization as an essentially independent and self-contained process, critical sociologists focus on the close relationship between childhood socialization and other aspects of social structure. In American society, for example, childhood socialization in the family follows one or the other of two broad modes.[49] One pattern is oriented toward obedience and is referred to as repressive or conformist socialization. The other is oriented toward independence and is referred to as permissive or self-directed socialization. Repressive socialization emphasizes the punishment of wrong behavior; permissive socialization emphasizes the reward and encouragement of good behavior. Participatory socialization attempts to leave children relatively unsupervised and encourages them to make decisions on their own; repressive socialization involves close supervision and encourages exact obedience to very specific rules.

There is evidence that the mode of childhood socialization has important consequences for later life. Carmi Schooler has found that children raised by participatory socialization resist strong authority in later years and are capable of dealing with very complex and ambiguous situations. Children raised by repressive socialization, on the other hand, value authority and feel uncomfortable with ambiguous situations.[50]

Participatory and repressive socialization modes tend to correspond to different kinds of family organization. In working-class families, sex roles tend to be sharply defined. The father is the breadwinner, and the mother is the housekeeper. Socialization consists largely of teaching traditional roles and conveying traditional expectations to the child.[51] Middle-class families are more likely to undertake joint activities, and their goals are more varied and changing. Melvin Kohn has found that the values of conformity or self-direction that parents use to socialize their children are the values that the fathers receive at their workplaces.[52] This suggests, as critical scientists have argued, that social class is a powerful structural factor affecting both culture and socialization in important ways. Indeed, some studies have argued that the New Left of the 1960s can be understood partly as a consequence of changing socialization processes which were a response to changes in the class structure of American society.[53]

If socialization is a process through which culture is transmitted to a new member of the society or, conversely, the means through which a new member assimilates a culture, it is reasonable to inquire into the characteristics of the culture and its suitability for new members as well as for existing members.[54] If the culture violates some fundamental characteristics or tendencies of human beings, then serious difficulties can arise. If the culture is fundamentally incompatible with a satisfactory human existence, then we can predict widespread disaffection and even revolt. If this were the case, it might be necessary to make fundamental changes in a society and its culture in order for young people to grow up effectively. Simply changing socialization techniques would not be sufficient.

In his classic study *Culture Against Man,* Jules Henry concluded that it is necessary to distinguish between the culture of life and the culture of death in contemporary Western society. For most people, he felt, the term "science" has become synonymous with destructive systems—that is, with death. Many people associate nuclear energy with destruction, but the culture of death includes much more than the work of mathematicians, physicists, and chemists. Biologists and physicians, Henry observed, engage in research related to biological warfare. Sociologists and anthropologists engage in systems analyses involving the integration of weapons, radar systems, people and machines, as well as in other studies involving such problems as the makeup of bombing crews. Economists work on global strategies for economic warfare as well as military logistics and the economics of weapons and contract allocations. Perhaps half of the American scientific talent, he estimated, constitutes the "well-fed, comfortably-housed culture of death." [55]

And the culture of life? It resides

> in all those people who, inarticulate, frightened and confused, are wondering "where it will all end." ... The forces of death are confident and organized while the forces of life—the people who long for peace—are for the most part scattered, inarticulate and wooly-minded, overwhelmed by their own impotence.[56]

What is the young parent to do? Does one socialize one's children to participate in the culture of life or the culture of death? And what does the child do who might prefer one, but is destined to be socialized for participation in the other?

One outcome of this dilemma is a socialization process that produces marginal persons.[57] This is a person who must live in two cultures that are not only different, but antagonistic. Children of immigrants, for example, are socialized to their parents' culture at home but are exposed to a different set of values in the dominant culture of the society in which they live. The very notion of a dominant culture implies that there exist other cultures that are not dominant. Cultural differences characteristically reflect differences in rewards and opportunities. In contemporary American society, certain socialization practices serve to channel nonwhites and women into roles that are subordinate to those of whites and men.

Not only does the dominant culture encourage socialization leading to inferior roles for some people, but the people occupying inferior positions often learn to accept their inferiority as natural, thus reinforcing the dominant culture in their own patterns of socialization. A mother who prepares her daughter for a good marriage rather than for a good occupation or profession, believes that she is doing what is best for her child, but she is helping prepare her daughter for a lifetime of dependency. For many years before the civil rights movement of the 1960s, black parents encouraged their children to avoid encounters with whites, in order to avoid exposure to prejudice. These children received little encouragement to challenge expressions of racial prejudice. The long-term effects of prejudice can have a destructive effect on the self-esteem and self-confidence of minority group children. Many studies have documented wide differences in levels of aspiration between Mexican-American or black minority groups, and women on the one hand, and white Anglo-Saxon males on the other. Other studies suggest that the cumulative effect of discriminatory socialization is manifest in a lack of orientation toward problem-solving, lack of self-esteem, and low aspiration, all of which combine to adversely affect learning and performance. In short, the problem of socialization is much broader than the selection of appropriate techniques for inducting the young into an ongoing society. There are serious questions about the very nature of society and the culture patterns that are to be transmitted.

Tribesmen reproduce, through their daily activities, not simply a group of human beings; they reproduce a tribe.[58] What tribesmen do is not a consequence of the natural characteristics of newborn persons in the tribe; it is a result of a socialization process. The tribe is a specific social form within which a particular group of human beings engages in specific activities in a specific manner. Similarly, slavery is a specific social form to which people in a given society submit only under particular material and historical conditions, although it may appear to persons living within that society that the master-slave relationship is natural and eternal.

The examples of tribesmen and slaves, it has been suggested, help us understand how wage-workers reproduce the people, social relations, and ideas of modern industrial society.[59] We are reminded that the capitalist system is "neither the natural nor the final form of human society; like the earlier social forms, capitalism is a specific response to material and historical conditions." [60]

The socialization process must be understood as a requirement of the dominant culture. Producing new commodities, opening new markets, and creating new workers are seen as three aspects of the same activity. Workers are not paid the full value of what they produce; the remainder is retained by employers.

A new labor force is created precisely in order to produce new commodities; the wages received by these laborers are themselves the new market; their unpaid labor is the source of new expansion. ... However, capital is not a natural force; it is a set of activities performed by people every day; it is a form of daily life; its continued existence and expansion presuppose only one essential condition: the disposition of people to continue to alienate their working lives and thus reproduce the capitalist form of daily life.[61]

Toward a Critical Synthesis

Professor Irving Zeitlin has provided the outlines of a synthesis of the theoretical orientations of Marx, Mead and Freud.[62] He observes that, although Mead is critical of socialization practices, he gives no sustained attention to the problems of domination and coercion. He does not consider the price an individual pays for the socialization process. Furthermore, since Mead was not primarily concerned with social structure, his conception of society seems to be somewhat naive politically. He sometimes leaves the impression that society can solve its problems with improved technology and methods of communication.

Zeitlin observes that we learn much about the concept of domination from Marx and about the concept of repression from Freud. Although Freud saw an insoluble antagonism between the individual and civilization, there was a violent reaction to his pessimism on the part of such neo-Freudians as Erich Fromm, Karen Horney, and Harry Stack Sullivan. These writers argued that the ego does not face an abstract, unchanging civilization, but a social world constantly in the process of change. Since Freud did not make this clear, they felt that his analysis was unnecessarily conservative. Herbert Marcuse, however, argued that the neo-Freudians were in error. He insisted upon the validity of Freud's fundamental proposition that all historical forms of the reality principle involve the repression of human instincts. There may always be a degree of human resistance to prevailing roles, relationships, and institutions. While these structures determine what a person will be, the converse is also true. Human beings determine and shape their own destiny.

Summary

Socialization refers to the set of processes by which a dominant culture is transmitted to an infant. From the perspective of the infant, it refers to the set of processes through which this culture is absorbed. In this sense, socialization is learned behavior. Instinctive behavior refers to a complex pattern of behavior, such as nest-building in birds, for which some species are programmed biologically. Imprinting is a form of behavior occupying an intermediate position between learned and instinctive behavior. Instinctive behavior and imprinting are processes found to some extent in all animals, including human beings.

Among the significant theorists of the socialization process are Charles Horton Cooley, who developed the theory of the "looking-glass self"; George Herbert Mead, who wrote about the "generalized other," the "I" and the "Me," and preparatory, play and game stages in the development of self; Sigmund Freud, who developed the concepts of ego, id, and superego; B. F. Skinner, who experimented in operant conditioning; and George Homans, who developed a social exchange theory. From a critical perspective, the socialization process can be seen as a requirement of the dominant culture.

Professor Irving Zeitlin, a critical social theorist, has provided the outlines of a synthesis of the theoretical orientations of Marx, Mead, and Freud. He sees Mead as a dialectical thinker who, while critical of socialization practices, gives no sustained attention to problems of domination and coercion. Marx tells us much about the former concept and Freud about the latter, Zeitlin notes.

It may well be the case that the individual can never be totally socialized. There is always a degree of human resistance to social pressure. These shape the individual, but they are, in turn, shaped by individual human beings.

For Further Study

For a good summary of the similarities and differences between humans and other animals, see W. H. Thorpe, *Animal Nature and Human Nature* (New York: Doubleday, 1974). James Downs also focuses on such differences in *Cultures in Crisis* (New York: Glencoe Press, 1971). The significance of feral children for our understanding of human nature has most recently been discussed by Lucien Malson and Jean-Marc Gaspard in *Wolf Children and the Problem of Human Nature* (New York: Monthly Review Press, 1972).

A classic symbolic interactionist view of socialization is presented by Erving Goffman in *The Presentation of Self in Everyday Life* (New York: Doubleday, 1959). For several interesting and valuable articles on socialization written from a phenomenological perspective, see Jack D. Douglas, *Understanding Everyday Life* (Chicago: Aldine, 1970). A nonsociological formulation of the positivist position is B. F. Skinner's *Beyond Freedom and Dignity* (New York: Knopf, 1971). Skinner has had enormous influence on positivist sociologists. You may also wish to look at Skinner's *About Behaviorism* (New York: Knopf, 1974). A good example of how the functionalist perspective has been applied to the study of family socialization can be found in Marion J. Levy's *The Structure of Society* (Princeton: Princeton University Press, 1952).

For an excellent discussion of how language influences both thought and behavior, see Basil Bernstein's *Class, Codes and Control: Theoretical Studies toward a Sociology of Language* (New York: Schocken, 1975). The most sophisticated empirical support for the critical perspective on socialization comes from Melvin C. Kohn's national and comparative studies of the relationship between class and child-rearing values. These were reported in *Class and Conformity: A Study of Values* (Homewood, Ill.: Dorsey Press, 1969). A number of recent studies of family socialization and sex role conflict are reported in *Family, Marriage, and the Struggle of the Sexes,* ed. Hans Peter Dreitzel (New York: Macmillan, 1972). For a discussion of occupational socialization, see Ronald M. Pavalko, *Sociology of Occupations and Professions* (Itasca, Ill.: F. E. Peacock, 1971), pp. 80–109.

For an interesting critical view of repression—"a process by which those in power try to keep themselves in power by consciously attempting to destroy or render harmless organizations and ideologies that threaten their power," see Alan Wolfe, *The Seamy Side of Democracy: Repression in America* (New York: David McKay, 1974). Finally, everyone should read Jules Henry's posthumously published masterpiece *Pathways to Madness* (New York: Vintage Books, 1973). "This book," Henry writes in his preface, "is written for children. I hope it will help reduce the misery in their lives; and I hope some parents, because they have read it, will be able to save themselves some suffering by avoiding some mistakes with their children. Some may be made aware that usually we do not know what we are doing to them."

Notes

1 George A. Pettit, *Prisoners of Culture* (New York: Scribner's, 1970), pp. 18–19.

2 Ibid., pp. 19–20.

3 Ibid., pp. 21–22.

4 S. A. Barnett, *Instinct and Intelligence: Behavior of Animals and Man* (Englewood Cliffs, N.J.: Prentice-Hall, 1967), p. 135.

5 Ibid., pp. 135–36.

6 Hans Hass, *The Human Animal* (New York: Putnam's, 1970), p. 64.

7 W. H. Thorpe, *Animal Nature and Human Nature* (Garden City, N.Y.: Anchor Press/Doubleday, 1974), p. 228.

8 Ibid., pp. 240–41.

9 Rene A. Spitz, "Hospitalism: An Inquiry into the Genesis of Psychiatric Conditions in Early Childhood," in *The Competent Infant: Research and Commentary,* eds. L. Joseph Stone, Henrietta T. Smith, and Lois B. Murphy (New York: Basic Books, 1973), pp. 775–86.

10 Harry F. Harlow, "Love in Infant Monkeys," *Scientific American* 200 (June, 1959): 68–74.

11 Harry F. Harlow, and Margaret K. Harlow, "The Affectional Systems," in *Behavior of Nonhuman Primates,* vol. 2, eds. Allan M. Schrier, Harry F. Harlow, and Fred Stollnitz (New York and London: Academic Press, 1965), pp. 287–334.

12 Lucien Maison, *Wolf Children and the Problem of Human Nature* (New York and London: Monthly Review Press, 1972), p. 10.

13 Ibid., p. 54

14 Ibid., pp. 63–67.

15 Ibid., pp. 68–71.

16 Ibid., p. 80.

17 Kingsley Davis, "Extreme Social Isolation of a Child," *American Journal of Sociology* 45 (January, 1940): 554–64; Kingsley Davis, "Final Note on a Case of Extreme Isolation," *American Journal of Sociology* 50 (March, 1947): 432–37. A condensed version has been prepared by David T. Spears, *Human Society* (New York: Macmillan, 1965), pp. 204–208.

18 Charles Horton Cooley, *Human Nature and the Social Order* (New York: Scribner's, 1902).

19 Ibid., p. 150. (Goethe, *Tasso*, Act 2, Scene 3.)

20 Ibid., p. 152.

21 Ibid., p. 168.

22 George Herbert Mead, *Mind, Self and Society,* ed. Charles W. Morris (Chicago: University of Chicago Press, 1934), pp. 135–226.

23 George Herbert Mead, "Cooley's Contribution to American Social Thought," in *George Herbert Mead on Social Psychology,* ed. Anselm Strauss (Chicago and London: Phoenix Books, The University of Chicago Press, 1964), pp. 293–307.

24 Bernard N. Meltzer, "Mead's Social Psychology," in *Symbolic Interaction,* eds. Jerome G. Manis and Bernard N. Meltzer (Boston: Allyn & Bacon, 1967), p. 6.

25 Ibid., p. 11.

26 Mead, *Mind, Self and Society,* pp. 174–79.

27 Ibid., pp. 176–78.

28 Dennis H. Wrong, "The Oversocialized Conception of Man in Modern Sociology," *American Sociological Review* 26 (April, 1961): 183–93.

29 Sigmund Freud, *The Ego and the Id,* rev. and ed. James Strachey, trans. Joan Riviere (New York: Norton, 1960), p. 4.

30 Sigmund Freud, *New Introductory Lectures on Psychoanalysis,* trans. James Strachey (New York: Norton, 1964), p. 73.

31 Freud, *The Ego and the Id,* p. 15.

32 Freud, *New Introductory Lectures,* p. 77.

33 Ibid., p. 63.

34 Meltzer, "Mead's Social Psychology," p. 12.

35 George Caspar Homans, *Social Behavior: Its Elementary Forms* (New York: Harcourt, 1961), p. 18.

36 Ibid., p. 19.

37 Ibid., pp. 19–20.

38 Ibid., p. 13. Also *see* G. C. Homans, "Human Behavior as Exchange," *American Journal of Sociology* 63 (May, 1958): pp. 597–606 for Homans' original statement on this subject.

39 B. F. Skinner, *Beyond Freedom and Dignity* (New York: Knopf, 1971), p. 199.

40 Ibid., p. 199.

41 Kurt W. Back, *Beyond Words* (New York: Russell Sage Foundation, 1972).

42 Albert B. Robinson, and Nancy M. Robinson, "Longitudinal Development of Very Young Children in a Comprehensive Day Care Program: The First Two Years," in Erwin Flaxman, ed., *Educating the Disadvantaged* (New York: AMS Press, 1973), pp. 133–142.

43 Robert L. Hamblin, David Buckholdt, Daniel Ferritor, Martin Kozloff, and Lois Blackwell, *The Humanization Processes: A Social, Behavioral Analysis of Children's Problems* (New York: Wiley, 1971), pp. 136–37.

44 Ibid., p. 138.

45 Ibid., pp. 163–216.

46 Edwin Knoll, "Hasty 'Landmark,'" *Southern Education Report* (September–October, 1965): 3.

47 "Joint hearing before the Subcommittee on Children and Youth and the Subcommittee on Employment, Manpower, and Poverty," Committee on Labor and Public Welfare, United States Senate, Ninety-second Congress (Washington, D.C.: Government Printing Office, 1972).

48 Walter Williams and John Evans, "The Politics of Evaluation," in Peter H. Rossi and Walter Williams, eds., *Evaluating Social Programs* (New York and London: Seminar Press, 1972), pp. 247–64.

49 Urie Bronfenbrenner, "Socialization and Social Class through Time and Space," in E. E. Maccoby, J. M. Newcomb, and E. L. Hartley, eds., *Readings in Social Psychology* (New York: Holt, 1958); *see also* Melvin L. Kohn, *Class and Conformity: A Study in Values* (Homewood, Ill.: Dorsey Press, 1969).

50 Carmi Schooler, "Social Antecedents of Adult Psychological Functioning," *American Journal of Sociology* 78 (September, 1972): 299–322.

51 Mirra Komarovsky, *Blue Collar Marriage* (New York: Random House, 1962).

52 Melvin Kohn, *Class and Conformity; see also*, Melvin L. Kohn and Carmi Schooler, "Occupational Experience and Psychological Functioning: An Assessment of Reciprocal Effects," *American Sociological Review* 38 (February, 1973): 97–118.

53 Richard Flacks, *Youth and Social Change* (Chicago: Markham, 1971); *see also* George R. Vickers, *The Formation of the New Left: The Early Years* (Lexington, Mass.: D.C. Heath, 1975).

54 See, for example, Paul Goodman, *Growing Up Absurd* (New York: Vintage, 1960).

55 Jules Henry, *Culture Against Man* (New York: Random House, 1963), p. 476.

56 Ibid., p. 476.

57 See, for example, Robert E. Park and E. V. Stonequist, *The Marginal Man* (New York: Scribner's, 1937).

58 See, for example, Fredy Perlman, "The Reproduction of Daily Life," in Arthur Lothstein, ed., *All We Are Saying: The Philosophy of the New Left* (New York: Putnam, 1970), pp. 133–54.

59 Ibid., pp. 133–34.

60 Ibid., p. 134.

61 Ibid., p. 154.

62 Irving M. Zeitlin, *Rethinking Sociology* (New York: Appleton, 1973), pp. 251–56.

A Postscript

As this book goes to press, we and many other observers of the American social scene have become aware of a strange mood among university students and many other adults in this country. The word "conservative" is often used to describe this mood, but it scarcely does justice to its subtleties and is probably completely misleading. Certainly the calls for liberation of women, blacks, Chicanos, Indians, and others reveal a most unconservative dissatisfaction with the status quo in this country.

Abroad—in Europe and elsewhere—there seems to be an increasing political movement toward the left, but there seems to be no constraint to be loyal or deferent to the power centers of socialism, either in the Soviet Union or in the People's Republic of China. Clearly, what has occurred in the United States cannot be characterized as a political movement toward the left, even in this contemporary, nonaligned idiom.

Some discerning commentators have attempted to explain the American phenomenon as a delayed reaction to the Watergate years. Final acceptance of the shocking truth that persons holding the most honorific places in American society were capable of deception and outright criminality seems to have led slowly to a curious malaise—a sense that no one in public life can really be trusted. Social issues, proposed policies, traditional political labels, even traditional logic in the discussion of social affairs—all have become suspect. There has emerged an unaccustomed preoccupation with ethical, moral, and religious concerns that is strangely anachronistic in the heartland of physical science and computer technology.

Since its inception, American sociology has been dominated by a theoretical and methodological focus that is heavily positivist in orientation. Primary attention has been devoted to pure sociology or work on applied problems, while critical approaches have been dealt with, at best, peripherally, and at worst in the rhetoric of cold war polemics. The theoretical and methodological concerns of phenomenology and dialectics continue to have an alien sound, even to many of the best-trained American sociologists.

Indeed, for many advanced students and even instructors, some of the material in the preceding pages may constitute a first exposure. But this is hardly the fault of individual students or professors. It is a consequence of traditional sociological education in this country. For those who have become familiar with analogous curricula in other parts of the world, the philosophical, theoretical, and methodological issues we have raised will be seen as indispensable for a responsible introduction to sociology.

We hope that this will not be seen as a kind of ethnocentrism in reverse—a denigration of things American and a glorification of all that is foreign. If we seem to be partisans, we are. But we are not partisans of a chauvinistic nationalism of any description. We do not raise a banner of irrationality or side with the forces of murkiness against those of clarity and science. And if we present a range of methods and theoretical orientations, it is not in the interest of a watered-down eclecticism. Like Karl Marx, we hope that we and our readers can effectively criticize positivist philosophy, while respecting the useful and constructive features of positivist sociological science.[1] We hope that we can do the same for phenomenological and critical sociology as well.

To deviate from the contemporary party line of hardnosed positivist respectability these days is to risk being labeled doctrinaire, or worse. To be doctrinaire is somewhat like being ideological. It is always an infirmity of the other guy. The sociologist whose phrase, "the end of ideology," started an enormous controversy among social scientists many years ago, has, more recently, explained that the phrase was meant to connote simply that "the older political ideas of the radical movement had become exhausted and no longer had the power to compel allegiance or passion among the intelligentsia." [2]

Daniel Bell could see no "positive viewpoint" to replace Marxism, which he felt had become severely discredited among Western intellectuals because of the excesses of Stalin and a "shattering of the belief that the Soviet Union was progressive merely because it called itself socialist." [3] Actually, however, there was, and is, such a replacement for some disenchanted intellectuals—the ideology of meritocracy.

In another work, Professor Bell tells us that the "initial logic" of what he calls the contemporary post-industrial society is a meritocracy. This is a society in which "differential status and differential income are based on technical skills and higher education." [4] This, to be sure, is an ideology quite different from the Marxist ideal, which called for distribution of societal products according to the formula, "From each according to his ability; to each according to his needs." It is also different from the formula, "To each according to his wealth or power—no matter how derived." The latter is a relatively accurate description of the ideology of classical capitalist society. Bell finds the meritocratic ideology congenial and somehow just. In a strange sort of way, the new capitalists are those who possess "human capital," embodied in their own persons. That is, they have high I.Q.s and a considerable amount of prestigious professional training. And the university, which "once reflected the status system of society, has now become the arbiter of class position. As the gatekeeper, it has gained a quasi-monopoly in determining the future stratification of the society." [5]

If one accepts the ideology of meritocracy, it becomes necessary to oppose populist demands for equality—for example, such demands as open admission to universities and equal opportunities. But all of this ultimately reduces to ideological nonsense. The most prestigious institutions in our society tend to be those with access to the largest amounts of wealth. With the ever-increasing spiral of tuition and other fees, it is clear that the most marketable human capital, in the form of physicians, lawyers, engineers, and accountants, will be derived increasingly from the sons and daughters of the upper classes. Beyond this, the central issue is not one of placing unqualified persons into positions or professions requiring advanced education and training; the basic issue is one of inequalities in the rewards available to those who do not meet requirements specified by the gatekeepers of power. In the last analysis, the gatekeepers are not the universities, but those who can ultimately determine which universities shall survive, and the conditions under which they shall be allowed to survive.

As Norman Birnbaum expressed it some years ago,

> the "educational and scientific estate" ... is an appendage of the system of power. Insofar as men of knowledge are elevated to power by virtue of their knowledge, they cease to function exclusively as men of knowledge, but function as men of power ... there are no purely technical or cognitive criteria for political decisions ... such decisions always involve choices of political values ... they alter the balance of power in one way or another (if only by maintaining it).[6]

We have not attempted to describe in any detail relationships among various methods, theories, philosophical orientations, and the system of power in our society. One cannot do everything in a prologue. We do hope that our efforts in this volume and elsewhere will lead to discussions and explorations that will allow students and their teachers to understand somewhat better the position of others with whom they may disagree.

We pause now in at least two senses. In the first place, as we have mentioned, this book is envisioned as the first half of a work that will extend the ideas discussed here to the full range of topics usually covered in a conventional American introduction to the discipline of sociology. Second, consistent with our conviction that the entire social universe is in a constant process of change, we are convinced that this and other works in the social sciences should begin a dialogue, if the social sciences are to continue to be meaningful and effective.

Notes

1 See Ehud Sprinzak, "Marx's Historical Conception of Ideology and Science," *Politics and Society* 5, no. 4 (1975): 395–416.

2 Daniel Bell, *The Cultural Contradictions of Capitalism* (New York: Basic Books, 1976), pp. 41–42.

3 Ibid., p. 41.

4 Daniel Bell, *The Coming of Post-Industrial Society* (New York: Basic Books, 1973), p. 409.

5 Ibid., p. 410.

6 Norman Birnbaum, *Toward a Critical Sociology* (New York: Oxford University Press, 1971), p. 378.

Index

Capitalism *(cont'd)*

and culture, 241–42
and the end of feudalism, 208–09
law of capitalist development (definition),
89
and Protestant religion, 108
relations between wage-workers and
owners, 185
and social history, 84
and socialization processes, 272
as a system of commodity production,
73–75
Capitalism and Modern Social Theory
(Giddens), 73–75, 94
Capitalist class, 75, 83
Capitalist society
definition of, 71
and the generation of poverty, 72
and the New Left, 89
Carnap, Rudolph, 123, 145
Carnegie Corporation, 33
Caro, Francis, G., 60, 69
Carr, E. H., 197
Cartwright, Dorwin, 131, 146
Catholics
and suicide, 30–31
Catton, William, R., Jr., 26, 40, 41
Causation, 2, 3
and contradictions, 80
and critical sociology, 80
and dialectics, 80
and historical analysis, 80
and poverty, 15–16, 21
and random sampling, 28
and scientific law, 23, 24
Cavalcanti, Pedro
Cave, Plato's Allegory of the, 151–52
Census
and surveys, 125
Chemistry, 1, 3, 5, 106
Chicanos
liberation of, 279
Children
autistic, 267–68
and changes in occupational structure, 89
feral, 256–58
of immigrants, 271
and imprinting, 252–53
and the looking glass self, 260–61
middle class, 232–33
and misery, 275
raised in "foundling home", 252–54
raised in isolation, 258–59
raised in "nursery", 252–54
raising of, 16

values of, 89, 232–33
working class, 233
China, People's Republic of, 279
Christoffel, Tom, 71, 72, 94
Churchill, Lindsey, 160, 175
Churchman, C. West, 224
Cicourel, Aaron, 98, 99
Circulation of elites, 106–07
Cities
Chicago 90, 98
cost of living in American, 90–91
Houston, 90
Phoenix, 98
San Francisco, 98
urban affairs, 58
urban high schools, 3
Civil rights
interest groups, 133–34
Clark, Kenneth, 65, 69
Class and Conformity: a Study of Values
(Kohn), 270, 275, 278
Class consciousness, 83, 84
Class Inequality and Political Order (Parkin),
217, 219, 225
Class structure, 75–76, 82, 87, 93
and the educational system, 88–89
power in, 88
Class Structure of the Advanced Societies,
The (Giddens) 83, 94, 223
Class struggle 75–76, 83
and the educational system, 88–89
Clients, 16–17, 55, 63, 65
Clinical approach
definition, 51, 54–55
and definition of social problems, 55–56
hospital administration, 54–55
and values, 65
Cohort study, 126–27
Cole, G. D. H., 102, 119
Cole, Stephen, 144
Coleman, James S., 32–33, 36, 41, 131, 146,
160, 175, 192, 193, 199
Collective orientation, 111
College, John J., 8
Coming Crisis of Western Sociology
(Gouldner), 94
Commodity
as cell of capitalism, 194–95
definition of, 74
in a materialist dialectic, 184
production, 73–75
Common sense, 179–80
Common sense world, 154
and biographically determined situations,
155–56
Communication, 109

Communist Manifesto, The (Marx and Engels), 93
Communities, 35
Competition, 74–75
    definition, 212
Computers, 53
    versus human role players, 133
    intelligence, 133
    (see simulation)
    and time compression, 133
Comte, Auguste, 6, 25–26, 28, 36, 41, 101–03, 106, 109, 117–19
Concepts, 7, 91–92
    abstract, 124
    becoming, 182
    being, 182
    (see commodity)
    culture, 202
    definition, 99
    and dialectics, 195
    domination, 273
    and generating hypotheses, 27
    of intelligence, 125
    and logical positivism, 124
    nothing, 182
    as operational definitions, 124, 142
    socialization, 202
    social structure, 202
Conditioning, 250
Conflict
    black-white, 83
    and contradictions, 92
    definition, 212
    slaves and masters, 185
    wage workers and owners, 185
Conner, Ross F., 61, 69
Consciousness
    (see class consciousness)
    and phenomena, 151–52
    and phenomenology, 151–54
Conservatism, 35, 61–62, 66, 161
    in America, 279
    and Freud, 273
    and functionalism, 110, 221
    and Hegel, 183
Constructs, 154
Contradictions
    according to Hegel, 183
    being and nothing, 182
    and class conflict, 76
    and conflict, 92
    definition of, 190
    development through, 189–90
    and qualitative change, 181
    wealth and poverty, 72
    within society, 80, 92

Cook, Thomas D., 61, 69
Cooley, Charles Horton, 161, 210–11, 224, 259–60, 261, 266, 274
Cooperation
    definition of, 212
    and law, 102
    necessity for, 162
Cornforth, Maurice, 188, 194, 197–98, 199
Correlation coefficient, 140–41, 142, 143–44
Coser, Lewis A., 45, 46, 67, 172
Cottrell, Leonard S., Jr., 112, 120
Coulson, Margaret A., 201, 203, 210, 223, 224
Courtship, 56
Crime
    and unequal distribution of power and wealth, 239
    Watergate years, 279
Critical sociology, 5–6, 7, 8
    versus applied sociology, 7
    and concepts, 202
    and culture, 243
    and poverty, 89–91
    versus pure sociology, 78, 91–92
    research, 82
    and socialization, 269–72
    and social structure, 205–19, 223
    task of, 72
Crombie, A. C., 40
Curiosity, 16
Cultural norms
    definition, 233
    (see folkways; mores)
Cultural relativism
    definition, 228, 242
Culture
    and advertising, 242
    autonomy of, 237–38
    of death, 271
    definition of, 227
    dominant, 233–34, 242, 271–73
    emergent, 237
    high, 233–34
    of life, 271
    as a map, 202
    opposition, 241
    and participant observers, 168
    popular, 233–34
    of poverty, 15–16, 64–65, 239
    residual, 236–37
    in the service of commodity production, 241–42
    shock, 228
    and social change, 241
    white collar, 82–83

Darwin, Charles, 47, 103, 187

Das Kapital (Marx):
[see Capital (Marx)]
Data, 7
    creating meaning of, 150
    to curb lawlessness, 50
    derived through subjective theories or
        methods, 150
    descriptive versus projective, 50
    in natural sciences, 36
    and positivism, 125
    to predict economic depressions, 50
    raw, 143
    to relieve unemployment, 50
    in social sciences, 36–38
    in theory, 123
    wrong kind, 49–50
Davis, Kingsley, 256, 258, 259, 276
Davis, Robert, H., 133, 134, 146
Death of White Sociology, The (Ladner), 93
Definition of the situation, 163
Deitchman, Seymour J., 66
Demerath, N. J. III, 67, 197
Democracy
    in the typographers' union, 192–93
DeSterke, Hetty
Deviance, 161
    and applied sociology, 238
    and functionalism, 238
    participant observation and, 171
    research on, 238
Dewey, John, 161
Dialectics
    and academic specialties, 195
    and American sociology, 279
    assumptions of, 188
    and critical sociology, 80
    and George Herbert Mead, 269–70
    and history, 192–94
    versus positivism, 179, 187–88
    relation between part and whole, 194–95
    and thinking, 181
    and understanding society as a whole,
        195–96
Differentiation
    as a basic social process, 103
Diffuseness, 111
Dilthey, Wilhelm, 36, 37, 42
Discrimination, 34, 64
Division of Labor in Society (Durkheim),
    103–04, 119
Douglas, Jack, 40, 274
Downs, James F., 227, 243, 244, 274
Dramaturgy, 163
Dreitzel, Peter, 275
Drug addiction, 239
Duncan, Hugh Dalziel, 231, 245

Durkheim, Emile, 6, 29, 30, 31, 32, 36, 40, 41,
    77, 103, 104, 105, 109, 119,
Dynamics, 25

Economics, 1, 156
    and dialectics, 195
    and operant conditioning, 265–66
    and social exchange theory, 265–66
Economic indicators, 59
Economic Opportunity Act of 1964, 58, 59
Economists, 12, 16
Education, 3–4
    dialectical analysis of, 189
    and power, 281
    and social structure, 206
Ego, 263–65, 274
Eighteenth Brumaire of Louis Bonaparte
    (Marx), 2, 9
Einstein, Albert, 46
Elementary Forms of Religious Life
    (Durkheim), 104–05, 119
Elementary situations, 196
Elites
    circulation of, 106–07
    definition, 106
    and high culture, 233–34
Engelhardt, H. Tristam Jr., 156, 174
Engels, Friedrich, 73, 93, 94, 184, 198, 223
Engineering approach, 51, 54
    definition, 51
    and definition of social problems, 55–56
    and Project Camelot, 53
    and social policy, 59
    and values, 65
Environment
    and heredity versus rational choice, 103
    and language, 231–32
    obtaining resources from, 111
    and symbols, 231–32
Epoché, 153
Equality
    of condition, 88
    meaning of, 87
Ethics, 55, 63
    in contemporary America, 279
    and scientific sociology, 107
Ethnicity, 235
    and subcultures, 235
Ethnocentrism
    versus cultural relativism, 228
    definition, 228, 242
    in reverse, 282
Ethnomethodology
    definition, 157, 160, 171
    and laws of human behavior, 179
    and method, 157

Ethnomethodology *(cont'd)*

and previous understandings, 157–60
as a theoretical perspective, 160–61
Evaluation research, 60–61, 67, 269
Evans, John, 269, 278
Evolution
(see social evolution, theory of)
Exchange and Power in Social Life, (Blau),
120, 223
Exchange value
definition, 74
Experience
for Husserl, 152
Experimental methods, 27
ex post facto design, 269
and John Stuart Mill, 129–30
method of agreement, 129
method of concomitant variation, 130
method of difference, 129
method of residues, 130
and theory, 123
Experiments, 3, 27
with autistic children, 267–68
child care, 252–54
feral children, 256–59
of effectiveness of Operation Head Start,
269
with flatworms, 250
on group atmospheres, 131–32
Hawthorne studies, 55
laboratory, 131–32
optimal socialization, 266–67
on productivity of workers, 49
Rhesus monkeys, 254–55
social, 125, 129–30
social isolation, 255
Exploitation
and expressive symbols, 230
and social exchange theory, 116–17
and symbolic interactionist theory, 164

Facts, 1, 2, 3, 97
and bias, 36
and constructs, 154
and methods, 98
social, 29
*False Promises: The Shaping of American
Working-Class Consciousness* (Aronowitz),
241–42, 244, 246
Family, 56, 59, 62
black 64–65, 85–86, 240–41
broken, 239
and changes in production and social
relations, 229
and the culture of poverty, 239

and *gemeinschaft* relationships, 211
incomes, 90
as an institution, 215
joint, 229
and neurosis, 191
participant observer study of, 168
and social structure, 206
Farberman, Harvey, A.,
Fear
as a human motive, 105
Feelings
as phenomena, 152
Feigl, Herbert, 123, 145
Fellin, Phillip, 144
Feral children, 274
Kaspar of Nuremberg, 256
Amala and Kamala of Midnapore,
256–58
Victor of Aveyron, 257–58
Ferritor, Daniel, 267, 268, 277
Feuer, Lewis, 73, 94
Feuerbach, Ludwig, 183
Filmer, Michael Phillipson, 150, 172, 173
Filstead, William, 173
Fink, Eugene, 151, 174
Finkelhor, David, 71, 72, 94
Flacks, Richard, 270, 278
Flaxman, Erwin, 266, 277
Folkways
definition, 105, 233
example of, 233
Folkways, (Sumner), 105–06, 119
Forces of Production:
in capitalist society, 184
definition, 73, 92
in feudal societies, 184
in slave societies, 184
Formation of the New Left, The (Vickers), 89,
95
Franklin, Benjamin, 36
Franklin Institute, 52
Freeman, Howard E., 67
Freud, Sigmund, 191, 263, 264, 265, 273,
274, 277
Freund, Julian, 107, 119
Friedenberg, Edgar Z., 40
Friedman, Milton, 16
Friedrich, Carl J., 183, 198
Fromm, Erich, 273
Functional interdependence, 104
Functionalism, 109
critique of, 110, 113, 114
revision of, 113
Functions
latent (see latent functions)
manifest (see manifest functions)
and society, 104, 109–10

Gallagher, Mary Beth, x
Gallup, George, 126
Game
      expression, 164
      scientific, 4
      simulation, 131
Gardner, Burleigh B., 54, 68
Garfinkel, Harold, 157, 158, 159, 160, 171,
      174, 175, 179
Gaspard, Jean-Marc, 274
Gay-Lussac's Law, 24
Gemeinschaft
      definition, 211
Generalized other, 261–62, 274
      game stage, 262, 274
      play stage, 262, 274
      preparatory stage, 261, 274
Genes, 1
Genovese, Eugene D., 85, 86, 95
German Ideology, The (Marx), 73, 94
Gerth, Hans H., 37, 42, 108, 119, 120
Gesellschaft
      definition, 211
Gestures, 162
Gibus, Jack P., 40
Giddens, Anthony, 73, 74, 83, 94, 223
Gilbarg, Dan, 71, 72, 94
Ginsburg, Helen, 12, 13, 18, 38, 39, 42
Gintis, Herbert, 88, 95, 189, 197, 199
Glass, John F., 67
Glassner, Barry, 173
Glick, Edward Bernard, 133, 146
Goals
      capacity to change, 134
      for human beings versus computer
            programs, 134
      interest group, 134
      irrational versus rational, 134
God, 22, 28
      as an expressive symbol, 230
      and serfs, 207
      and society, 101
Goethe, Johann Wolfgang von, 260
Goffman, Erving, 163, 164, 175, 214, 215,
      216, 217, 222, 225, 274
Golden, M. Patricia, 144
Goode, William J., 128, 145
Gorman, Benjamin L., 220, 221, 224, 225
Gorman, William, 59, 60, 68
Gouldner, Alvin W., 8, 51, 52, 68, 77, 94, 112,
      118, 120, 161, 175
Graham, Frank Porter Child Development
      Center, 266
Greenberg, Daniel S., 40
Greenberger, Martin, 133, 146
Greene, Kenyon, B., 224
Gross, Bertram M., 66

Groups, 17, 66, 92
      and the actions of individuals, 210
      autocratic, 131, 132
      definition, 210
      democratic, 131, 132
      as elements of social structure, 222
      interest, 50, 133–34, 217
      laissez-faire, 131, 132
      primary, 211, 222
      secondary, 211, 222
      and symbols, 231
Grugan, Arthur, 151, 174
Grundrisse (Marx) 223, 224
Guaranteed Income, 45–46, 88
Guetzkow, Harold, 132, 146
Gurley, John, 71, 72, 89, 94
Gurwitsch, Aron, 155, 174

Hamblin, Robert L., 267, 268, 277
Hammond, Phillip G., 8, 33, 41
Harlow, Harry F., 254, 255, 276
Harlow, Margaret K., 255, 276
Harrington, Michael, 11, 12, 18
Harris, Louis, 126
Hartley, E. L., 270, 278
Haskell, Martin R., 165, 173, 175
Hass, Hans, 251, 275
Hatt, Paul K., 128, 145
Hawthorne Plant, Western Electric Company,
      55
Hegel, George Wilhelm Friedrich, 182, 183,
      184, 186, 187, 195, 198
Helmreich, William B., 173
Henry, Jules, 271, 275, 278
Heredity
      and environment versus rational choice,
            103
Herzog, Elizabeth, 15, 18
High Schools
      conventional courses in, 62
      status in, 32, 33
Hinrichs, Harley H., 60, 67, 69
History, 1, 2
      of American society, 84, 88
      and biography, 78–79
      creators of, 58
      creatures of, 58
      and critical sociology, 72, 80
      and dialectical theories of social change,
            181
      and dialectics, 188, 192, 195
      of education, 88
      and functionalism, 110
      of human society, 104
      of inequality, 72
      and the present, 6
      research, 83–91

History (cont'd)

    of scientific thought, 3–4
    social, 83–86
    of society, 26, 206
    as the unfolding of reason, 182
    and variations in minimum subsistence,
      90
Hitler, Adolph, 52
Hobbes, Thomas, 102
Hofstadter, Richard, 105, 119
Homans, George C., 114–17, 120, 190, 223,
    265, 274, 277
Hoos, Ida, 62, 63, 69, 224
Horney, Karen, 273
Horowitz, David, 8
Horowitz, Irving Louis, 53, 54, 68
Horton, Paul B., 237, 245
Housing, 64
Huff, Darrell, 141, 146
Hughes, H. Stuart, 103, 119
Human behavior, 1
    biological determination of, 249–52
    determinants of, 149
    and payoffs, 265
    and the transformation of nature, 73
    volitional, 150
Human beings
    versus apes, 187
    instincts, 249–52
    limits on actions of, 202
    motives of, 105
    needs of, 205
    versus other animals, 73, 161–62, 230,
      274
    as passive objects, 149
    and Plato's allegory of the cave, 151–52
    reaction versus action, 162
    as tool-using animals, 250
    and the use of symbols, 162
    varieties of, 79
    will and volition in, 149
Human engineering, 58
Human Factory, The, 8
Human relations, 49
Humphreys, Laud, 173
Hunger
    as a human motive, 105
Hunt, Chester L., 237, 245
Husserl, Edmund, 150–53, 159, 171, 173
Hypotheses
    definition, 27
    generation of, 150

"I", 163
    and the "me", 262–63, 274

and other people, 260
Id, 264–65
Idealism
    definition, 182
    and social change, 186–87
Ideal types, 107
Ideology, 16, 280
    and the dominant class, 76
    end of, 280
    and Marxism, 77
    of meritocracy, 280–81
Ideology and the Development of Sociological
    Theory (Zeitlin), 118
Illness
    and mental hospitals, 216–17
Imperialism
    and expressive symbols, 230
Impression management, 163–64
Imprinting
    characteristics of, 251
    definition, 250–51, 273–74
    in human infants, 251–52
    and sexual behavior, 251
Income
    and the Industrial Reserve Army, 90
    unequal distribution of, 16
Inconsistency, 196, 197
India, 58
    pattern variables in, 112
Indians
    liberation of, 279
Individuals, 1, 3, 48, 92, 201
    meaning of, 259–60
Industrial Reserve Army, 75, 90
Industrial societies, 83
Inequality
    in rewards, 283
Inequality: A Reassessment of the Effect of
    Family and Schooling in America
    (Jencks, et al), 87–88, 95
Information
    contests, 164
Instinctive behavior, 249–50, 273
Institutions
    economic, 16, 215
    educational, 88–89, 215
    family, 215
    as elements of social structure, 222
    feudal, 180
    and functionalism, 221
    generalizations about, 194
    as imperfect reflections of ideal forms,
      183
    modern capitalist, 180
    and normality, 161
    and other parts of a social system, 192

Institutions *(cont'd)*

political, 16, 215
religious, 234
slave, 180
social, 16, 47–48, 103, 179
total, 215–17
Insurgent Sociologist, The, 8
Integration
as a basic social process, 103
as a functional prerequisite for society, 111
Intelligence
changes in, 266–67
of children raised in isolation, 258–59
and class position, 282–83
concept of, 125
of feral children, 256–58
and I.Q. tests, 125, 267
measurement of, 125
Interchangeability of Standpoints, 155–56
Interest groups, 50
in mental hospitals, 217
in American society, 133–34
International Journal of Sociology The, 8
Internation simulation, 132–33
Interpretation, 27
Interval scales, 135, 136
Interviews, 97, 125
I.Q. tests, 33, 125
and class position, 283

Jews
under the Hitler regime, 52
and suicide, 30–31
Journal of Social Issues, 8
Journals, 4

Kant, Immanuel, 151
Kennedy, John F., 11
Keppel, F. P., 33, 42
Kidder, Louise H., 128, 145
Knoll, Edwin, 268, 277
Knowledge, 4, 5, 8
and dialectics, 197
and power, 58, 281
relevant, 46, 156
for its own sake, 49, 101
scientific, 27–28
and scientific method, 21
and social structure, 206
about society, 101
(see stock of knowledge at hand)
about the subject in an Odyssey, 195
Knowledge for What? (Lynd), 49–51, 68
Kookelmans, Joseph J., 172

Kohn, Melvin L., 233, 245, 270, 275, 278
Kolakowski, Leszek, 196, 197, 199
Komarovsky, Mirra, 67, 270, 278
Korbel, John, 133, 146
Korean War
and prosperity, 90
Korzoff, Martin, 267, 268, 277
Kosik, Karl, 194, 199
Kovanda, Karel, 194, 199
Kuhn, Thomas S., 3, 4, 8, 9, 40

Labor
division of, 104
by joint families, 229
as an interest group, 133–34
productivity of, 105
and the socialization process, 272–73
time, 74
typographer's union, 192–93
Labor and Monopoly Capital (Braverman), 93
Laboratories, 3, 16
Ladner, Joyce, 93
Laissez-faire, 47
groups, 131–32
Language
and behavior, 275
and thought, 231, 275
LaPiere, R. T., 128, 145
Larsen, Otto N., 26, 40, 41, 67
Larson, Richard F., 220, 221, 224, 225
Latent Functions:
definition, 114
Latin America, 35, 54
Law
and class struggle, 185
of contemporary American society, 179
and cooperation, 102
dialectical, 179
and dialectics, 195
and ethnomethodology, 179
in feudal societies, 180, 207, 208
generality of, 180
of human behavior, 5, 101, 179
in modern capitalist societies, 180
moral basis of, 104
and necessity, 208
phenomenological, 179
positivist, 179
repressive, 104
restitutive, 104
scientific, 123
in slave societies, 180
and the social contract, 102
as a social institution, 47
of social order, 102
and social structure, 222

Natural science methods *(cont'd)*

and human actions, 106, 117
and phenomenological sociology, 149–50
positivism, 101, 118
and pure sociology, 71, 80, 81
and sociology, 21, 57, 81, 125
Natural science paradigms, 8
and human behavior 101
Natural Standpoint, 152
Negro
definition, 35
Neubeck, Kenneth,
Neurosis, 191–92
Newcomb, J. M., 270, 278
New Left, 89
and changing socialization processes, 270
and the educational system, 89
and white students, 89
New Left Review, 9
Newton, Isaac, 46
New Utopians, The: A Study of System Design and Social Change (Boguslaw), 220, 225
Nicolaus, Martin, 66, 184, 197, 198, 206, 223, 224
Nijhoff, Martinus, 151, 154, 173, 174
Nisbet, Robert, 40
Nixon, Richard, 269
Nominal Scales, 135–36, 143
Normal Science, 3
Noumenon
definition, 151
Novick, David, 67

Objectivity
and critical sociology, 80–81
definition, 80
versus value neutrality, 80
Observation, 26, 27
participant, 167–71
unit of, 162
Occupations
blue collar, 89
structure of, 89
white collar, 89
Odyssey
as a literary device in *Capital*, 195
as a literary device in *Phenomenology of the Spirit*, 195
Offenbacher, Deborah, x
Operant conditioning
activity, 265
contingencies, 266
definition, 265
operant, 265
Operating units, 220

Operational definitions, 124–25
Operation Head Start, 268–69
Orcott, Guy, H., 133, 146
Ornati, Oscar, 38, 39, 42
Order and Change (Leslie, Larson and Gorman), 224
Ordinal Scales, 135–36, 143
Organizations
bureaucratic, 108
as power configurations, 17
studied by participant observers, 168–71
Oversocialized conception of man, 263
Our Generation, 9

Panel Study, 126–27
Paradigms, 3, 4, 8
and new facts, 150
Parents
socialization of blacks, 272
socialization of women, 272
values of, 232–33
Pareto, Vilfredo, 106, 107, 109, 119
Park, Robert E., 161, 271, 278
Parkin, Frank, 217, 218, 225
Parsons, Talcott, 65, 69, 78, 108, 110, 111, 113, 119, 120, 161, 190, 214, 221, 223, 225
Participant Observation, 166, 167–71, 172
analysis of data, 170–71
field notes, 170
practice of, 168–71
rules for, 168
selecting a research site, 170
Street Corner Society (Whyte), 167–68
Particularism
in India, 112
versus universalism, 111
Pasanella, Ann K., 67
Pascal, R., 73, 94
Pathways to Madness (Henry), 275
Pattern-maintenance, 111
Pattern variables, 113
Pavalko, Ronald M., 275
Pearsonian Product-Moment Correlation (see correlation coefficient)
Perlman, Fredy, 272, 273, 278
Peterson, Richard, A., 197
Pettit, George A., 250, 275
Phenomenological reduction, 153
Phenomenological sociology
definition, 149–50
and deviance, 238
versus positivism, 149–50
and socialization, 266–67
and social structure, 223

294

Index

Power *(cont'd)*

  relations of, 179, 180
  and social control, 233
  and social exchange theory, 116–17
  and symbols, 231
Practice of Social Research, The (Babbie), 144
Prediction
  and human behavior, 163
Prejudice, 34
  and the phenomenological perspective, 151
Principle of Cumulation, 34
Process of creating institutions, 215–17
  dialectical, 181
  meaning of, 180
Production
  (see forces of production; relations of production; mode of production; commodity production)
Project Camelot, 52–54, 66, 68
Propositions
  factual, 123, 124, 125
  formal, 123, 125
Protestant Ethic and the Spirit of Capitalism (Weber), 108, 119
Protestants
  and culture, 234
  religion, 108
  and suicide, 30–31
Psathas, George, 150, 160, 172, 173, 175, 224
Psychoanalysis
  (see ego; Id; superego)
  use of dialectical methodology in, 191-92
  repression, 263
  resistance, 263
  and socialization, 263–65
Psychoanalysis and Feminism (Mitchell), 93
Psychodrama, 165–66, 172
Public assistance
  negative consequences of, 45–46
  non-degrading forms of, 45–46
Public opinion poll, 125
Public Opinion Quarterly, 126
Pure sociology, 5, 7, 8, 57
  versus applied sociology, 71, 91–92
  and concepts, 202
  versus critical sociology, 78, 91–92
  definition, 39
  diversity within, 36
  and poverty, 38–39, 71
  and Project Camelot, 53–54
  and social ideals, 48
  values, 57, 71
  and *verstehen* 37–38
Purpose
  in human actions, 107

Qualitative Change, 180–81
  and contradictions, 181
  and history, 192
  and psychoanalysis, 191–92
  and quantitative change, 187, 188–89
Quality
  in India, 112
  versus performance, 111
Questionnaires, 125

Race Relations, 34
  black-white conflicts within the working class, 83
Radcliffe-Brown, A. R., 109
Radical America, 9
Rainwater, Lee, 65, 66, 69, 85, 95
Rand Corporation, The, 52
Raser, John R., 130, 133, 146
Ratio Scales, 135, 136, 143
Rawick, George, 84, 85, 86, 95
Reality, 97
  and language, 231
  multiple, 156
  non-empirical, 153–54
  and phenomenology, 156
  and positivism, 156, 157
  and sense impressions, 150
  social and natural, 98
  and sociological methods, 98
  and sociological theories, 98
Redfield, Robert, 161
Reich, Wilhelm, 191, 192, 199
Reitz, Jeffery, 67
Relations of Production
  in capitalist society, 75
  definition, 73, 92, 184
  in feudal society, 75
Relevance, Structures of, 156
Reliability
  and concepts, 142
  definition, 125
Religion
  Catholics, 30–31
  ceremonies, 104
  communal rites, 104
  in contemporary America, 279
  and culture, 234
  festivals, 104
  as an integrating force in society, 104
  moral codes, 103
  as part of the superstructure, 78, 185
  versus positivism, 101, 107
  Protestant, 108
  and social indicators, 59
Research, 1, 2, 5, 7, 29, 32, 34
  bias in, 36
  and the client, 52–54

Research *(cont'd)*

on deviance, 238
dialectical, 88
on education, 88
evaluation, 60–61
funds, 53
methods, 7
military sponsored, 66
participant observer, 167–71
on parts versus whole of society, 103, 105
phenomenological, 179
positivist, 101
Project Camelot, 52–54
on religion, 108
self-evident assumptions in, 153–54
social benefit of, 63
social change, 82
structural change and individual behavior, 82
into subjective meanings, 150
survey, 98
Resources
human labor, 206, 209
natural, 206, 208
technological, 206, 209
Respondents, 97
Rethinking Sociology (Zeitlin), 118, 120, 153, 172, 174, 224
Review of African Political Economy, 9
Review of Radical Political Economics, 9
Revolution
against feudalism, 186
American, 209
and contradictions, 186
cultural, 198
English, 208
French, 209
permanent, 198
political, 77
prevention of, 83
scientific, 4
and the social contract, 103
Reynolds, Janice M., 145
Reynolds, Larry T., 145
Rickman, H. P., 36, 42
Riddle, David S., 201, 203, 210, 223, 224
Ritzer, George, 4, 9
Riviere, Joan, 263, 277
Rivlin, Alice M., 133, 146
Robinson, Albert B., 266, 277
Robinson, Nancy M., 266, 267
Rogers, James Harvey, 106, 119
Role
complementarity, 220
definition, 164, 172, 214

as element of social structure, 222
enacted, 214–15
examples of, 214
and J. L. Moreno, 164–66
for non-whites in American society, 271
normative, 214–15
of participant observers, 168–71
perceived, 214–15
reciprocity, 215, 220
and socialization, 271
subordinate, 271
theory, 164–65
Role playing
and acting, 214
and all-people simulations, 131–32
applications of, 166
definition, 166
and ethnomethodology, 166
and symbolic interaction, 166
Roll, Jordon, Roll (Genovese), 85–86, 95
Roper, Elmo, 126
Rosenberg, Bernard, 8
Rossi, Peter, 61, 62, 67, 69, 269, 278
Roszak, Theodore, 235, 245
Rousseau, Jean-Jacques, 102, 119
Rowen, Henry, 60, 69
Rules of Sociological Method (Durkheim), 29

Sampling
random, 27–28, 136–37
representative, 97, 98
statistics, 136–37, 143
stratified random, 137
Sapir, Edward, 231, 244
Scaling
(see nominal scales; interval scales; ordinal scales; ratio scales)
definition, 135
Schild, E. O., 131, 146
Schneider, Louis, 188, 198, 238, 243, 245
Scholars, 49–50, 52
Schonfield, Andrew, 66
Schooler, Carmi, 270, 278
Schooling in Capitalist America: Educational Reform and the Contradictions of Economic Life (Bowles and Gintis), 88–89, 95, 197
Schrag, Clarence E., 26, 40, 41
Schrier, Allan M., 255, 276
Schuessler, Karl F., 67
Schumaker, John A., 135, 138, 146
Schutz, Alfred, 154–57, 171, 174
Schutz, Ilse, 155, 174
Schwartz, Richard D., 145
Science, 1, 3, 5, 6, 21
and culture, 271
definition, 23, 39

Science *(cont'd)*

    and human activities, 21
    and multiple realities, 156
    and practical life, 28
    and research into subjective meanings,
       150
    underlying assumptions of, 23
Science, applied, 5
    automobile assembly line, 48
    development of piston engines, 46
    versus pure science, 46–47, 54
Science, biological, 29
Science, natural, 1, 2
    versus social science, 36
Science, physical, 29, 49, 53, 279
Science, pure, 5
    versus applied science, 54
    laws of motion, 46
    quantum mechanics, 46
    theory of relativity, 46
Science, social, 1, 29, 49
    data in, 36–38
    and experimental method, 27
    lack of purity in, 50
    and Marxism, 77
    role of, 50
Science and Society, 8
Science of Logic, The (Hegel), 182, 198
Scientific Law
    definition, 23
    and invariable relationships, 24–25
Scientific Management, 48
Scientific Method, 1, 3, 7
    definition, 21
    and human beings, 36
    and knowledge, 21
    and sociology, 21
    and the visibility of facts, 154
Scientific Revolution: (see Revolution,
      Scientific)
Scientific Standpoint (Husserl), 152
*Seamy Side of Democracy, The: Repression in
      America* (Wolfe), 275
Sechrest, Lee, 145
Self
    (see Looking Glass Self; generalized
      other; "I")
    Image of, as the basis for action, 162–63
Selfishness, 105–06, 201
Self-Orientation
    versus collective orientation, 111
Selznick, Philip, 224, 243
Sensations
    and other people, 22–23
    and thought, 22

Sense Perceptions
    reality of, 156
Seppilli, Tullio, 214, 225, 227, 230, 243, 244
"Sesame Street", 61
Sex
    and equality, 87
    and human needs, 205
    and imprinting, 251
    and neurosis, 191–92
    and occupations, 83
    new values and norms, 236
    ratio, 56
    roles, 16
    and survey research, 98
Shaffer, Ann, 61, 69
Shaw, J., 66
Sheldon, Eleanor B., 59, 66, 68
Sherwood, Clarence C., 67
Shils, Edward A., 214, 225
Shostak, Arthur, 8
Silverman, David, 150, 172, 173
Simpson, George, 29, 30, 32, 104, 119
Simulations
    all-computer, 133–34, 143
    all-people, 131–32, 143
    definition, 130, 143
    internation simulation, 132–33
    mixed people-computer simulation,
      133–34, 143
    PLANS, 133–34
Situations
    defined as real, 213
    definition of, 213–14
Skinner, B. F., 265, 266, 274, 277
Slavery, 84–86
    conflict between masters and slaves, 185
    and family structure of blacks, 85–86
    slaveholders, 86
    slaves as forces of production, 185
    as a social form, 272
Smith, Henrietta T., 252, 276
Social Behavior: Its Elementary Forms
    (Homans), 120
Social change, 7, 16, 66
    (see contradictions)
    and Comte, 25–26
    without contradictions, 190
    and critical sociology, 80, 81, 92
    and culture, 235–37
    and deviance, 161
    dialectical, 180–81
    and education, 189
    and functionalism, 110
    and idealism, 186
    and Karl Marx, 73
    and materialism, 186

Society *(cont'd)*

societies; Mass society)
agricultural, 206, 209
capitalist, 75, 209
destruction of, 76
division within, 75–76
evolution of, 103
feudal, 75, 207, 208–09
feudal vs. capitalist, 180, 186
and groups, 209
and human history, 79
national, 53
nature of, 101
as an organism, 79, 102–04, 210
parts versus whole, 79
preliterate, 206
and presidential elections, 97
purpose of, 201, 221
reconstruction of, 76
and self, 162–63
slave versus feudal, 180
as a social contract, 102
structure of, 79
as a system of forces, 106
tasks necessary for survival, 109–10,
    111–12, 161
Society, 9
Society for the study of social problems, 8
Sociodrama, 166, 172
Sociological Imagination, The (Mills) 2, 9, 58,
    68, 78–79, 94, 97, 99
Sociologists, 2, 3, 4, 5, 7, 12, 13
    (see Applied Sociology; Critical Sociology;
        Positivism; Poverty; Pure Sociology)
    and alternate approaches to sociology,
        91–92
    and immediate social problems, 57, 63
    positivist, 125, 243
    and poverty, 21
    task of, 102
    Whitman, Walt, 165
Sociology, 2, 4, 8
    (see Applied sociology; Critical Sociology;
        Methods, sociological;
        Phenomenological sociology; Pure
        sociology; Theory, sociological)
    American, 123, 142, 150
    and astronomy, 26
    definition, 3
    European, 123, 142
    managerial, 49
    the nature of, 16, 81
    and the positivist stage, 25
    as a science, 6
    and the scientific method, 21

and social change, 92
the task of, 5, 78–79, 81, 101
teachers of, 91
values in, 81
verstehen, 107
white, 93
Sociology (Broom and Selznick), 224, 243
Sociology (Horton and Hunt), 237–38, 245
Sociology in Action (Shostak), 8
Sociometry
    and psychodrama, 165–66
    and role playing, 166, 172
    and sociodrama, 166
    sociograms, 165
    sociometric test, 165
Solovay, Sarah A., 29, 41
Somerville, John 180, 185, 188, 191, 197–99
Soviet Union, 279
Space
    free places, 216
    group territories, 216
    personal territory, 216
Spanish-Americans, 13–15
Special Operations Research Office, 52
Specificity
    versus diffuseness, 111
Spencer, Herbert, 102–08, 119, 210, 224
Spitz, Reve A., 252–55, 268, 276
Spaulding, J. A., 29, 30, 32, 41
Spears, David T., 258, 276
Sprinzak, Ehud, 282, 284
Stachey, James, 263, 277
Stalin, Joseph, 77, 280
Standard deviation, 139, 144
Statics, 25
Statistics
    average deviation, 138, 143
    averages, 137–39, 143
        mean, 137–38
        median, 138
        mode, 137–38
    correlation coefficient, 140–41, 142,
        143–44
    descriptive, 135–36, 143
    and manipulation of variables, 27–28
    published, 29–32
    and scales, 135–36, 143
    statistical inference, 136–37, 143–44
    traps, 141–42
    t-test, 139–40
    variability, 138, 143
    variance, 139, 143–44
Statistics (Weinberg and Schumaker), 137–39
Status
    among American adults, 34
    and the educational system, 88–89